# of order?

Police relationships with black communities in Britain and the United States are fraught with tensions. Blacks insist that the police are racist and brutal in their treatment of black people; police officers counter that blacks are disorderly and in need of control. In this book, the contributors assess these conflicting claims and investigate whether the situation is, as many believe, out of control.

Out of Order? is the first book to look comparatively at the policing of black people in both Britain and the United States. Utilising historical and contemporary research, it analyses the policing that black communities have been subjected to and examines the effect this has had both on the communities and on the police themselves. It argues, for example, that the police have associated the ideas of 'crime waves' and 'social disorder' with black people in order to justify increases in their resources, and the extension of their legal and political powers. Drawing on a wide range of research and critical perspectives the contributors (from both sides of the Atlantic) present a new evaluation of a problematic relationship.

Pr   CASHMOR
readi   **Out of Order? Policing Black People**
and f
conce

London: Routledge   0415037263

...rovocative and informative ...ment of Order/ will be required ...ng for students of criminology, sociology and social policy, ...ry for all those interested in policing generally, especially those ...ncerned with the policing of minority groups.

Out of order?

Policing black people

Edited by
Ellis Cashmore
and
Eugene McLaughlin

London and New York

First published in 1991
by Routledge
11 New Fetter Lane, London EC4P 4EE

Simultaneously published in the USA and Canada
by Routledge
a division of Routledge, Chapman and Hall Inc.
29 West 35th Street, New York, NY 10001

Typeset in Baskerville by
NWL Editorial Services, Langport, Somerset

Printed and bound in Great Britain by Mackays of Chatham PLC, Kent

British Library Cataloguing in Publication Data
Out of order?: policing black people.
  1. Great Britain, United States, Police, Black persons
  I. Cashmore, Ellis II. McLaughlin, Eugene
  363.20973

Library of Congress Cataloging in Publication Data
Out of order?: policing black people / edited by
  Ellis Cashmore and Eugene McLaughlin.
    p. cm.
  Includes bibliographical references and index.
  1. Police–Great Britain. 2. Police–United States.
  3. Discrimination in law enforcement–Great Britain.
  4. Discrimination in law enforcement––United States.
  5. Blacks-Great Britain. 6. Afro-Americans. 7. Great
  Britain–Race relations. 8. United States–Race relations.
  I. Cashmore, Ellis. II. McLaughlin, Eugene, 1959–
  HV8208.097 1991   90-27272
  363.2'32 – dc20   CIP

ISBN 0–415–03726–3

Contents

Contributors

Ellis Cashmore is professor of sociology at the University of Tampa and author of several books, including *United Kingdom?* and *The Logic of Racism*.

Eugene McLaughlin is lecturer in criminology and social policy at the Open University.

Trevor Carter was Head of Equal Opportunities at the Inner London Education Authority until its abolition in March 1990. He was also Founder of the Caribbean Teachers' Association and served on the government inquiry into the needs of ethnic minority children which produced the Rampton and Swann Reports. He is also the author of *Shattering Illusions: West Indians in British Politics* (1986)

Ruth Chigwada lectures in criminology at Birkbeck College, London University.

Jean Coussins is director of social policy at the British Commission for Racial Equality.

Homer Hawkins is associate professor of sociology at Michigan State University.

Tony Jefferson is reader in criminology at University of Sheffield and author of many books on policing, including *Policing the Crisis*.

Michael Keith is lecturer in geography at Queen Mary and Westfield College, London University.

Tim Rackett is a graduate research student in the Department of Politics and Sociology, Birkbeck College, London University.

John Solomos is senior lecturer in social policy at Birkbeck College, London University, and author of several books, including *Black Youth, Racism and the State.*

Richard Thomas is professor of sociology at Michigan State University.

Introduction

Ellis Cashmore and Eugene McLaughlin

The police. Has there ever been a group treated so well with so little obvious return? Over the past decade, the British police numbers have risen by 15 per cent with even more rises forecast for the future. According to recent estimates, an increase of 1,000 new officers a year is the going rate. In London, police numbers have grown by nearly 20 per cent. Government spending on the forces of law and order has by far outstripped inflation – as have police salaries: in 1988, the police won a pay claim of double the public-sector average, contributing to a rise in real earnings of 41 per cent since 1979. Perhaps more importantly, the Home Office has regularly – and often quite tamely – conceded to the police's periodic re-equipment grants and, controversially, extended legal powers through the 1984 Police and Criminal Evidence Act and the 1986 Public Order Act. The Home Office has also slowed the pace of civilianization of administrative and clerical aspects of police-work in order to maintain police overtime and has so far resisted the demands for the introduction of an 'officer class' at the behest of the police. At a less visible level, the police have been allowed to encroach on many areas previously outside their remit. Their statements have acquired a moral authority previously associated with only the church. The police have eclipsed the medical profession in several areas, imprinting their ideas on the health and sickness of society on the public consciousness with an unrivalled power and urgency.

If a bargain has been struck with governments resulting in an increase in police powers, it would seem to be a highly unequal one, for, in return, the police have collected statistics showing, with a minor dip in 1988, a 'crime wave' that has grown to vast proportions. Such statistics have stoked public concern and sustained pressure on politicians for further police resources.

This idea of a crisis has been widely promulgated and accepted, usually uncritically, by the media and many academics. Given the public anxiety over 'law and order' that has been expertly nurtured by recent governments in Britain, the police's demands can be seen as a form of blackmail; a highly effective form of blackmail too, if the police's growing political voice is anything to judge by. Which politician really dares to call the police's bluff and demand some tangible evidence that the resources, physical and moral, being handed over to the police are yielding some social return? In an atmosphere alight with the expectation of a breakdown in law and order, few would risk crossing the very agents who supposedly stand between order and chaos. In 1988 senior police-officers warned the government that if more resources were not forthcoming the police could lose control of the streets. More resources were forthcoming. When the then Home Secretary, David Waddington, crossed the Police Federation over the issue of rent allowances, his speech was effectively boycotted at the 1990 Federation Conference. By contrast, the Chairman of the Police Federation, Mr Alan Eastwood, received rapturous applause when he finished his speech by asking the key question 'It is time to speak up for Britain's bobbies. Mr Waddington, Mrs Thatcher, we ask you – what price loyalty?' The import was clear.

The credibility of police arguments is enhanced by the mass media's incessant depiction of crowd violence, child abuse, street crimes, burglary and – most seriously for our purposes – the supposed threat posed by an increasingly 'superfluous' and 'unruly' black underclass. The public, having been inundated with media scaremongering, wants more stability in the social order and expects the police to secure it for them. The police accept the responsibility; but want more power as a *quid pro quo*. Historically, they have been begrudged this. But over the past decade, they have manoeuvred themselves into a position from where they can *demand* it. If both the middle class and 'respectable' working class want security, then the police can promise to deliver. But only if they have the political weight they desire.

In objective terms, the United Kingdom is not overwhelmed by crime in its inner cities when compared to many European cities and certainly not when compared to a great many US cities. So it is rather intriguing to know that, according to the Home Office, the British fear crime more than their European and American counterparts. As *The Times* has bemoaned, Britain is a 'crime-obsessed society'. This is most probably because they have had their anxieties stretched to breaking point by a near-hysterical media, themselves responding to every twitch from the police. And over the past decade the police have twitched mightily over the issue of black people.

In the post-war period, the police have suggestively played with the idea that black people present some kind of threat, though without actually identifying them as being responsible agents in some great surge of lawlessness. After the critical year of 1981, when disorder broke out in major British cities, the police, aided by a hyperbolic mass media, were able to nail down their problem much more precisely. Blacks, particularly young blacks, were a new force in British society and one which, unless checked, could undermine the nation's stability. A rush of lurid editorials, academic theses and television documentaries tended to confirm the police's premise: blacks were a problem.

Here was the resource that the police wanted and needed to fire their drive for more legal power, professional autonomy and moral credence. They used the widespread fear of a society out of order to justify their insistence on more political power, a power that sometimes bordered on political privilege. As concern over this new 'crisis' mounted, the police did little to allay fears. Quite the opposite: they fuelled concern further by making pronouncements on the nature of the crisis and what needed to be done about it. Through the media they also released statistics to show the real extent of the crisis. The police were also expertly assisted by certain academics, many of whom disagreed with police tactics, yet continued to agree with the diagnosis that there was indeed a crisis that needed to be tackled. *How* it was to be tackled was a point of contention. That it actually existed was not.

The question with which we opened this introduction is actually misleading. As we will attempt to show in the next chapter, 'Out of order?', the police have given quite a lot back in return for the many favours dispensed by governments, usually with public approval. They have contained the alleged crisis admirably, not resolved it: it would be tactically inexpedient for the police to claim a solution to such a problem. Further rewards are available to the group saddled with the burden of managing a redoubtable and seemingly insoluble crisis. The police have generally resisted the urge to state that they are 'winning' the fight against crime and disorder. Such a claim would diminish their claim for more officers, more equipment and more legal powers. As we will see in the next chapter, the police have placed no real stress on the conquest of the crisis: the best they have arrived at is limiting its damaging effects on the rest of society. It may jar with many to suggest that policing has become a politically privileged activity and that scares over the black presence in Britain have been of great utility to the police. But this is precisely the line taken in this chapter and it establishes a framework for understanding how the police have established themselves as a pre-eminent social institution. Black people have been an extremely unwilling resource in the efforts of the police to gain such pre-eminence. The police have used them and the threat that many people believe they pose to justify and even rationalize their largely successful claims for greater power and privileges.

In Chapter 2, John Solomos and Tim Rackett examine the policy debates that were triggered off by the inner-city disturbances of the 1980s. Their contribution addresses two key issues. First, they analyse the political debates that emerged concerning the origins of the disturbances, and second, they consider the impact of the unrest on the policy agenda. The chapter concludes by attempting to assess prospects for a change in the structural position of black communities in the 1990s. They warn that if policy changes are not enacted to alleviate the deprivation and social injustice suffered by black people in Britain, tough policing will have to remain the order of the day.

Richard Thomas and Homer Hawkins provide a comparative dimension for this column in their consideration of the policing of black neighbourhoods in the United States. They document how policing systems were established as a form of white social control over black communities. After considering the historical origins of what they describe as the 'white policing syndrome' they consider the forms of police control that were constructed to control newly-urbanized black communities in the latter half of the nineteenth century. They then proceed by addressing the nature of the relationship between the police and black communities in the twentieth century and consider the impact of black political power on previously white-dominated police departments.

We take up this theme in Chapter 3 on black recruitment in the United States: the transformation of police-forces from being all white to having, in certain instances, a considerable black presence. Central to this chapter is the contention that the appointment of black police-chiefs was more than just a public-relations exercise. The recruitment of black police-officers of all ranks reflects a wider incorporation of a certain stratum of blacks into US society. This stratum of black state functionaries have a role not just in legitimating the system, but also have the responsibility of controlling the black underclass who have been excluded from participating in the American Dream.

Together these two views from the USA contain messages for Britain, where the issue of black recruitment to the police-force has been on the agenda since the publication of the Scarman Report. There has been an almost unqualified official acceptance of the desirability of having more black officers and recruitment drives have been organized all over the country in what has been an abysmally unsuccessful campaign to attract more black candidates. Similar campaigns were initiated in the USA following the recommendation of Scarman's American counterpart, the Kerner Report in 1968. In numerical terms it was quite successful, thanks in no small part to the legislative weight lent to it by federal affirmative action. The American experience is instructive to those for whom more ethnic minority officers appears to be a positive move. Positive for whom? Not necessarily for black communities because black representation in the police is no necessary guarantee of social justice.

The American experience provides an interesting counter-point to British police-forces' attempts to recruit more black officers, attempts that were stepped-up very seriously after the 1981 disturbances. Despite sustained drives aimed at attracting ethnic minorities, the police have not been inundated with black candidates. In fact, there is a continuity in the resistance of blacks to joining British police ranks. Only 1 per cent of the force in 1990 was black, despite the fact that blacks represent approximately 4 per cent of the economically active population. The most senior position held by a black officer at the time of writing (1990) was superintendent: there was just one black incumbent of such a position; there are 1,513 white superintendents. Out of 2,303 chief inspectors, two were black. The British police-forces are having less success than their American colleagues in attracting black officers and boosting them into senior positions. The chapter 'Black Cops Inc.' invites the reader to decide whether the British motives for trying to increase black recruits are fundamentally the same.

In Chapter 5, we address the issue of police accountability in Britain. The chapter documents the struggle over increasing the democratic accountability of the police that took place during the first half of the 1980s. Central to this struggle were the experiences and demands of Britain's black communities. The chapter also documents how such struggles and demands were effectively neutralized in the latter half of the decade despite continuing concern about unaccountable policing practices. The conclusion considers the advent of a single European market in 1992 and the implications for first, police accountability and second, the civil liberties of black people in Britain.

The civil liberties of black women in particular are addressed in Chapter 6. Ruth Chigwada considers the issue of the policing of black women, arguing that black women are more likely to come into contact with the police than white women for a series of reasons. First, black women are perceived as being more likely to commit criminal acts. Second, the media portrays black women as social deviants and they are therefore subject to more intervention. Third, because of the colour of their skin their rights of citizenship are always open to questioning, and finally they are vulnerable because of the police's utilization of mental health legislation.

Trevor Carter and Jean Coussins address the struggle that took place in the 1980s over the presence of police in schools. They examine the context within which police in schools became so controversial. In their conclusion they argue that the police must reassess the manner in which they deal with other social institutions and must recognize the rights of those institutions to limit and monitor the nature of the contact with the police. In this sense this chapter is a micro-analysis of the controversial issues surrounding multi-agency policing debates that emerged in the course of the 1980s.

Tony Jefferson argues that in order to produce an understanding of race and police-work it is necessary to unravel the complexities of that phrase at a series of levels. First, it is

necessary to construct a political economy of police-work in order
to catalogue the structural features of the relationship between
police and black people. Second, it is necessary to consider how
contemporary processes interact with structural features to
determine police–black relations in this particular historical
conjuncture. Third, the issue of race and crime must be addressed.
Finally, it is necessary to examine the attitudes, perceptions and
experiences of black people. Throughout this chapter one of the
important themes that emerges concerns the policing of the
powerless.

Two burning issues that fall inside the 'policing the powerless'
relationship and which will continue to blaze away for some years
to come concern the Broadwater Farm 3 and the control of racist
attacks. There have been repeated demands for a judicial
re-examination of the cases of the three men found guilty of police
constable Keith Blakelock's death during the Broadwater Farm
disorders. Concern has spiralled after the overturning of other
convictions. The three Broadwater Farm convictions were based
on limited evidence after a problematic police investigation and,
even then, after a denial of counsel to the three accused. Should
the case be reopened, the central questions about policing those
without power will remain.

And what of those who feel insufficiently protected by the
police, yet lack the resources to give their grievances legitimacy?
Commissioner of the Metropolitan Police, Sir Peter Imbert, and
his predecessor, Sir Kenneth Newman, hammered out the
message plain and clear: racial attacks would be made a police
priority. A significant publicity campaign launched in early 1989
designed to increase the reportage of crimes of racialist violence
gave credence to this. Yet, Asian community groups are still
demanding more action from the police to deal with such crimes.
Community groups also question the police's conceptualization of
the problem. It is not so much a problem of under-reportage, but
one of the police's tendency to 'de-racialize' – ignore the racist
motivations and take account of only the objective features of
violent incidents. The police continue to resist this accusation.

Michael Keith's chapter specifically focuses on how particular
understandings of the nature of collective disorder came to serve
as euphemisms that justified the selective oppression of one
section of British society. The author illustrates how key official

discourses were constructed around ideas such as 'violent conflict', 'riots', 'symbolic locations' and 'no-go areas' to justify and legitimize policing changes in the 1980s. Through the hegemony of such discourses, it is argued, the basis of police–black conflict was also mystified.

On this point a new 'symbolic location' has entered official parlance – Stonebridge Estate, Harlesden, North London. After a confrontation between police and black youth on the estate in June 1990 the media was full of pathological conceptualizations of the estate and its 7,000 predominantly black residents. According to media reports the estate was the 'most lawless and dangerous manor in the city' where paramilitary policing was the order of the day; it was a drug-infested contagion of 'crime, isolation and despair', ' gangsterism' and 90 per cent unemployment. This was the nearest that the British media have got, so far, to associating a black community in Britain with Charles Murray's feared black underclass of US cities. The pathological status of this ultimate 'no-go' fortress was reinforced by the announcement that the only solution was to raze the estate to the ground and build homes 'fit for humans to live in'. The parallels between this and the Pruitt–Igoe experiment in St Louis during the 1950s are inescapable. Pruitt–Igoe was the site of a large-scale housing project that was supposed to improve race relations in the city. But it became a dumping ground for poor blacks who had to endure all manner of social problems. Such was the outcry that twelve years after its construction the apartment blocks were literally blown up. If the panic about Stonebridge is anything to go by, Britain's equivalent may not be too far away.

The police may justifiably claim that they are on the front line and hence have to deal with society's most unpleasant tendencies in places like Stonebridge. They also claim, this time not so justifiably, that such tendencies are generated by society at large, then passed over to them. Society expects to be protected from crime, shielded from disorder and sheltered from upheaval. As the proceedings of the annual Police Federation conferences indicate, many police officers feel beleaguered as a result of such expecta-tions. None of the chapters in this volume extends too much sympathy to the police in this respect. Overwhelmingly the police are seen less as losers, more as beneficiaries. The reasons for this is not that all the contributors have axes to grind. It is simply that, when distance is placed between the analyst and the topic under consideration, new perspectives emerge. The police may feel beleaguered; but in many situations they have actively contributed towards this, often for political reasons. As has often been stated, the British police win by appearing to lose.

One small instance of this is the almost perpetual argument that many of the service functions of the force could be handed over to auxiliaries, releasing police for duties they have increasingly insisted are more important – not so much observing the law but maintaining order. Trained street wardens or community guardians could replace some officers. This would clearly make for a more efficient division of labour. But it would also shrink the wide range of powers the police have garnered for themselves over the years and, so, reduce their political power. Not surprisingly, the police have grudgingly acknowledged the rationality of such devolution, yet resisted it fiercely on the grounds of the unique nature of the British policing tradition. A stock response to the proposal is that the community would not gladly settle for a second-rate corps of auxiliary workers who lack the training and expertise of real police officers and hold a more limited legal remit. There is an answer to whether this is so; though the police would not be too eager to learn it. The 'wrong' response from the public may endanger the police's authority in this and all other matters. Ceding power in street patrols may be the thin end of an unwanted wedge. So the police are prepared to take the flak over their ineffectiveness in some matters, just so long as their overall powers are not eroded. This is a theme that will recur in many of the chapters. It is one that issues a stringent challenge to all those interested in policing generally and, more specifically, to those concerned with the policing of minority groups.

Chapter 1

Out of order?

Ellis Cashmore and Eugene McLaughlin

> The mechanism for destroying the colonized cannot but worsen daily. The more oppression increases the more the colonizer needs justification.
>
> (Albert Memmi)

> The crisis is: only that there is being generated the idea that there *is* a crisis.
>
> (Robert Bunyard, Commandant of Bramshill)

THE CRISIS CONSPIRACY

Conspiracy theories are usually viewed as poor and improbable ways of explaining events. But, in the case of the British police's use of 'crisis' as part of their push to secure professional independence and political influence, pieces of a plot were drawn together to produce what might be seen as, at kindest, a convenience, at cruellest, a connivance.

The idea of linking immigrants with crime, unruliness and disorder is by no means a novel one. The Irish in the nineteenth century and Jews between 1880 and 1914 were popularly associated with habitual criminal activity, and moral panics were generated about foreigners and aliens, premised on racist caricatures (Holmes 1979; Swift and Gilley 1985; Williams 1985; Davis 1989). Young blacks over the past twenty-odd years have been accorded a similar distinction: officially defined as a social problem and given special treatment, which has in turn, emphasized their problematic status. Coming from populations over which the English had, in imperial eras, ruled, black people had a paradoxical presence: they were regarded as inferior, but had at least a legal claim to equality with their former 'masters'. John Solomos, in *Black Youth, Racism and the State* (1988), shows in detail how social policy both created and attempted to avert the alleged 'crisis' of black youth. The police were, of course, part of the more general attempt.

We do not have to know the precise motives of the police to appreciate that black youth have been of enormous help to them in their attempt to secure political influence and professional autonomy. Attributed with the status of a social problem with no apparent practicable solution, black youth were the object of some very special attention by the police up to and beyond the watershed year of 1981, as study after study indicated (see, for instance, collections in Cashmore and Troyna 1982; Troyna and Smith 1983; PSI 1983). Black youth, being materially powerless with limited formal access to political representation, were manna, a perfect resource. The police used them symbolically to demand, determine, justify, legitimate and, at key moments, rationalize their drive for power. At one level, the police have been enforcing their control of this segment of the black population through, for example, swamping operations, drug sweeps, selective enforcement of drug laws and paramilitary policing tactics. At another, they have, with the help of the popular media, been masterfully stretching society's nerves: depicting a social problem of frightful proportions and, in doing so, accessing power and resources to manage it (Hall *et al.* 1978; Sim 1982). Throughout the 1970s and 1980s the concern about black youth and their supposed 'heritage of violence' as 'muggers', 'drug barons', 'steamers', 'Yardies' and 'posses' has been handled in such a way as to engender public support for police strategies, especially as most of the stereotypes have been uncritically accepted and, at times, supported by politicians and the mass media. Why?

Our answer lies in the concept of crisis. It has power to instil a sense of danger or chaos in the popular imagination; and an unlikely alliance of academics, politicians of all persuasions, the mass media and the police themselves has built a rough orthodoxy about the existence of such a crisis. For the past twenty years or so, most of the arguments about the ability of the police to guarantee order have been conducted against a backdrop of crisis. During this period, academics in Britain began to consider the role of the police in relation to a more general malaise. *Policing the*

Crisis (1978) was the title of the most authoritative analysis of the relationship between the police, the state and the multiple problems afflicting British society from the 1970s onwards. Phil Scraton, by the middle of the 1980s, was arguing in *The State of the Police* (1985) that law and order was 'out of control.' John Lambert referred to 'The crisis in policing' (1984) whilst John Lea and Jock Young asked a pressing question in the title of their book, *What is To Be Done about Law and Order?* (1984).

The assumption in these and in many other pieces of work that have proliferated on policing in Britain from the 1970s onwards is that there is a crisis, one which affects and is affected by the police but which extends far beyond the police themselves, to every area of society. It is an assumption that takes substance from the media, in the 1980s and early 1990s full of images of petrol bombs hurtling towards police lines, police-horses charging into demonstrators and armed and armoured police-officers patrolling not just inner-city 'front lines' but also traditional Yorkshire mining villages, fields around Stonehenge, outside factories, university student unions, acid house parties, football grounds and town halls. From the early 1970s anxieties have been raised by chief police-officers like James Anderton, who has interpreted every episode as part of a conspiracy to overthrow democracy in Britain.

'Crisis' is one of those concepts that knits together the otherwise diversionary philosophies of Left and Right, haves and have-nots, them and us. Quite apart from the police themselves, politicians and policy-makers have sought to justify their politics and policies by reference to the assumed disintegration of values and the collapse into disorder and anarchy that it entails (Box 1987: 150). Tom Nairn believes the concept of crisis has permeated British thought and action for virtually the whole of the twentieth century. As he puts it, 'since 1910 it has been all "crisis"' (1979: 44). But it has taken on a new relevance since the early 1970s. Such is the agreement about its existence, that it is now established 'fact'. This has proved to be an inspired starting-point for the police's irresistible and unerring progress towards autonomy and influence. However one defines the crisis and whether or not it actually exists are not so important as the police's use of the widespread belief that it exists.

The crisis may have the status of the emperor's new clothes:

existing only so long as everyone's explicit agreement holds up. Unlike the clothes, a sole voice will not be enough to dispel what has now become an orthodoxy. The police are enthusiastic parties to this orthodoxy and, as we will show, have utilized the idea of a crisis to address a series of problems they needed to solve en route to autonomy. Problems such as those people who have demanded more democratic accountability and a reduction in police powers were successfully negotiated by police-forces whose prime mandate was to restore law and order. 'I sense and see in our midst an enemy more dangerous, insidious and ruthless than any faced since the Second World War', declaimed Anderton in 1982, adding that the subversive aim of this 'quiet revolution', as he called it, was to turn the police into 'an executive agency of a one party state' (Anderton 1982). Anderton's major effort in his position as Chief Constable of Greater Manchester, was to resist this apparent trend. In the process, he consistently urged the removing of political and financial fetters and the release of the police from virtually all controls of governance. As Michael Brogden has noted: 'If the functionaries are able to dramatize the connection between the organization goals and social values within the dominant ideology greater expenditure and more autonomy may be obtained' (1982: 86).

Such strategies have been analysed by Steven Box in *Power, Crime and Mystification* (1983). He argues that the police shock the community they allegedly serve by substantiating fears, then using them for their own purposes. 'The state's attempt to reform the police into a reliable force against its domestic enemies would only be bought at a price demanded by the police', observes Box (1983: 116). The price exacted has:

1 Enhanced political influence, with police acting in a consultative capacity on issues which are quite unrelated to the service functions of the police and not necessarily related to police expertise: for example, on questions of morality (including homosexuality and AIDS), housing (inner-city planning), education (wanting schools to accommodate police visits), censorship (pornography being a central topic), race relations (all aspects) and health and sickness (especially mental illness).

2 Hastened professionalization along similar trajectories to the medical and legal professions: making esoteric knowledge claims that only highly-trained and disciplined members of the occupational group have the necessary expertise to deal

adequately with troublesome and even life-threatening problems; the claim includes the stipulation that only those privy to the knowledge and expertise are equipped to judge or even evaluate standards and behaviour. This has complemented the influence outlined in (1) by blocking off the possibility of any reciprocal influence: political intervention in police matters has been discouraged and nullified. It could be argued that police-chiefs have now acquired unique discretionary power unheard of in other professions.

3 Affirmed internal control not only by discouraging, but actually invalidating, intervention from outside groups, including politicians: so specialized is policing, that no-one outside the occupation can comprehend its peculiar complexities; errancy or irregularities in the force therefore must be handled internally – the police are virtually self-policing.

4 Strengthened the police's negotiating position *vis-à-vis* central government: this is manifested in several spheres, such as in the police's ability to avoid the financial constraints imposed on other welfare- and education-oriented occupations and professions (for a breakdown of comparative expenditures, see Brogden, 1982: 86); and in their successful attempts to resist accountability to local government in the face of contrary efforts.

5 Increased physical powers: a major result of the strengthening of negotiating position is the ability to justify increased expenditure on labour and technology, usually by reference to the growing demands of a society in turmoil; the costs of paramilitary policing have been offset by a government convinced of its necessity.

Documenting what is effectively a process of empowerment helps us understand why, when questions about the police's ability to command public support or maintain public order are asked, the police themselves join the chorus. They have even taken lead roles, loudly warning of the chasms opening up in British society and the dangerous factions that need to be quelled if order and stability are to be maintained and consensus restored. As Keith MacDonald has observed:

> For them [the police] community integration is not just a warm feeling, but also a means to a tangible end, that they are highly

motivated to achieve. If there is genuine social disintegration
and reintegration is required, who better to undertake such a
task?

(1976: 52)

What concerns us here is not the truth or falsity of police claims
about a crisis, but the functions they have served in the police's
effort to secure and legitimize political influence and professional
autonomy. The problematic is not the objective reality of the
streets; more germane to our analysis is the way in which this
reality has been presented and used by the police.

The concept of crisis with black youth at its centre has been of
great utility to the British police and our purpose in the remainder
of this chapter is to elaborate how the ideas have been articulated
and how the police have responded to them. We will argue that
the police have drawn legitimacy from a largely supportive public,
convinced that a crisis of law and order is upon us and equally
convinced that the police should take appropriate measures to
deal with it. We will also devote some attention to the most
important sign that the police have achieved a position of
unparalleled independence and influence: a paramilitary presence.
The final ideological break with the 'traditional' British method of
policing and the inclination towards methods favoured by colonial
forces is indicative of the political leverage gained by the police
over the past decade. We trace the sources of influence and the
consequences. Police reaction to events that may seem only mildly
troublesome, most notably the acid house parties of 1989, the Poll
Tax demonstrations and soccer disorder of 1990, now include the
deployment of suppression apparatus, previously used only in the
north of Ireland and other colonial contexts. The parallels, we will
suggest, are revealing. But our next task is to address some
general questions about police legitimacy.

LEGITIMIZING CONTROL

Commentators such as Michael Stephens (1988) and Robert
Reiner (1985a) argue that the legitimacy conventionally afforded
to the police has evaporated during the past twenty years. This has
come about, they reason, because of the more overtly political role
the police occupy; a 'politicization' that has resulted in, as

Stephens puts it, a 'diffuse change in the attitudes of the public to the police', namely 'a decrease in the public's evaluation of the acceptability of police action' (1988: 4).

Our argument rests on a different interpretation of events. The civil disturbances of the 1970s and 1980s in English inner cities may well have been precipitated by a change in police attitudes, a change that was certainly accompanied by a gearing up of equipment for both intelligence and confrontational purposes (see Bunyan 1982). We would also agree that the police have increased their political influence. But we are sceptical about whether this has led to a decline in legitimacy in the eyes of the general public. It could be argued that the general population is at least ambivalent and in most cases even supportive of the police in their dealings with groups that have been defined as threatening, subversive and unwanted, particularly young blacks. There is little evidence to suggest that the white majority were ever tolerant of political and cultural diversity or that they frowned on attempts to put ethnic minorities 'in their place' (Cesarani 1990). The assimilationist approach has usually been favoured. In many circumstances, harsh policing responses have been supported by significant sections of the population in the same way as those sections have also supported crackdowns on dole-scroungers and drug-dealers. In this sense, the legitimacy of the police has been enhanced rather than reduced.

In a highly fragmented and differentiated society, a crisis for any one group can be a source of reassurance for the others. It is in such a situation that the police have built the foundations of their own legitimacy. They have done so with the backing of a central state that confers power on those agencies that contribute to the maintenance of a common set of values – a consensus – and, ultimately, social order. The police may have lost sympathy among some segments of the population, most notably those subject to policing, yet there are correspondent gains: they are generally accepted and, indeed, in certain instances, vigorously supported, especially in their efforts to establish a hard assimilationist line for ethnic minorities. As John Rex (1988: 116) has noted: 'while most white people in Britain feel that they can ultimately rely on the police to defend them, for many young blacks they seem an alien force or an occupying army'.

If there is a tendency in modern Britain for the majority of people to share the values that are purportedly upheld by the police, we must ask: why? Is it because they are utterly manipulated, or because they genuinely and voluntarily lend their consent? Paul Gilroy and Joe Sim provide a clue when they observe that: 'The majority of citizens may never have an unsatisfactory encounter with the police'; and 'Popular sentiment about crime which develops without the experience of being a victim and without any contact with the police is obviously prone to panic and manipulation' (1987: 98). They also argue that panics over law and order and the identification of culpable villains are recurring features of British society. The police draw legitimacy from public concern over such matters and can usually justify tightening their control in a drift towards a more authoritarian society. Furthermore, a powerful police agency has the means to create conditions under which public concern about law and order can occur. Public opinion is capable of being manipulated in such a manner that the stirring of anxieties about social problems and disorder strengthens the mandate of the police for implementing new strategies.

> This unity of purpose, an ideological as well as political expression, is not unique to the 1980s but is an inherent feature of the development of the rule of law and its criminal justice system. It has been informed and characterized by a rhetoric of law and order which identifies all opposition to the established order as a 'threat' to the state.
>
> (Scraton 1987: 182)

This is an overwhelmingly effective process: defining specific groups or functions as threatening to the state pushes them beyond the legitimate pale and solidifies the 'unity of purpose'. The groups in question are made to appear pathological and much more threatening than they actually are. Resistance by such groups may exist, but we would argue that it is containable and, in many circumstances, beneficial to the social order. By officially designating what is wrong and threatening, the state reminds the rest of society what they should not be. In this sense, a certain resistance is useful to the state. Black resistance, in particular, has been expertly manipulated and turned to police advantage.

As Emile Durkheim (1973: 68–9) argued, all societies need criminals to induce conformity and order. They also need rules and mechanisms for detecting and apprehending transgressors of them. *Ergo* the police. So the police and the whole control apparatus of which they are part can quite plausibly insist that they always act in the interests of the common good. The 'common good' may reek of rhetoric, but, throughout history, some form of overt force, or threat of force, has been employed as a means of social control and been accepted as useful, if not essential, to the keeping of order. Yet, in itself, this is inefficient and expensive, requiring surveillance and territorial control, plus extensive resources, including weapons and the personnel to use them – like township policing in South Africa or the holding of the north of Ireland. Because of this, the police rely on their authority: their legitimacy derives from a general acceptance of their propriety, the laws and rules they enforce, the values they stand for, the morality they are supposed to support and the order they maintain. It is through this process that the police can come to directly represent the 'common good'. The sight of the police may strike fear into some, but it merely reminds the majority that they should continue to exercise their internal control. As Smith and Gray have argued:

> as long as most people conform at least when some pressure has been brought to bear upon them by other agents, the police can effectively deal with the few remaining cases. They are the last resort in a long process of social control.
>
> (1985: 10)

Some might call this policing by consent, others preferring policing by manipulation. Neither does full justice to its dual-sided nature. We need to make sense of the fact that people tend to accept the opinions of those in positions of authority (including the police); they also tolerate substantial material inequalities and, because of this, are relatively easy to control, or at least influence. The ability of the police to command authority is based partly on the formal power with which they are vested, but also on the wide constituency of support they enjoy. As Brogden has noted: 'public attitudes and policing practices do not seem to be far apart' (1982: 201). Wide constituency does not mean total, of course, and there are many groups for whom police power is a problem. But these groups are the powerless minorities. Those who are most difficult to control typically reflect opinions, or oppose inequalities and

make stringent efforts to escape control. They may even have
ideas that run counter to dominant ideologies. These are precisely
the groups for whom hard policing is reserved: surveillance,
weapons and prisons are some of the components involved in
implementing control over such groups. Licence is then taken to
re-establish authority and order on what are depicted as lawless
and disorderly factions with control, surveillance and, if seen as
appropriate, repression.

As the paramilitary drift indicates, the options available to the
police in their execution of their duties include escalating
militaristic violence. They have been able to secure this option
without effective disapproval largely because they have generated
sufficient professional and political power to be able to define
what is and is not necessary for the efficient policing of Britain.
One of the main ways any police force defends its own existence
is by exaggerating the threats posed by various groups. The
British police have persuasively won the right to do this, and often
in defiance of such pressure groups as Liberty and the Community
Relations Councils. Defying such groups has been possible
because 'high and recurring levels of public support' have 'created
an atmosphere within which the acquisition (and prospective use)
of new riot equipment seems generally acceptable' (Brewer *et al.*
1988: 37–8).

It may seem alarmist for Gabrielle Cox, the former Chair of the
Greater Manchester Police Authority, to express concern about
'the inner cities becoming the subject of "township policing"'. It
may also seem to be an exaggeration for Paul Harrison to argue
that Stoke Newington police-station is an isolated fortress from
which 'the police sally forth like commandos, equipped with all the
latest technology, into enemy held territory' (1983:12,281). But
there is something portentious about criminologist P.A.J.
Waddington's advocacy of the police's use of sjamboks (the
Afrikaans word for rhino whips), lathi (hardwoodsticks used by the
Indian police) and 'sting sticks' for dealing with civil disturbances
(1989). Whilst coming from different directions these commentators arrive at a similar conclusion: that the type of policing
practice reserved for black people in Britain derives from the model
established in former colonies. As a consequence of the manipulation of the idea of crisis, this model does not seem to have incurred
the disapproval of the white majority in Britain. In the next section

we will examine the evolution of this model of differential policing.

POLICING THE DOMESTIC COLONIES

The restructuring of the British economy and the colonial situation that resulted in black migration to Britain in the late 1940s and 1950s provided the context within which black immigrants would be received by the imperial 'mother country'. The presence of what Sheila Patterson, writing in 1965, described as the 'supreme and ultimate' strangers was, from the outset, defined as a problem by various government departments. For example, the Colonial Office was anxious to distance itself from having to take responsibility for the new arrivals because it was concerned how the treatment of migrants by the native population could affect its relationships with the dominions. The Home Office was concerned that large-scale migration would result in 'undesirable elements' coming to Britain whilst other civil service departments were expressing concern about where the new arrivals would settle and work (Rich 1986: 163). As early as July 1950 demands for a 'colour bar' and immigration controls were made and calls were made, at the 1957 and 1958 Conservative Party conferences, for legislation to be implemented to allow the deportation of 'undesirable immigrants' (Richmond 1961: 234).

What did happen in order to deal with settlement problems of the new arrivals was the effective 'application of indirect rule methods' used in the colonies utilizing indigenous social welfare agencies. Initially, the government took no direct part in the settling process, partly in order to minimize government expenditure but also to retain a distance. Instead, the voluntary agencies and churches took a prominent role, viewing the situation as one of 'strangers facing problems in settling down in Britain rather than as citizens suffering discrimination' (Hill and Issacharoff 1971: 1). In the absence of direct government intervention, all issues relating to the migrants were addressed to a Colonial Office reluctant to be involved.

Characteristic of this combination of colonial paternalism and indigenous welfarism was the development of mediating bodies premised on notions of consultation and liaison to deal with the migrants. In the immediate post-arrival period, these mediating bodies actually excluded the immigrants from the debate about their needs. At the first meeting of the Nottingham Consultative Committee for the Welfare of Coloured People in 1954 there was no black person present. The same thing happened in Sheffield in 1959. It was also during this period that the various social services and agencies coming into contact with the new migrants appointed 'liaison' officers. 'Not, it should be noted, a Race Relations Officer to ensure that no citizen had his rights diminished on grounds of race', writes John Rex (1986: 103), 'but a liaison officer to maintain liaison with an "alien element" in the population.'

This type of mediation was formalized when the government became actively involved in race relations in the 1960s. While stringent legislation was passed to control the number of immigrants eligible for entry to Britain, an integrationist policy for those settled in the country was promoted by the government through liaison and consultative bodies. Paul Rich has described this process as the replication of 'traditional Colonial Office policy of seeking to rest colonial rule on stable and identifiable community structures' (1986: 161). Structures were created and encouraged which allowed representatives of the black community to be identified with whom the government and other social service agencies could liaise and consult. The problem with such colonial structures is that only community representatives who accepted the status quo would be recognized, consulted and liaised with. It has been argued that, as various governments continued to pass immigration control laws, these community organizations and representatives were given the role of acting as apologists for white society and the government, explaining the necessity for such laws and promoting integrationist and assimilationist policies (Sivanandan 1983; Humphry and John 1971; Nandy 1967). The problem was that:

> The loose definition of integration which implies 'change' on behalf of the part of the immigrant, none on the part of the host community, invites a colonialist-paternalistic response by white authorities which stresses teaching the immigrant to conform and his learning to change.
>
> (Lambert 1970: 185)

In classic colonial manner, the structures of representation and participation which were created were premised on consultation, liaison, integration and assimilation, as opposed to full rights of democratic citizenship. Within this colonial structure only certain interests could be represented, those which agreed with what Howe (1988) had described as the 'whispering in the ear of authority' approach. The formalization and institutionalization of this approach meant that every social-service agency and government department had an identifiable set of community leaders and representatives it could liaise with and developed liaison/ consultative structures for dealing with the "natives". It is little wonder that Howe (1988: 16) and Sivanandan (1983: 118) began to refer to the black communities in Britain as 'domestic colonies'.

We argue that this domestic colonial context is crucial to understanding how the relationship between the police and the black communities in Britain developed. The very presence of black people in Britain was defined as problematic by both the government and the wider society. This status was compounded by the construction of structures of representation and participation premised on colonialist and social welfarist ideas. Simultaneously, the government agency ultimately responsible for the day-to-day regulating of 'problem' populations was consolidating and expanding upon its autonomy. As a consequence, a very particular relationship was established between the police and black communities. An idea of what that relationship would look like can be gained by looking at the seaport black communities which existed in Britain prior to the Second World War.

Public concern was expressed about the black 'colonies' of Liverpool and Cardiff before the Second World War and they were defined as an unwanted presence by the various levels of government, including the police. In 1919 there were racial disturbances in Liverpool, Cardiff, Newport, Tyneside, Glasgow and east London. The general response to the riots was the demand for black seamen to be repatriated. In Liverpool the initial police response to the situation involved moving 700 black men to the Bridewell prison for their safety. However, *The Times* of 13 June 1919 reported that the authorities in Liverpool decided: 'that coloured men should be moved quickly from the Bridewell and other places in the city and placed in an internment camp pending repatriation'.

In 1925 the passing of the Special Restriction (Coloured Alien Seamen) Order enforced compulsory registration with the police if documentation of British citizenship was not produced. Ron Ramdin argues that during the inter-war years this Order had 'an all pervasive effect on the black community' (1987: 491). As a consequence he locates this as the period when the police became a problem for the black communities because of the way in which they chose to respond to racist attacks as well as their harassment of these communities in the enforcement of the 1925 Order.

Rich confirms this, arguing that the 'police effectively became the key local spokesmen warning of consequences if the course of deportation was not taken' (1986: 125). Concern was expressed about 'mongrelization' and miscegenation that could result from the black presence. Research carried out in Liverpool in 1929 pathologized 'half-caste' children, whilst studies in Cardiff and elsewhere focused on the connections between black men, crime, prostitution and disease (Richardson 1961: 238–9). In 1929 the Chief Constable of Cardiff argued that similar legislation to that of the 1927 South African Immorality Act should be passed to prohibit 'inter-racial' sexual intercourse.

We can identify the themes which would later manifest themselves in the post-war relationship between the police and the black communities. The black presence was continued to be defined as a vexatious one, fears over the consequences of the black presence were manipulated and utilized and there were continual allegations of racist police behaviour. Such issues came to the fore in the immediate post-war years when there was racial violence in Liverpool in August 1948 with the police being accused of not arresting the white attackers but instead seeing the cause of the violence as the black presence (Cashmore 1989: 79–80).

The problem status in policing terms was expressed in relation to the consequences of large-scale immigration. There was the continued association of black males with social problems 'in which issues of sexuality and miscegenation were often uppermost' (Gilroy 1987: 79). The Metropolitan Police began to identify the presence of 'coloureds' in immoral activities in the early 1950s with the Home Office sending a memorandum to all chief constables in March 1957 asking for information on the number of immigrants in their area, the state of the integration process, living conditions, level of crime, illegitimacy rates and involvement in brothels (Howe 1988: 19). The riots in Nottingham and various parts of London in 1958 also confirmed the presence of black people as a potential public-order problem for the police. In the post-mortem on the riots, one of the central explanations was that: 'the quantity of the friction is determined by the number of coloured immigrants' (Glass 1960: 144).

Their handling of the riots also raised questions about the fairness of the police in dealing with the new immigrants. In May 1959 Herbert Hill, the Labour Secretary of the National Association for the Advancement of Coloured People, conveyed his impressions of Notting Hill: 'I was particularly disturbed by the many allegations against the police. The coloured people in this district are upset and anxious about abuses of police power' (*New Statesman*, 9 May 1959: 635–6). The allegations were that black people were being beaten up in police-stations, harassed by police officers on the streets and having their clubs and homes raided by police officers who did not have search warrants. In addition it was alleged that not only did the police afford no protection from racist attacks, but that police-officers sided with white racists in such situations. Hill warned: 'Repeatedly one is given a sense that these people feel completely deserted, and that, if effective and reasonable forms of protest and redress are not provided, irrational forms of protest and explosions of anger are inevitable' (ibid.).

The role of the police in relation to black people reflected the relationship between black people and British society generally. That relationship was premised on imperially-based conceptions of why black people were in Britain and what their role within British society should be. The police were to play a crucial role in attempting to implement government ideologies in relation to integration and assimilation. Building on Lambert's point, we would argue that one agency of the state was crucially placed to implement 'colonialist-paternalist' definitions of integration which 'stresses teaching the immigrant to conform and his learning to change' (1970: 185). That agency was the police and their integrationist role was to have a soft and a hard side.

The police made contact with black people using the same liaison and consultation structures mentioned above. There was an urgency in doing so as they 'were the medium through which most of the scanty information reached Whitehall' (Deakin 1970: 249). After the riots of 1958, a chief superintendent of the Metropolitan Police was given the responsibility for liaising with the black communities in London. this liaison and consultation role was encouraged and expanded throughout the 1960s. In January 1964 the Home Office and the Metropolitan Police agreed that officers should become a part of the general immigrant consultative structures that were developing. In 1966, Roy Jenkins became Home Secretary and inquired as to what measures Chief Officers in areas with immigrant communities were taking to 'promote integration of coloured immigrants into the community' (Deakin 1970: 252). A circular from Jenkins in July 1967 gave impetus to the police. By the end of 1967 the Metropolitan Police had established a full community-relations department and by 1969 had approximately 100 liaison officers (Merricks 1970: Roach 1978). The purpose of such liaison and consultation was to explain the role of the British police to immigrants because, as far as the police were concerned, immigrants did not understand their function. Ironically, one police-officer writing on police–immigrant relations unwittingly recognized that immigrants were fully cognizant with one model of British policing, colonial policing, that led them to expect brutality, harassment, fabrication of evidence, graft and corruption when encountering the police (Dear 1972: 141).

As with all the other structures of liaison and consultation the annual Chief Constables' reports on such liaison and consultation gave a hint that there were problems. In these reports, there are constant references to the fact that whilst 'responsible' community leaders and organizations were co-operating with the police, other 'irresponsible' ones were not. As Michael Hill and Ruth Issacharoff, in their analysis of the arrangements, made clear: 'there is no evidence that the opportunities provided for informal consultation between police and immigrants through community relations committees have made any difference' (1971: 185).

Whilst the police, along with the other state agencies, had created colonial-type structures of consultation and liaison with identifiable community representatives, the whole problem of what interests were being represented was obvious. The soft integrationist line was being peddled by the police to receptive community leaders in the consultation structures; on the streets the police were peddling a harder version to the non-receptive sections of the black communities.

By the mid-1960s further evidence began to emerge about how inner-city black neighbourhoods were being policed. In 1965 the West Indian Standing Conference published a study of police/black relations, which argued that: 'threads of objectionable prejudice seem to be interwoven into the fabric of police and immigrant relationship. It must be maintained that many instances have proved that the police are malicious and exceptionally hostile' (Hunte 1965: 244). In addition concern was again expressed about the apathetic police response to racist attacks. Kelso Cochrane was murdered by a gang of white youths in Kensal New Town, London, in May 1958 – his killers were never brought to justice. Thus a pattern was established whereby the police protection afforded to black people, in any form, was minimal. Stuart Bowes, writing in 1966, was highly suspicious of the lack of police protection.

> The inadequacy of police protection for 'coloureds' in Notting Hill during the disturbances could have been deliberate (in part intended to develop the atmosphere in which government limitation of immigration could be achieved), but it could not have been because the Metropolitan police were incapable of providing anything better.
>
> (1966: 64)

Darcus Howe (1988) has pointed to the overall lack of concern on the part of white society about the policing of the black communities that was taking place during this period. While the 1959–62 Royal Commission examined the causes for public concern about policing, there was a 'blanket silence' on the issue of police–black relations. Howe has argued that this: 'could only serve to reinforce in police officers that their malpractices in the domestic colonies had the sanction of official society and the public at large' (1988:16).

In 1970 John Lambert documented how various state agencies were expecting black people to assimilate into a society that was openly hostile to their presence and how those who did not do so were being defined as a problem to be controlled. He ominously argued that the only way that this could be achieved would be through the construction of 'a whole gamut of state machinery and legislation of a violent, oppressive racist kind' (1970: 186). Policing strategies were being developed to deal with those sections of the black population which were openly rejecting the assimilationist approaches.

Howe (1988) has argued that, in the 1970s, police-officers behaved like 'colonial governors'. The result of the attempt by these 'governors' to impose colonial rule was a struggle for the control of the streets of the black areas, which, in the 1970s, saw an escalation in the number and seriousness of confrontations between the police and black youth. Concern began to be expressed about the supposed criminality of black youth and this developed into a 'crisis' about the crime-ridden nature of Britain's inner cities and the 'prowling' black mugger. Hall *et al.* (1978) have shown how, in this period, black youth became a metaphor for every fear and anxiety that existed in British society. Through the manipulation of those fears, the police justified their hard policing of Britain's inner cities: 'The emphasis on black crime became a useful means to bolster the standing of the police, enhancing support for the organisation at a difficult moment and winning popular consent which could no longer be taken for granted' (Gilroy 1987: 96).

In order to strengthen control of black youth, policies similar to what Lambert feared were implemented to confine black people to their own areas, which, in turn, were aggressively policed by the use of specialist squads, such as Special Patrol Groups, and saturation tactics, such as Swamp'81. The eventual consequences of that policing and indeed British society's treatment of black people were the civil disturbances of the early 1980s: 'in 1981 all frequently voiced fears that young people – above all, young black people – would rise up against the police and lay claim to a respect which had been denied them became a dramatic reality' (Kettle and Hodges 1982: 251).

If 1981 was something of an *annus mirabilis* for race relations in Britain, it was also the beginning of a change in public perceptions of policing. Clearly, the police were inadequately equipped to deal with the changing demands of what was seeming to be an increasingly lawless Britain. It seemed logical that the police should acquire appropriate hardware, techniques and the discretion about when to use them. Riot gear, CS gas, plastic bullets, water cannons, surveillance systems and guns: these were all justified by senior police officers in the name of responding to the intensifying crisis.

After the 1981 disturbances, the police reconsidered their approach to maintaining public order. The odour of programmatic convenience hung over the police's response: it complemented almost too perfectly the drive for autonomy and influence already underway. In 1979 the Police Federation had demanded of the government that it endorse the upgrading of riot-equipment and provide the police with more extensive public-order powers. In 1980 key Chief Constables had pressed for a more aggressive approach to public-order policing and produced a public-order manual which recommended the upgrading of riot training and equipment. After the St Paul's district of Bristol erupted in April 1980 and the police decided to withdraw from the area, the Home Secretary, William Whitelaw, initiated a review of police arrangements for handling disturbances. This review stressed the importance of enhancing the effectiveness of mutual aid arrangements, transport and communication provisions, protective equipment, riot-training and community relations. It was emphasized that:

> The effective preservation of order depends in the long term on the consent of the community. While the use of sophisticated riot equipment might be effective in quelling disorder in certain circumstances, it could also lead to the long term alienation of the public from the police. . . . Similar considerations would apply to the development of paramilitary riot squads within police forces or a paramilitary national reserve force.
>
> (Quoted in Northam 1988: 176)

Thus it was stressed that order rested on consent not coercion. Maybe so; but the police, after the widespread disturbances of 1981, were presented with a peculiar set of difficulties, for there were clearly areas of Britain's inner cities where consent was meaningless. The Association of Chief Police Officers (ACPO), representing the separate police forces, met the Home Secretary and officials and ministers of the Home Office in September 1981; it was an emergency meeting to discuss the spiralling problem of public order. The result was an acceptance by the government that the police were not equipped to handle unrest on the scale

seen at Brixton and elsewhere and an acknowledgement that they
needed to study other police forces which had experience of
containing widespread civil disorder. A process of government-
authorized paramilitarization which had its origins in the
conflictual first decades of the twentieth century and which was
tentatively upgraded in the 1970s received a major boost as a
result of the 1980–1 disturbances (Bunyan 1982; BSSRS 1985:
Morgan 1987).

THE RULE OF FIST

There was one model that the British police could turn to, one
which we would argue is integral to British policing - policing in
the colonies. We find the roots of this in Britain's very first colony
and one of its most recent. Between 1780 and 1840, Ireland was,
according to Palmer, a 'policing laboratory', where Sir Robert
Peel experimented with his ideas. His embryonic Royal Irish
Constabulary (RIC) was an armed force run on strictly military
lines with the sole aim of maintaining law and order in the colony.
Peel's new police force came into its own when the British were
confronted with the problems of how to maintain law and order
in their other colonies: 'Ireland, so often the pioneer and
paradigm in British colonial experience, provided the model: it
was on the lines of the Royal Irish Constabulary that colonial
governments built their paramilitary police' (Arnold 1977: 102).
As Palmer notes: 'The RIC model was chosen to maintain public
order, political control and administrative efficiency in the
colonies' (1988: 542). Officers of the RIC were used to set up
forces throughout the British Colonies and those from colonial
forces were sent to Ireland for training, so that: 'By the end of the
(nineteenth) century, Britain had established a virtual worldwide
imperial policing system' (Palmer 1988: 544).

The history of the British empire is, in one perspective, a
venerable story of unfolding destiny, Britannia ruling a quarter of
the world as if by divine right. In another perspective, it is a
tragedy in which the dictates of greed and profit guided the British
will to dominate, exploit and rule. Given that the dominated,
exploited and ruled were not necessarily desirous of being so,
dissenting subjects in the colonies were treated to either rough
justice or violent suppression.

Some of the most horrific passages in recent history have occurred in the maintenance of law and order in British colonies. Amritsar, India, 1919: British troops fired for ten minutes into a dense crowd of Indians hemmed-in by a walled enclosure, killing 379 and wounding 1,200 unarmed protesters. Dublin, 1920: British forces killed 12 and injured 60 civilians in one day. Belize, British Honduras, 1934: 500 rebels, again unarmed, fought a pitched battle with the police. St Kitts, West Indies, 1935: striking sugar workers, unarmed, were fired on by police, who killed three and injured more. Grenada, West Indies, 1937: police killed 12 strikers and wounded 50. Barbados, 1937: four people killed, 47 injured, after police fired into unarmed crowds of demonstrators. Jamaica, 1938: police and troops put down unrest, killing 12 and wounding 171. These are some of the more vivid recent examples in which the British colonial authorities have confronted resistance and re-established their law and order. In all these situations, the police assumed roles usually associated with the military. It was in the last British colonies, the north of Ireland and Hong Kong, that the domestic forces found their inspiration in the 1980s.

The complex manner in which the experiences of the Royal Ulster Constabulary in the north of Ireland provided the initial knowledge and lessons for British police officers, whether it was in terms of organizational innovations, accessing exceptional legal powers, operational strategies or weaponry, has been well documented (Ackroyd *et al.* 1977; BSSRS 1985; Faligot 1983; Hillyard 1988). Just as important, according to Gerry Northam, was one of the colonial forces which was set up on the lines of the RIC – the Royal Hong Kong Police (RHKP). Northam describes the Hong Kong policing model as being 'the distillation of British colonial policing as practised in the most important remaining outpost of the empire'. It was designed for 'suppressing rebellions by Chinese Communists, indigenous trade unions or anybody else who had the nerve to take on the colonial power of the British abroad' (1987: 39). During the 1966–7 turbulence in the colony this 'thin green line' earned itself the prefix 'Royal' for the efficient manner in which it suppressed those who challenged British rule. It also provided the force with the grounds for unveiling its upgraded paramilitary capabilities and justified the further refinement of these capabilities.

To the UK, 1981–2 was what 1966–7 was to Hong Kong: a mandate for introducing new methods of policing with little public resistance. The disturbances revealed that the British police were 'ill-equipped, poorly trained and badly led' (Graef 1989: 55). The RHKP was approached with a view to advising ACPO. Hong Kong's Director of Operations, Richard Quine, travelled to Britain, with minimum publicity, to brief ACPO on his force's approach. Gerry Northam argues that the RHKP effectively provided the ideas for Britain's paramilitary development. Many of the features of the RHKP were transposed to Britain: a computerized system of communications provided minute-by-minute command and control networks; riot-suppression units comprising platoons of officers drilled to congregate in various formations and defend or attack in different modes; and an armoury of batons, firearms, CS gas, etc. Of particular importance was the specialized training: Hong Kong officers were given ten-week programmes covering all kinds of disorder, crowd-control and riot-suppression.

The colonial connection was further strengthened when Brigadier Michael Harvey, a veteran of Korea and Oman, and former adviser to the British Army in the north of Ireland, became Scotland Yard's self-defence adviser after 1981. Just as important as the importation of techniques and technology was what Northam calls 'the habit of mind which determined the whole process of empire' (1988: 131). This has been expressed in master–servant type relationships, the police instructing and the colonial populations obeying. The colonial policing tradition has disregarded any reference to public opinion and employed an unsubtle pragmatism. This was necessarily reflected in the internal structure of colonial police forces where the Commissioners enjoy complete autonomy.

In the light of the RHKP advice and the deliberations it promoted, ACPO made what Northam regards as 'the most significant shift in police strategy Britain had known for a century and a half' (1988: 41). A working group was set up to review the policing of public order. Two years later, the Community Disorder Tactical Options Inter-Force Working Group, consisting of six senior officers, submitted its report, which encouraged, and actually prompted, a significant ideological shift in police strategy. Prior to the committee's investigation, ACPO had expressed reservations about anti-riot policing's 'acceptability to public opinion and their political masters' (Northam 1988: 41). The intervening two years presumably dispelled the doubts. Commenting on the committee's findings and the national manual that was prepared to complement them, ACPO President Kenneth Oxford, the then Chief Constable of Merseyside, talked positively of tactics 'which are capable of dealing swiftly and effectively with large-scale street disorder, and which at the same time are clearly appropriate responses to the levels of violence experienced involving the use of no more than the necessary minimum force' (Quoted in Northam 1988: 43).

Here was perhaps the first open indication that the British police were prepared to abandon the traditionally clear distinction between themselves and the army. If public order was to be preserved in the face of collective violence, then fire would be met with fire. To date, there seems to be little evidence that this philosophy has antagonized the general public. Quite the contrary, in fact: for the ten years preceding 1981, television viewers had witnessed almost first-hand the north of Ireland, Saltley (1972), Bristol (1980) and other sites of confrontation, where the police had laboured, usually without success, to control hostile crowds. Roger Graef makes the point that viewers saw only the police's version of events: 'For reasons of safety, most television shots are taken from behind police lines and give no balanced idea of the provocation from the other side' (1989: 47). Graef uses this to support his plausible view that 'most people support police tactics in public order incidents' (1989: 48).

Given the role of the media in the presentation of civil disorder, it was not surprising that television cameras were assembled en masse at the Orgreave coking plant in South Yorkshire in May 1984 when approximately 1,500 riot-trained police-officers wielding high-tech equipment confronted 800 miners. Many people were injured and there were 83 arrested in the bloodiest single episode of the 1984–5 coal dispute. Mounted police charged pickets without obvious provocation to project a new, robust image of the police-force. In addition, throughout the dispute the police laid siege to dissenting communities – there were to be no 'no-go' areas in the heart of England. Through the employment of bail and bind-over conditions the police were able to restrict freedom of movement and freedom of protest. Those subject to such conditions were effectively restricted to their homes and to specified parts of the country. In a dispute lasting over a year, there were three deaths and 9,810 arrests yielding 4,318 convictions. Forty-two different police-forces, co-ordinated by a National Reporting Centre, worked a sum of 40 million hours at a total cost of £200 million (Fine and Miller 1985). After their humiliation at Saltley in 1972 and their loss of control during the 1980–1 inner-city disturbances, the coal dispute was a victory for the police. Anthony Arblaster has identified the precise nature of this victory. He argues that the controversial actions of the police during the coal dispute were not necessarily required by the government: 'They are the actions of police who see a golden opportunity to extend their powers and harass those whom they see as their opponents' (1984: 183).

In 1985, a series of 'front line' disturbances saw the police in action again; this time, more prepared technologically and strategically. There were deaths: two Asians in Handsworth, Birmingham; one black woman and a police officer in Tottenham, London. The confrontations were bloodier than ever. They were also about power: the police were, by this stage, objectively much more powerful than they were in 1981. Politically, they were empowered to deal with situations of potential or actual unrest with more autonomy and the physical resources and riot-trained know-how to be able to handle such situations more effectively. During the disturbances plastic bullets were deployed, though not used. Answering criticism of this deployment, Sir Kenneth Newman called it 'a practical option for restoring peace and preventing crime and injury' and issued notice to the people of London that he would repeat the tactic should the situation demand it (*London Evening Standard*, 7 October 1985).

The magazine, *New Society*, caught the crisis mood in one of its editorials: 'Mainland Britain has never come closer, within most people's memories, to a total, if temporary, collapse of consensual civil government than it did in Tottenham' (11 October 1985). The acknowledgement by a left-leaning publication that Britain was in a grip of a crisis dovetailed perfectly with the police's interpretation of events. In the wake of Broadwater Farm, another operational review was carried out which assessed the changes that had taken place in public-order policing tactics since 1981 (Metropolitan Police 1986). This review recommended further training and equipment as well as the utilization of Territorial Support Groups for dispersing large crowds. Most significantly, the Home Secretary, Douglas Hurd, gave permission for the police to purchase 24 bullet-proof vehicles and 80 armoured personnel carriers. He also gave his full support to the right of the police to use plastic bullets and CS gas to maintain order on the streets of Britain.

The role of the police in the preservation of law and order had effectively been redefined. Sir Kenneth Newman, between 1983 and 1987, made this explicit when he observed that policing inner-city ghettos had much in common with policing terrorism. Newman had been head of the Royal Ulster Constabulary (RUC) and was practised in working in what he called 'symbolic locations' – areas in which there was little or no support for police. Part of Newman's plans was to target particular areas of London and to re-establish police control of them, at the same time removing low-priority elements, such as mundane crime, from the police's remit (Kettle and Shirley 1983).

Special attention was given to target areas, both in terms of overt control and community liaison and consultation. From some perspectives such 'hard' and 'soft' approaches were contradictory; in others the community-based exercises were perfect foils for the quasi-military tactics in that they helped prepare a virtual intelligence network in the communities involved. In 1986 it was revealed that the Metropolitan Police had compiled dossiers on twenty London housing estates identified as 'high', 'medium' and 'low' in order of their potential for serious disorder. The formula for determining this included factors such as ethnic mix, environment and hostility towards the police. Intelligence from the community was obviously essential in collating such dossiers (Bridges 1983a).

Between 1985 and 1990, the police showed its preparedness to resort, as a matter of course, to colonial-style paramilitary policing methods. The exceptional had become the normal. Incidents at Manchester University Student Union and Stonehenge in 1985 saw hard policing, and at RAF Molesworth 1,000 regular police assisted by 600 Ministry of Defence police and 1,500 Royal Engineers descended on a CND camp in what the police described as a 'sanitation' exercise. The News International Dispute in 1986/7 also witnessed the deployment of officers in full riot-gear, as well as shield units, snatch squads, mounted police and, for the first time, riot-trained female police officers, to deal with pickets.

The colonial influence also became even more pronounced in black neighbourhoods at the end of the 1980s. Between 1986 and 1987, three London 'anti-drug' operations saw the police employing highly aggressive, military-style tactics in black neighbourhoods. Despite the reservations about the wisdom of using military codenames that were expressed after the disastrous Swamp'81, the 1986–7 operations were named 'Condor', 'Broadlands' and 'Trident'. In September 1986, under the codename 'Operation Delivery', the police swamped the St Paul's area of Bristol 'in a grossly insulting and intimidating racist attack (Mentor 1988: 76). In June 1987 riot-equipment was deployed during two days of clashes between the police and black youths in Chapeltown, Leeds. During the 1987 Notting Hill Carnival the police implemented control tactics first used in the News International dispute. Sophisticated surveillance vans, armoured landrovers with gun ports, riot-squads and armed police-officers were successfully deployed to quell disturbances that broke out at the end of the carnival. Allegations were made that during the carnival the police deliberately changed their tactics, as they had done in 1976, in order to 'try out' the strategies and equipment which had been 'blooded' at Wapping (*Guardian*, 2 September 1987). Official credence was lent to such allegations by Sir Peter Imbert, the Commissioner of the Metropolitan Police, when he stated:

> It is a difficult and delicate balance, but it has to be acknowledged that it is necessary to be prepared to win on such occasions; hence the need for officers to be equipped and properly trained to deal with serious disorder in a professional manner.
>
> (*The Independent*, 10 September 1987)

During February and March 1988 operations 'Vulture' and 'Falcon' resulted in riot-clad police officers armed with sledgehammers making another drug raid, this time on the Mangrove Club in Notting Hill. In 1989, in three separate incidents, police donned riot-gear and implemented military tactics in situations that hardly threatened civil order. In

Wolverhampton in May 1989, 120 officers in riot-gear raided a public house in a mostly black housing estate and arrested 20 people, 12 for drug offences. 'Crack' with a street value of £500 was recovered along with a small quantity of cannabis. There were strained black–police relations in the area as a result of the death, in controversial circumstances, of Clinton McCurbin in April 1987. The police-raid resulted in 250 officers being deployed to pacify the housing estate. After this successful pacification exercise Deputy Chief Constable Paul Leopold confidently stated: 'We have the ability, equipment and the will to deal with these people' (*Sun* 26 May 1989). Within a month, police reacted with riot equipment and tactics to demonstrations in London and Dewsbury, Yorkshire, both involving mainly Asian youth. The first was a Muslim protest against Salman Rushdie; the second was an anti-racism rally.

In August 1989, the Metropolitan Police reclaimed one of the most famous symbolic locations – the Notting Hill Carnival. In addition to attempting to neutralize those members of the carnival's organizing committee who opposed hard policing, the police prepared for another showdown with black youth. Five thousand officers were deployed, including all 28 Territorial Support Groups and plain-clothes anti-steaming/anti-mugging squads. They were once more backed up with sophisticated surveillance techniques and marksmen armed with plastic and lead bullets. The heavy police presence and the decision to shut down the sound systems early provided the police with the reason to execute their battle plans. As bottles and stones were directed towards the police an 'early resolution' operation, refined in the light of Orgreave, Wapping and the previous carnivals, was implemented. A panoply of military tactics and techniques involving 600 officers in full riot-gear and police-horses was used to deal with the trouble.

It was later reported that the operation had been the culmination of months of planning and that three options had been decided when trouble broke out. First, the use of a limited response to isolate the trouble, second, flooding the carnival with officers if the trouble continued and, finally, deploying plastic bullets and CS gas if the disturbances got out of control (*The Times*, 30 August 1989). Options one and two were put into effect. The Metropolitan Police were determined to reclaim this important symbolic location and did so (*City Limits*, 14 September 1989).

On 29 September 1989 the Metropolitan Police reclaimed another significant symbolic location – Broadwater Farm. 'Operation Kingfisher' involved between 400 and 800 officers, many in riot-gear and wielding axes and sledgehammers, occupying the estate for a weekend. Certain community representatives, journalists and a criminologist were invited to witness the operation and the arrest of twenty-four people for petty drug offences. The Broadwater Farm Defence Committee was in no doubt that the exercise was a 'badly disguised attempt to criminalise our community' whilst the Residents' Association issued a statement claiming that: 'The police used the hype surrounding drug problems as an exercise to impose their massive presence, to intimidate the local residents and to stage a publicity coup.' In late 1989 both Moss Side, Manchester, and Liverpool 8 were also subject to highly publicized drug-raids. Once more the supposed links between black people, crime and moral danger were being reaffirmed.

These operations suggest that any reluctance the police might have about using riot-gear and tactics have disappeared. Reservations were expressed by the Police Federation about officers' legal rights in trying to control disorder and, at one point, it warned that police officers could refuse to follow orders in serious disturbances. While officers are legally entitled to use 'reasonable force' to arrest people committing crimes during disorder, that does not necessarily entitle them to remove crowds, with or even without disturbance control equipment. In January 1989, officers from east London's Territorial Support Group refused to undergo public-order training after expressing uncertainty about their legal rights. The move followed a decision by the Director of Public Prosecutions to recommend charges against twenty-six officers for assault, perjury and conspiracy to prevent the course of justice as a result of alleged offences during incidents at News International's Wapping plant in 1987. This indicates a concern within the force, but not necessarily one about the paramilitary drift, just about the legal position of officers engaging in this type of policing.

CONCLUSIONS: POLICING AND THE RESTLESS SOCIETY

The 1970s saw the political context change to an environment more conducive to police demands. Conducive enough to accommodate the view that: 'It is only right that the police should shape public opinion on important questions.' ACPO president Goodson justified this by reference to the fact that 'they are the professionals and have first-hand experience' (*The Times*, 23 April 1980). As Day and Klein (1987: 114) have argued, such professionalization: 'explains crime and crime control as technical-apolitical matters that are best left in the hands of trustworthy experts'.

During this period, concern about black youth was constructed into a larger-than-life political icon. Both police and black youth became reified as if by a process of molecular bonding. Convenient myths, stereotype images and sheer dogma were the orders of the day (Hall *et al.* 1978: 38–52; Gilroy 1987: 88–99).The police in the 1970s and early 1980s were able to use the potential and actual resistance of black youth and other groups to push for changes they desired. Those changes were manifold and had the effect of distancing the police from the local political process and enhancing the force's independence. What is interesting in this period is the absence of any intrusion by the Home Secretary in any issue, save to protect the independence of chief police-officers. When the Home Office did make programmatic statements on controversial issues, its arguments tended 'to mirror those of the police institution', as Brogden puts it (1982: 118). In restoring stability to a society seemingly mired in crisis, the police were seen to be representing the interests of the government and central state; so any substantial critique would have undermined the authority of all parties.

One effect of what was becoming a virtual obsession with remedying the crisis was to sharpen the police's focus on the groups it had targeted as threats and, correspondingly, to blur its focus on crimes that were arguably more serious. CS gas and riot-shields are of little use against fraudsters, inside-dealers and other white-collar criminals. It is difficult to assess with any precision the effects this has on public perceptions of the police. A *Sunday Times* survey in January 1984 disclosed that 62 per cent of respondents endorsed the police's use of plastic batons, CS gas and water cannons against potentially violent demonstrators. Concern was expressed over ends rather than the means of achieving them. Even those who were not supportive drew short of questioning the validity of the police's problem. Graef reckons that there is an age division: 'Older members of the community may be reassured, but not the young on whose trust the future of policing by consensus depends' (1989: 83). Of crucial importance is the capability of the police to mobilize legitimacy through their role as crisis managers. Hall has expressed concern at the 'manner in which the technical factors associated with the problems of policing an increasingly restless society have become a legitimate basis for far-reaching administrative restructuring of the police function' (*Guardian*, 5 January 1980). And Michael Brogden sees the 'politicization' of the police hinging on 'the economic and ethnic crises of the Bristol, Brixton, and the Liverpool riots, the industrial foci of Saltley Coke Depot and secondary picketing; and the political re-emergence of the IRA' (1982: 22).

What such views fail to emphasize is that the actual events were not elements of a 'crisis' of 'restless society': they were made to appear that way because of the police's handling of them. Of course, Brixton, Saltley and the other episodes happened. But so did Liverpool in 1948 (the first post-war 'race riot'), Dagenham in 1968 (a major dispute over sex discrimination) and any number of strikes between 1965–9 (when the annual number of days lost because of industrial dispute averaged 3.95 million, the highest since the war). These were not regarded as necessarily symptomatic of a crisis. Yet, in a context receptive to police claims, at a stage when the police were pushing hard for autonomy and influence, comparable events were reproduced by police and their critics alike as reflecting a deeper malaise. The events are not under our investigation; the utility derived from them by the police is. Powerful and powerless alike seem to have been persuaded of the necessity of an autonomous police, of the move towards increased paramilitarism and of the absolute importance of keeping Britain's inner- city streets free of muggers and, worse still, rioters.

Slow-rioting, the process whereby black youth and the police will be involved in continuing clashes on the streets of Britain's inner cities, will be confined and contained and will be capitalized on. This will justify more political power and independence for chief police officers, at one end of the organization, and a greater demand for weaponry by rank and file officers at the other. It seems unlikely that the police will reverse the trend of the last ten years and decrease fire-power. Britain has moved to a situation where, over the past two decades, armed police units have begun to patrol the streets on a full-time basis (Ackroyd *et al.* 1977: 138–41; Mainwaring-White 1983: 117–33; *Daily Telegraph* 15 July 1989). Now that the 'hallowed' distinction between civil and military power has been clouded, there is always the possibility that the police may continue to take cues from the colonial experience and team up with the militia when confronting 'emergency' situations. This would have the negative effect for the police of undermining its ability to control any civil situation (Ackroyd *et al.* 1977: 114). The more realistic alternative is for the police force to continue to stress the primacy of the police in controlling public disorder. As a consequence, force spokespersons can pressure for more and more equipment and labour power and justify these by reference to the supposedly hostile environment in which they have to operate. Waddington (1988: 113) has expressed concern about 'the ratchet effect' of acquiring more and more weaponry to meet crisis policing needs. He argues that it is much 'more difficult to reverse direction once an escalatory step has been taken'. As we have documented, during the last two decades such escalation has resulted in colonial policing methods being imported for use on the streets of Britain.

The entire prognosis is based on the rejection of the crisis scenario in which turmoil is seen to precipitate a deterioration of public confidence in the police. Realities are often constructed not from empirical facts or scientific observations, but from convenient myths, stereotype images, dogma and baseless fears. People's beliefs in them depend on their source. Our argument suggests that the police have commanded authority and their views have sufficient legitimacy to persuade the population that a crisis of colossal proportions is afoot. Far from losing public confidence, the police have strengthened it by demonstrating a hard-edged toughness and resolution in its efforts to maintain order in the face of all manner of threats, the main one of which has been black youth.

The atmosphere, as we have noted, has changed such that Britain now largely accepts the police as a paramilitary force. The exceptional has become the normal. Perceptions of the police as crimebusters have changed; protectors of order might be more apposite in the 1990s. Such is concern over stability and order that the police's crime-fighting role may become secondary to their more talismanic duties. People value their stability and react when they feel it is threatened: they may feel it is threatened more seriously by large-scale disorder than by the occasional burglary or shoplifting. As Eric Hobsbawm (1987) has argued, liberal and left thinkers have failed to comprehend how important the concept of 'social order is to the majority of men and women, how terrible the fear of its disintegration into disorder, uncertainty or anarchy'.

Stephens argues that the police have an 'over-concern with public order and control' which he believes is nearing the status of an 'obsession' (1988: 40). Now that the police have manoeuvred themselves into a position where their views are virtually beyond question, there seems little likelihood that this obsession will subside. More likely is a further utilization of the threats supposedly posed by black youth and any other convenient groups in the crisis that supposedly afflicts contemporary Britain. Those charged with the responsibility of confronting this crisis, who have profited so much from public anxieties over its consequences, are unlikely to abandon such a serviceable idea when there is more to be gained from its perpetuation. Kai Erikson once offered a timeless insight and we end by endorsing it:

> If the police should somehow learn to contain most of the crimes it now contends with . . . it is still improbable that the existing control machinery would go unused. More likely the agencies of control would turn their attention to other forms of behaviour, even to the point of defining as deviant certain styles of conduct which were not regarded so earlier.
>
> (1966: 27)

Chapter 2

Policing and urban unrest
Problem constitution and policy response

John Solomos and Tim Rackett

INTRODUCTION

The 1980s were an important period in the racialization of debates about law and order, crime and policing in British society. This was so in at least two ways. First, the politicization of the black youth unemployment issue helped to focus attention on the inter-relationship between 'race', unemployment, urban unrest and crime. Second, the riots during 1980–1 and 1985 forced the issues of 'black crime' and violence on the streets onto the main-stream political agenda. The widespread coverage given to the issue of 'race' in connection with the riots helped to open up a wider debate about issues such as 'mugging' and 'black crime'.

Civil disorder and unrest were recurring phenomena in many inner-city areas during the 1980s. In 1980, 1981 and 1985 major riots in Bristol, London, Liverpool and Birmingham commanded the headlines and became a key theme in policy debates about the future of the inner cities. It is also the case that in *each* year since 1980 there have been examples of serious street disorder. These outbreaks of disorder have presented a major challenge to the Conservative Government's image as the guardian of public order. More importantly, however, they have given added urgency to the long-running debate about the future of Britain's inner cities. The sight of violent confrontations on the streets of major cities helped to stimulate yet further the acrimonious political debate about how to regenerate depressed inner-city localities (Robson 1988).

This chapter explores the political and policy debates surrounding the major outbreaks of urban unrest during 1980–1 and 1985, and the ever-present threat of more violent disorder.

After providing a brief overview of the chronology of urban unrest during the 1980s, the chapter concentrates on two main themes. First, the political debates about the origins and causes of the unrest are assessed, and second, the impact of the unrest on the policy agenda is examined. This entails a review of the impact of the Scarman Report, and other important policy documents, on the agenda of both the government and other political institutions. Finally, the chapter concludes by providing some reflections about the prospects during the decade ahead.

THE POLITICS OF RACE AND POLICING

The 1970s witnessed a complex process by which sections of the black communities in Britain's inner-city areas, particularly young blacks, came to be seen as intimately involved in (a) particular forms of street crime and (b) confrontations with the police which represented a challenge to the maintenance of law and order (Solomos 1988). This process of racialization involved the construction of complex images of 'race' as a causal factor in the development of violence and disorder in British society. It also provided a clear example of the ways in which 'race' can easily become a symbol to which are attributed a variety of meanings.

A good example of this process occurred during the aftermath of the 1980–1 riots in Bristol, Brixton, Toxteth and elsewhere. In March 1982, the Metropolitan Police decided to release a racial breakdown of those responsible for street robberies, a statistical breakdown which it had not published previously, although it had been collating such statistics for some time (Scotland Yard, Press Release, 10 March 1982; *Guardian* 11 March 1982). The police statistics showed a marked rise in street robberies, but the crucial statistic which the press and the media picked on was concerned with the 'disproportionate involvement' of young blacks in street crimes such as 'mugging', purse snatching and robbery from stores. The press reaction to the press release varied from sober commentaries on the nature and limitations of the statistics, sensational headlines about 'black crime', to the *Sun's* 'The Yard blames black muggers'. But a common theme was the argument that the statistics, along with the riots during 1980–1, were further evidence of the consequences of letting in alien communities to settle in the very heart of Britain. The *Daily Telegraph* articulated this argument succinctly:

Over the 200 years up to 1945, Britain became so settled in
internal peace that many came to believe that respect for the
person and property of fellow citizens was something which
existed naturally in all but a few. A glance at less fortunate
countries might have reminded us that such respect scarcely
exists unless law is above the power of tribe, or money, or the
gun. But we did not look; we let in people from the countries
we did not look at, and only now do we begin to see the result.
Many young West Indians in Britain, and, by a connected
process, growing numbers of young whites, have no sense that
the nation in which they live is part of them. So its citizens
become to them mere objects of violent exploitation.

(11 March 1982)

Such an argument amounted to a direct link between 'race' and
'crime'. A similar tone was adopted by papers such as the *Daily
Mail* and the *Sun*, which went even further in their use of images
of 'mugging' – harking back to Enoch Powell's 1976 definition of
mugging as essentially a 'black crime'.

A year later the intervention of Harvey Proctor, the right-wing
Tory MP, helped to secure the release of similar figures by the
Home Office and led to a similar wave of articles in the press about
the 'rising wave' of crime in areas of black settlement. Since then
the Metropolitan Police have been much more reticent about
publishing such statistics, because of their potentially volatile
political impact.

Not surprisingly, however, the issue of the involvement of
young blacks in criminal or quasi-criminal activities remains a key
area of concern for the police and other institutions, both locally
and nationally. Because of this climate of official concern the
issues of 'crime' and 'violence' remain central to the full understanding of how contemporary ideologies about young blacks as a
social category were formed and how they are being transformed.

What is clear is that the successive shifts in political language
about the black youth question throughout the period since the
early 1970s have involved the issues of policing and 'black crime'
as a central theme. Whether in terms of specific concerns about
'mugging', 'street crime', or with more general concerns about the
development of specific subcultures, such as Rastafarianism, among
young blacks, the interplay between images of 'race' and 'crime'
has remained an important symbol in political language. Since the

late 1970s, and particularly after the 1980–1 riots, political debates about the 'black crime' issue have also been overdetermined by the phenomenon of urban unrest and civil disorder. But even within this context the issues of 'race, crime and the ghetto' remain the bedrock for the shifts in official ideologies and public debate about 'black youth'.

This also helps to explain the increasingly politicized nature of the response to black youth unemployment and violent urban unrest (Solomos 1988). The ideological construction of the involvement of young blacks in mugging and other forms of street crime provided the basis for the development of strategies of control aimed at keeping young blacks off the streets and keeping the police in control of particular localities which had become identified both in popular and official discourses as 'crime-prone' or potential 'trouble spots'. It also helped to bring to the forefront a preoccupation with the social and economic roots of alienation and criminal activity among young blacks. This was reflected in the debate about the impact of unemployment on young blacks, but it was also reflected in the increasing preoccupation of the police and other social control agencies with particular localities where relations between the police and sections of the black community were becoming tense and politicized.

This concern became apparent in the context of the responses of the police to the waves of urban unrest during the 1980s. The unrest raised important questions about the nature of policing and law and order in inner-city multi-racial areas, and it is to this issue that we now turn.

POLICING, LEGITIMACY AND URBAN UNREST

The first notable instance of urban unrest during the 1980s took place in the St Paul's district of Bristol on 2 April 1980. The immediate reaction to this event was one of shock and surprise, with public and media attention focusing particularly on the interplay between racial and social deprivation in the area (Joshua and Wallace 1983). A year later further serious violence occurred during the weekend of 10–12 April 1981 in the Brixton area of south London, which resulted in many injuries and widespread damage, and attracted enormous media attention.

Further disturbances took place in many parts of the country in

July 1981. On Friday 3 July a pitched battle occurred in Southall between hundreds of skinheads and local Asian people, and the police quickly became embroiled. On the same night in the Liverpool 8 district of Merseyside, an apparently minor incident sparked off rioting which lasted until Monday 6 July. The disorder in Liverpool 8 was particularly violent. For the first time ever in Britain, CS gas was fired at rioters by the police. Looting and arson was widespread, and the damage was estimated at some £10 million. On the night of 7–8 July 1981, disorder occurred in Moss Side, Manchester. During the following week disturbances were reported in places such as Handsworth in Birmingham, Sheffield, Nottingham, Hull, Slough, Leeds, Bradford, Leicester, Derby, High Wycombe and Cirencester.

Disorder again erupted in Brixton on 15 July 1981. At 2.00 a.m. 11 houses in Railton Road were raided by 176 police officers, with a further 391 held in reserve. The police had warrants to look for evidence of unlawful drinking and to search five houses for petrol bombs, although no evidence of either was found. During the operation the houses sustained very considerable damage – windows, sinks, toilets, floorboards, furniture, televisions and personal possessions were smashed. The resultant outcry led to an internal inquiry which exonerated those involved and stated that the police officers had been issued with sledgehammers and crowbars 'to effect speedy entry'. Compensation of £8,500 for structural damage, and further sums for damage to personal property, were paid by the Metropolitan Police. This raid, and the resultant violence on the streets of Brixton, convinced many people that the way policing is carried out is a vital factor in the context of urban unrest. An inquiry into the Railton Road raid by the Police Complaints Board discovered 'serious lapses from professional standards' and an 'institutional disregard for the niceties of the law' (Benyon and Solomos 1987).

Disorder was again evident in 1982 and in subsequent years, although on a reduced scale (Benyon and Solomos 1987). The attention of the news media was firmly focused on the Falklands, and so few accounts of disturbances in British cities were reported. It is clear, though, that urban unrest continued to occur in parts of London and Liverpool, and similar disorder seems to have taken place in 1983. The following year, the Metropolitan Police Commissioner, Sir Kenneth Newman, reported that during 1984 there were many mini-riots which had the potential to escalate to Brixton 1981 proportions and he added: 'London is nowadays a very volatile city.'

A MORI opinion poll in February 1985 reported that 64 per cent of those surveyed expected further riots to occur in British cities, and seven months later their fears were justified. In September and October 1985 serious urban unrest again became the focus of popular attention. The first eruption occurred on Monday 9 September 1985 in the Lozells Road area of Handsworth, Birmingham. The riot resulted in the deaths of two Asian men, Kassamali and Amirali Moledina, who suffered asphyxiation in their burning post office. One hundred and twenty-two other people, mainly police, were reported injured and the value of damaged property was put at £7.5 million. Further rioting occurred the next day when Douglas Hurd, the Home Secretary, visited the area. Other disturbances, widely regarded as 'copycat', were reported elsewhere in the West Midlands, for example in Moseley, Wolverhampton and Coventry, and in the St Paul's district of Bristol.

The Handsworth/Soho/Lozells area, with a population of 56,300, is regarded by Birmingham City Council as the most deprived district in the city. Unemployment is a major affliction, and at the time of the riots 36 per cent of the workforce in Handsworth was out of work, while the figure for people under twenty-four was 50 per cent. It is an area in which it was claimed that reasonably good relations existed between young blacks and police, as a result of the practice of community policing introduced in the late 1970s. However, at the end of 1981 a new superintendent instituted changes which included moving a number of the area's community police-officers to other duties and clamping down on the activities by local youths which had previously been tolerated.

These changes resulted in an increase in tension between youths and the police. In July 1985 two serious disturbances occurred in Handsworth, but both were played down and went unreported in the media. The context within which the eruption on 9 September occurred was thus one of deteriorating relations between young people, especially blacks, and the police, as well as one of widespread unemployment and social disadvantage. The tinder merely required a spark, which was provided when a black youth became involved in an altercation with an officer over a parking ticket. It was alleged that during the incident, at which more police arrived, a black woman was assaulted. Three hours later some forty-five buildings in Lozells Road were ablaze.

Brixton was the scene of the next outbreak of violent disorder, during the weekend of 28–9 September 1985. Seven hundred and twenty-four major crimes were reported, 43 members of the public and 10 police officers were injured, and 230 arrests were made. As in Handsworth, the event which led to the rioting involved police-officers and a black person. At 7.00 a.m. on 28 September armed police entered Mrs Cherry Groce's house in Normandy Road, Brixton, looking for her son. Two shots were fired by an officer, and a bullet damaged Mrs Groce's spine causing permanent paralysis. At 6.00 p.m. the local police-station was attacked with petrol bombs, and during the next eight hours large numbers of black and white people took part in burning and looting which caused damage estimated at £3 million. During the riot a freelance photographer sustained injuries from which he died three weeks later.

Two days after Mrs Groce was shot, rioting occurred in Liverpool 8. In this instance, the disturbances were precipitated when four black men were refused bail at Liverpool Magistrates' Court. During the summer there had been reports of rising tension in the area, and on 30 August a crowd demonstrated outside Toxteth police station and then attacked police-cars and the station itself. A number of assaults on police officers were also reported. As in Brixton and Handsworth, police relations with youths, and especially young black people, were a significant factor in the explosive mixture, and in Toxteth, too, the disorder was precipitated by an incident involving police-officers and black people.

The most serious of the disorders occurred at Broadwater Farm Estate, in Tottenham, London. The rioting began at about 7.00 p.m. on Sunday 6 October 1985, and during a night of extraordinary violence Police Constable Keith Blakelock was stabbed to death, 20 members of the public and 223 police-officers were injured and 47 cars and some buildings were burned. Guns were fired at the police, causing injuries to several officers and reporters, and the police deployed CS gas and plastic bullets, although these were not used.

As in Handsworth, Brixton and Toxteth, the context within which the disturbances occurred in Tottenham was one of deteriorating relations between the police and young people, especially blacks, and the trigger event involved police officers and black people (Gifford 1986). The chief superintendent for the area was a firm believer in community policing, and he put as his first priority the prevention of public disorder. However, it is clear that many of his police constables and sergeants did not agree with this approach. During the summer of 1985 there was evidence of increasing tension, and a prominent member of the Hornsey Police Federation was quoted as saying that rank-and-file officers 'desperately wanted to go in hard and sort out the criminals'. Some serious incidents occurred during this period on the Broadwater Farm Estate, such as an attack on police by youths which resulted in one officer sustaining a bad head wound, and there was also a series of attacks on an Asian-owned supermarket. Senior police officers appeared to play these incidents down, but black youths of the estate complained they were increasingly harassed by the police.

The incident which precipitated the riot began when police officers stopped a car driven by Floyd Jarrett, a 23-year-old black man well-known in the area. One of the officers decided to arrest Jarrett for suspected theft of the car, but after an altercation Jarrett was in fact charged with assaulting a police officer. On 13 December 1985 Jarrett was acquitted of this charge, and was awarded £350 costs against the police. While he was detained at the police-station a number of police officers used a key taken from the arrested man to enter his mother's home. During the police search of the house Mrs Cynthia Jarrett collapsed. The family alleged that her death was caused by a police officer who pushed her over; the police denied that this had occurred. On 4 December 1985 the inquest returned a verdict of accidental death. Mrs Jarrett was certified dead at 6.35 p.m. on Saturday 5 October, and news of the tragedy spread quickly around the estate during the evening. The next day, after sporadic incidents, violent disorder erupted at about 7.00 p.m.

Disorder occurred again in 1986. During the spring there were renewed reports of increasing tension in some areas. In Notting Hill, for example, there were allegations of assaults by the police, and the planting of drugs, while in Nottingham a number of forced entries into black people's homes and a series of street searches caused widespread anger. On the Broadwater Farm Estate virtually every black male under thirty was interrogated – over 350 people were arrested, although most were released without charge. In July 1986 the Metropolitan Police mounted a huge raid in Brixton, involving nearly 2,000 officers, aimed at selected premises in which cannabis offences were allegedly being committed.

In early September 1986 serious disorder occurred on the streets of the North Prospect Estate in the Devonport constituency of Plymouth. A large crowd of white youths set up burning barricades, and smashed windows, doors and fences on the estate. a few days later the Avon and Somerset Police organized a large raid in the St Paul's district of Bristol. Almost exactly one year after the Handsworth riots, 600 police moved into the area to search several premises in connection with drugs and drinking offences. The reaction was serious rioting and attacks on the police involving petrol bombs, bricks and stones.

THE POLICY IMPACT OF URBAN UNREST

Reactions to the riots have concentrated on a number of key variables that are said to characterize the localities in which the riots have occurred. Lord Scarman's report on the 1981 disorders highlighted the importance of unemployment, urban deprivation, racial disadvantage, relations between young blacks and the police, the decline of civic consent and political exclusion as the key issues. Other reactions have concentrated on the issue of the interplay between inner-city decay and racial disadvantage in contemporary Britain. Yet others have argued that the unrest can be seen as a symptom of the breakdown of law and order in British society (Gaffney 1987; Hall 1987; Keith 1987).

The main issues that were prominent in debates during 1980–1 were 'race' and 'law and order'. This was by no means an accident, since throughout the 1970s a powerful body of media, political and academic opinion had been constructed around the theme of how Britain was drifting into a 'violent society', and how the basis of consent was being shifted by the pressures of immigration and the growth of multi-racial inner-city areas.

A glimpse of the impact of the 1980–1 riots at this level can be achieved through two important debates in Parliament. The first took place in the midst of the July 1981 riots, and had as its theme: 'Civil Disturbances'. The tone of the debate was set by Home Secretary William Whitelaw's introductory statement in which he spoke of the need to (a) 'remove the scourge of criminal violence from our streets', and (b) the urgency of developing 'policies designed to promote the mutual tolerance and understanding upon which the whole future of a free democratic society depends' (*Hansard*, vol. 8, 16 July 1981: col. 1405). The 'scourge of criminal violence' was, Whitelaw argued, a danger to the whole framework of consent and legality on which the political institutions of British society were based. In reply Roy Hattersley, the Shadow Home Secretary, supported the call for the immediate suppression of street violence, but warned that the roots of such riots could not be dealt with until all people felt they had a stake in British society (ibid: cols. 1407–9).

The second debate took place on 26 November 1981, on the publication of the Scarman Report, and had as its theme: 'Law and Order'. The importance of the riots in pushing the law and order issue, and specifically policing, onto the main political agenda was emphasized by the Liberal leader, David Steel, who argued that 'urgent action' to prevent a drift into lawlessness was necessary from both a moral and political perspective (*Hansard*, vol. 13, 26 November 1981: cols. 1009–1). A subsequent debate on the same issue in March 1982 was also full of references to the experience of 1981, the impact of street violence, crime, decaying urban conditions, the breakdown of consent between the police and many local communities, and the spectre of 'more violence to come' if changes in both policing tactics and social policy were not swiftly introduced (*Hansard*, vol. 20, 25 March 1982: cols. 1107–81).

The need to support the police was accepted by both the Labour and Conservative speakers in the parliamentary debate on the riots, and was established as a benchmark for the official response to the riots long before the Scarman Report was published in November 1981. Any substantive disagreement centred around the issue of what role social deprivation and unemployment had in bringing young people to protest violently on the streets.

Intermingled with the discourses about race and law and order were constant references to unemployment, particularly among

the young, and various forms of social disadvantage and poverty
(Solomos 1988: 186–90). Throughout 1980 and 1981 debates
about the riots in the media, Parliament and in various official
reports hinged around the inter-relationship between racial, law
and order and social factors. The importance of this debate can be
explained, partly, by the political capital which the Opposition
could make from linking the social and economic malaise of the
country at large with violent street disturbances. Conversely,
throughout this period government ministers strenuously denied
that unemployment and social deprivation were significant causes
of urban unrest.

Although the Scarman Report is often taken to be the central
text which argues for a link between 'social conditions' and
'disorder', the terms of the debate were by no means set by
Scarman. During both April and July 1981 vigorous exchanges
took place in the press and in Parliament about the role that
deteriorating social conditions and unemployment may have
played in bringing about the riots. During the 16 July parliamentary debate on 'Civil Disturbances', Roy Hattersley's
formulation of this linkage provided a useful summary of the
'social conditions' argument. After some preliminary remarks
about the Labour Party's support for the police, he went on to
outline his opposition to the view of the riots as essentially
anti-police outbursts:

> I repeat that I do not believe that the principal cause of last
> week's riots was the conduct of the police. It was the conditions
> of deprivation and despair in the decaying areas of our old
> cities – areas in which the Brixton and Toxteth riots took place,
> and areas from which the skinhead invaders of Southall come.
> (*Hansard*, vol. 8, 16 July 1981: col. 1408)

Much of the subsequent controversy about this analysis centred on
the question of youth unemployment. Hattersley had suggested
that the riots were a 'direct product' of high levels of youth
unemployment, and a furious debate ensued in both Parliament
and the media about this assertion.

The final symbolic cue used to make sense of the 1980–1
protests is more difficult to categorize, but its basic meaning can
be captured by the term 'political marginality'. While a number of
discussions of the roots of urban unrest in the USA have noted the

salience of political marginality in determining participation in violent protests (Skolnick 1969; Fogelson 1971; Edelman 1971; Knopf 1975), this issue has received relatively little attention in Britain. Nevertheless, during the 1980–1 events and their aftermath the political context was discussed from a number of perspectives.

The Scarman Report, for example, located part of the explanation for the riots in the feelings of alienation and power-lessness which were experienced by young blacks living in depressed inner-city areas. A successful policy for tackling the roots of urban disorder was seen as one which sought to involve all the community in dealing with the problems of each area so that they could come to feel that they have a stake in its future (Scarman 1981: para 6.42).

Where such arguments did not fit in with the overarching themes of race, violence and disorder and social deprivation they were either sidelined or pushed into the sub-clauses of official reports. The Scarman Report, for example, contained the following policy proposal: 'I recommend that local communities must be fully and effectively involved in planning, in the provision of local services, and in the management and financing of specific projects' (Scarman 1981: para. 8.44). Such a move towards greater political integration was seen by Lord Scarman as essential if the gap between inner-city residents and the forces of law and order was to be bridged. But the concern with overcoming political marginality remained on the sidelines of the main public debate because it questioned the perception of the rioters as driven by irrational, uncivilized and criminal instincts. This did not, however, stop the question of political marginality and the need to reform existing policies from being raised at all, as can be seen subsequently by the attempts after 1981 to introduce measures both locally and nationally which were meant to address some of the grievances of the rioters and to ensure that further disturbances did not occur. Aspects of these measures are considered further on in the chapter.

POLICE RESPONSES

In the aftermath of the Scarman Report's publication police opinion was divided on the question of whether its proposals for reforming the police and the adoption of new methods of policing could be implemented, or whether such changes could insure against further violence and unrest. Sim (1982) has argued that the police were particularly worried by Scarman's recommend-ations that they should (a) tackle racial prejudice and harassment, (b) improve their methods of policing inner-city multi-racial areas and (c) develop new methods of managing urban disorder. He sees the police and sections of the media and right-wing parliamentarians as launching a counter-offensive to counteract criticisms of the police handling of the riots or their handling of the black community in general.

Certainly even before the publication of the Scarman Report the police and sections of the media were engaged in constructing a rather different explanation of the riots and of the participants in such events. From the very first confrontation in Bristol on 2 April 1980 the issue of race was a prime concern of the popular media. Under the headline 'Riot Mob Stone Police' the *Daily Mail* talked of 'mobs of black youths' roaming the streets (3 April 1980). This was a theme repeated in the coverage of the *Sun*, *Daily Star* and *Daily Express* during this period.

During both the Brixton riot of April 1981 and the nationwide riots of July 1981 the press was full of images, both pictorial and written, that emphasized that 'race' was somehow a central variable or even the main one. The strength of these images is particularly clear during July 1981 when headlines proclaimed the hatred that blacks had for the police, their alienation or detachment from the mainstream values of British society and the growth of racial tension in certain important localities. Among the early reports on the riots the *Daily Mail's* headline proclaimed simply: 'Black War on the Police' (6 July 1981). This was perhaps the most extreme, but the *Sun* was only marginally less direct when it talked of 'The Cities that Live in Fear', while the *Daily Mirror* proclaimed the words of Merseyside's Chief Constable, Kenneth Oxford, when it argued: 'This was not a race war. It was blacks versus the police.'

During July 1981 a number of accounts of the events focused on the issue of the family background of riot participants and the decline of 'firm parental control' over children. Kenneth Oxford made a number of statements which argued that the main responsibility for the riots lay with parents who either could not control their children or who did not care. The *Daily Telegraph* reported Mr Oxford as saying:

What in the name of goodness are these young people doing on the streets indulging in this behaviour and at that time of night? Is there no discipline that can be brought to bear on these young people? Are the parents not interested in the futures of these young people?

(8 July 1981)

According to this model the cause of the riots lay not in the conflict between young people and the police but in the failure of families to control the actions of their children. Such arguments were articulated with regularity throughout the period of the riots. Both the Prime Minister, Margaret Thatcher, and the Home Secretary, William Whitelaw, supported such arguments. *The Times* reported the Prime Minister as saying that if the parents could not control the actions of their children, what could the government do to stop them from engaging in 'hooliganism' and a 'spree of naked greed' (10 July 1981). At the same time the Home Secretary was reported as saying that the government was looking at plans to involve parents in 'the consequences of offences committed by their children' (*The Times*, 10 July 1981).

Such arguments were not necessarily linked to race, but, as we saw earlier, Lord Scarman himself partly explained the drift of black youngsters into crime and violence by reference to the weak family units of the West Indian communities. And during 1981 much media coverage was given to the supposed weakness of the West Indian family and the isolation of young blacks from both their families and society as a whole. Moreover, the history of political responses to black immigration is deeply infused with the notion that blacks were intrinsically a 'problem', either in social or cultural terms. Thus even when such arguments were not about 'race' *per se*, popular common sense helped to link the notion of 'weak family structure' to the West Indian communities; and it was a short step from this to explaining the riots as an outcome of pathological family structures.

Arguments around the question of the family were linked to other issues: e.g. the crisis of youth, the growth of violence in society generally, the phenomenon of 'youth hooliganism', the drift of young people into crime. Whether such images were based on factual evidence or not they succeeded in becoming part of the public debate about the 1980–1 riots and became even more important during 1985. By becoming part of public debate they helped to construct a model of the riots which saw them as the outcome of causes which were outside of the control of either the government or the police. They thus helped to deflect attention away from the 'broader social context' of Lord Scarman's report and towards specific social problems which undermined law and order.

WHAT KIND OF REFORM?

Despite widespread predictions of further unrest in the aftermath of 1981, the scale and the location of the 1985 riots seem to have surprised even some of the most astute commentators, Handsworth, for example, was presented even shortly before September 1985 as a 'success story' in terms of police–community relations. The outbreak of violence in this area was therefore widely presented as an aberration. Similarly the spread of violence in London to areas such as the Broadwater Farm Estate in Tottenham was seen as a break from previous experience, which had centred on areas such as Brixton.

There are many continuities between 1980–1 and 1985 in relation to the 'common-sense' images used in the press and television to cover the events. But responses in 1985 were different, at least in terms of degree, and probably in relation to the extent to which the riots were seen as a 'race' phenomenon by a wider body of opinion. The ambiguities and sub-clauses to be found in much of the press coverage during 1980–1 had at least acted as a countervailing tendency against the more extreme forms of discourse which blamed the riots completely on black people.

During the 1985 riots and their immediate aftermath, the imagery of 'race' was used by sections of the press without the sense of ambiguity which could still be found in 1980–1. The 'silence over race' was breached in 1980–1, but in 1985 debate about racial issues was taken a step further. Peregrine Worsthorne, for example, used the ferocity of the confrontations in Handsworth, Brixton and Tottenham to argue that there was a major question mark over the possibility of assimilating the 'coloured population' into mainstream 'British values' (*Sunday Telegraph*, 29 September 1985). To be sure, there was still a strong response opposing Enoch Powell's call for repatriation, from all shades of political opinion, but the racialization of public debate about the 1985 riots went much further than 1980–1.

In this context it was the externality of British Afro-Caribbeans and Asians which was highlighted rather than the racist institutions and processes which worked against blacks at all levels of society. The usage of 'race' during the September–October 1985 period took on new meanings, which had little if anything to do with the impact of racism as such, since the emphasis was on the cultural characteristics of the minority communities themselves. After Handsworth part of the press response was to blame the riot on rivalry between West Indians and Asians, and even after the arguments were criticized by local residents and community leaders they were used to 'explain' what happened. In addition, the questions of whether the cultures and values of the black communities, their family structures and their political attitudes 'bred violence' were constantly raised (van Dijk 1988).

The actual 'facts' of who was arrested during the riots, whether black or white, were hardly debated, since it was assumed that they were mostly black and mostly unemployed and involved with crime (Keith 1987). The imagery of the 'black bomber' used in Handsworth was extended to the notion that there were groups of alienated and criminalized young blacks who saw the riots as a chance to engage in an 'orgy of looting'. The Dear Report on Handsworth captures this image and links it to the social condition of young blacks:

> The majority of rioters who took part in these unhappy events were young, black and of Afro-Caribbean origin. Let there be no doubt, these young criminals are not in any way representative of the vast majority of the Afro-Caribbean community whose life has contributed to the life and culture of the West Midlands over many years and whose hopes and aspirations are at one with those of every other law-abiding citizen. We share a common sorrow. It is the duty of us all to ensure that an entire cultural group is not tainted by the actions of a criminal minority.
>
> (Dear 1985: 69)

This 'black' criminal minority was constructed not only into the leading force behind the riots, but sometimes as the *only* force. Indeed, throughout September and October 1985, and during the following months, the imagery of race continued to dominate debate both about the causes and the policy outcomes of the riots.

As pointed out earlier, the 'social causes' argument was another major plank of public debate about the 1980–1 riots, particularly in relation to the highly politicized issue of unemployment. During 1985 this issue was raised once again, though by then the extent of mass unemployment and urban de-industrialization and decay was more stark than it had been in 1981. Images of 'urban decay', 'tinderbox cities' and 'ghetto streets' linked up with the images of 'race inequality' and 'black ghettos' to produce an analysis more complex but contradictory.

An interesting mixture of the various images was provided by a story in the *Daily Telegraph* under the headline: 'Broadwater Farm: Like the Divis Flats with Reggae' (8 October 1985). The *Daily Mirror* described the estate as 'Living Hell', and quoted one resident as saying that 'You've no idea how awful daily life is' (8 October 1985). Such images were reworkings of arguments already used about Toxteth in 1981 and Brixton in 1981, but they were used more widely than in 1980–1. Even the *Daily Mail*, which deployed the clearest use of 'race' and 'outside agitator' type arguments, ran a major story on Broadwater Farm under the headline: 'Burnt-out hulks litter this concrete jungle. Despair hangs heavy' (8 October 1985). A number of stories using such imagery were run by both the quality and popular press during this period, but similar arguments are to be found in parliamentary debates (*Hansard*, vol. 84, 21 October 1985: cols. 30–46 and col. 388) and even in official reports produced by the police on the riots in Birmingham and London.

The 'cities of inner despair' were conceived as the breeding ground for disorderly protest, and however hard the government tried to break the causal link between the two it was forced to take on board the need to restore order not only through the police but through promises of help for the inner cities. Much as in 1980–1, the 'social causes' argument cannot be seen separately from the broader debate about the future of the British economy and society. The government's record on unemployment was a heavily politicized issue, and, just as in 1981, it vehemently denied any responsibility for the riots through its pursuit of free-market policies. But the government did find a way of accepting a link between the riots and social problems without bringing its main policies into the debate: namely by linking the growth of violent disorder to crime and drugs.

The emphasis on 'crime' and the 'criminal acts' of the rioters in the official responses to the 1985 riots took a general and a specific form. The general form relied on the argument that the riots were not a form of protest against the insufferable social conditions of inner-city areas or the actions of the police, but a 'criminal act' or a 'cry for loot'. This was an argument put most succinctly by Geoffrey Dear, Chief Constable for the West Midlands (Dear 1985) and by Douglas Hurd, the Home Secretary, in relation to Handsworth. But it recurred as a theme in official and press responses to the other riots. The specific form was built upon the notion that the outbreak of violence in Handsworth and Brixton, in particular, was brought about by 'drug barons' who saw the police attempting to curb their activities and control 'their territory'. Numerous examples of this line of argument can be found in Dear's report on Handsworth, and in press coverage during the riots.

Taking the specific argument about the role of drugs and 'drug barons' in stimulating the riots, this seems to have served two purposes. First, it distanced the riots from the social, economic, political and other grievances which had been linked to them, by locating the cause outside of the 'social problems' of inner-city dwellers and in the 'simple greed' of the drug barons to accumulate 'loot'. Second, just as Dear's image of a few hundred 'young black criminals' was used to explain what happened in Handsworth, the problem of drugs was used to explain what happened at a national level. The issue of drugs provided an everyday image, already a national issue through saturation media coverage and public debate, around which the police, the Home Office and other institutions could de-politicize the riots.

Responding to the Handsworth events, Douglas Hurd was moved to argue forcibly that such events were senseless and reflected more on those who participated in them than on the society in which they took place: 'The sound which law abiding people in Handsworth heard on Monday night, the echoes of which I picked up on Tuesday, was not a cry for help but a cry for loot' (*Financial Times*, 13 September 1985). The Chief Constable for the West Midlands, Geoffrey Dear, took this argument further by pointing out that the day before the riots a successful carnival had taken place, with the support of local community leaders. He drew the conclusion from this that the riot 'came like a bolt out of the blue' (*Guardian*, 21 November 1985). Such language focused attention on the individuals or groups who were 'breaking the law', 'committing criminal acts' and threatening the interests of the law-abiding 'majority'.

In terms of economic and social policies the impact of the 1980–1 riots was equally ambiguous and contradictory. Part of this ambiguity, as outlined above, resulted from the government's strenuous efforts to deny any link between its policies and the outbreak of violence and disorder. This denial was particularly important, since at the time the Thatcher administration was going through a bad period in terms of popular opinion on issues such as unemployment, social services and housing. While Lord Scarman was careful not to enter the political dispute between the government and the Labour Party on issues such as unemployment and housing, his call for more direct action to deal with these problems, along with racial disadvantage, posed a challenge to the political legitimacy of the policies which the government had followed from 1979 onwards. It also posed a delicate problem for the Home Secretary himself, since Lord Scarman had been appointed by him to carry out his inquiry. Having spent the whole summer denying any link between its policies and the riots, the government had to tread wearily in responding to the economic and social policy proposals of the Scarman Report when it was published in November 1981.

The parliamentary debate on the report showed the Home Secretary adopting a two-pronged strategy in his response. First, he accepted many of the recommendations of the report, particularly in relation to the role of the police. Additionally, he accepted the need to tackle racial disadvantage and other social issues. Second, he emphasized the government's view that, whatever broader measures were taken to deal with racial and social inequalities, the immediate priority was to restore and maintain order on the streets. When the Home Secretary talked of the need for the Government to give a lead in tackling racial disadvantage he therefore saw this as an issue for the longer term. On the other hand, he was much more specific about the reform of the police and the development of new tactics and equipment for the management of urban disorder (*Hansard*, vol. 14, 10 December 1981: cols. 1001–8).

In 1985, however, the government specifically rejected calls for another Scarman type inquiry, arguing that since the riots were a 'criminal enterprise' it was useless to search for social explanations or to have yet another report advising it about what to do. Implicitly the government was saying that it knew what the problems were, and how they could be tackled.

Some senior policemen, like Metropolitan Police Commissioner Sir Kenneth Newman, wanted to stress the link between the response of the police and other areas of 'social policy' (Metropolitan Police 1986). Within the context of this perspective it was necessary to develop complex forms of 'social policing' in which the actions of the police were linked to those of other agencies, such as social workers and youth workers.

The official government response, however, attempted to decontextualize the riots and see them as the actions of a small minority who were either criminalized or influenced by extreme political ideas. The dominant approach of the government attempted to emphasize two main arguments:

1 that the riots were 'a lust for blood', an 'orgy of thieving', 'a cry for loot and not a cry for help';
2 that the riots reflected not a failure to carry out the 'urgent programme of action' recommended by Lord Scarman in 1981, but were the outcome of a spiralling wave of crime and disorder in inner-city areas.

The logic of this approach, articulated by Home Secretary Douglas Hurd most clearly, was that the riots were both 'unjustifiable' and a 'criminal activity'. In a widely reported speech to police chiefs at the time of the disorders Hurd made this point clear:

Handsworth needs more jobs and better housing. But riots only destroy. They create nothing except a climate in which necessary development is even more difficult. Poor housing and other social ills provide no kind of reason for riot, arson and killing. One interviewer asked me whether the riot was not a cry for help by the rioters. The sound which law-abiding people heard at Handsworth was not a cry for help but a cry for loot. That is why the first priority, once public order is secure, must be a thorough and relentless investigation into the crimes which were committed.

(*Daily Telegraph*, 14 September 1985)

Such arguments resonated throughout the media and in the various parliamentary debates during September and October 1985. They become part of the symbolic political language through which the riots were understood by policy-makers and by popular opinion.

Since the 1985 unrest, and particularly after the 1987 general election, the government has announced a number of initiatives on the inner cities, and it has presented these as part of an effort to rejuvenate depressed areas on a sound basis. The evidence that has emerged since then, however, points to a major discrepancy between the government's promises of action and the allocation of resources to implement them (Robson 1988). It is perhaps too early to reach a conclusion on this point, but a repeat of the period of inaction between 1982 and 1985 seems to be evident, within the current political context. A number of local authorities have attempted to take more positive action to deal with the issues raised by the 1985 riots, but their experience has shown that such local initiatives are often severely limited by the actions of national government, the police and broader economic and political pressures.

In the years since 1981 the one consistent response to urban unrest has been the provision of more resources, more training and more equipment to the police. Instead of tackling the causes of urban unrest, the government has built up force to deal with the manifestation of those root conditions.

Increasingly the most strident political voices are raised in the name of free enterprise and law and order, not for equity and social justice. For the New Right and other influential sectors of political opinion the attempt to achieve racial equality through legal and political means is at best naïve political folly, and at worst a restriction on the workings of the market. The present political climate gives little cause for optimism that a radical change in governmental priorities in this field is likely (Solomos 1989).

The government's plan of *Action for Cities* (DoE 1988), issued after Mrs Thatcher's post-1987 election promise, says very little directly about racial inequality. It remains to be seen whether it will suffer the fate of numerous other initiatives on the inner cities and fade into obscurity. But one thing seems clear: during the past decade the government has been more intent on reducing the powers of local authorities than on providing for fundamental changes in the social conditions of the inner cities.

CONCLUSION

Finally, what of the prospects for the future? Certainly the experience of the past decade makes it difficult to be optimistic about the chances of a radical change in public policy in this field. As the predominant political ideas have shifted to the right, so the probability of the political action required at the national level to tackle the roots of racism and social disadvantage has diminished. The situation, however, is by no means static. The frequency of outbreaks of urban unrest during the 1980s indicates that the continued exclusion of black communities and other inner-city residents may result in the repudiation of political authority, manifest as civic indifference, as a refusal to comply with laws and directives or as open conflict and violence. While the excluded black and white citizens of urban areas seem set to continue to suffer deprivations and injustice, it cannot be assumed that they will do so in silence.

In recent years the Conservative administrations have proclaimed their intention of regenerating the inner cities, largely through free-market oriented programmes of action. Again there is little room for optimism that such strategies will substantially improve the position of the most deprived citizens of the inner cities. Unless radical action is taken, British cities seem poised to become yet more turbulent, brutalized and trouble-torn. The remedy of using tough policing is merely tackling the symptoms of the disorder, and is liable to exacerbate the underlying malaise.

What the outbreaks of urban unrest during the 1980s showed clearly is that political institutions have yet to address seriously the question of how to overcome the exclusion of large sections of the black population from equal citizenship and full political rights. Recent political developments do not show any indication that the present administration is prepared to make major initiatives in this area. Short of radical and imaginative reforms it is likely that during the 1990s there will be further outbreaks of violent urban unrest, and this will have major implications for the role of the police in British society.

ACKNOWLEDGEMENT

We are grateful to the Nuffield Foundation for providing a small grant which helped us to carry out the research on which this chapter is based. We are also grateful for helpful suggestions from John Benyon, Clive Harris and Michael Keith.

Chapter 3

White policing of black populations
A history of race and social control in America

Homer Hawkins and Richard Thomas

INTRODUCTION

For decades black leaders and their white allies lamented the problem of white police brutality against black citizens. Throughout the first few decades of the twentieth century it was common practice for white policemen to beat and even kill blacks with immunity. Local committees of the National Association for the Advancement of the Coloured People (NAACP) in numerous American cities were kept busy processing complaints from black citizens against white police brutality. In every major city where blacks lived in large enough numbers to be noticed and feared by whites, the white police-force was allowed and often encouraged to keep 'the niggers in their place'. In large cities the white police presence conveyed totally different racial meanings to the black and white communities. To the white community, white police in black communities provided the first line of defence against 'the black hordes'. To the black community, white policemen represented nothing less than a hostile occupation army. Young blacks, especially males, and not just those outside the law, grew up hating and distrusting the white police presence in their communities. While at the same time, many white males grew up dreaming of donning the blue uniform and going forth into black communities to test their mettle. In short, much of the white policing in black urban communities was little more than another form of white social control which had evolved over the centuries in response to whites' racial phobias of black people. White policing of urban blacks, therefore, has far deeper and wider implications than might appear on the surface. Rather, white policing of blacks in general has been a consistent pattern in the history of white racial dominance over blacks in America.

As we shall see, the whites who reduced Africans to slaves had set up policing systems to control them. Not even free blacks could escape the net of white policing fuelled by their ever-present fear of black rebellion. After slavery, white southerns felt a greater need for policing the emancipated blacks, since to their minds slavery itself had been the most effective means of controlling and civilizing a 'barbarous people'. As blacks made their way from southern plantations to southern and northern cities, they discovered that their mere presence triggered some subliminal urge in whites to police, watch and monitor them, to terrorize them into passivity and to keep them under control. And when racism and poverty reduced urban blacks to crime and pathology, and finally to urban rebellions in the 1960s, they found themselves once again surrounded by white police. The long history of white policing of blacks would not be seriously challenged – at least in most northern urban communities – until the emergence of black mayors and predominantly black city councils.

THE HISTORICAL ORIGINS AND DEVELOPMENT OF THE WHITE POLICING SYNDROME: THE ANTEBELLUM PERIOD

White racial dominance over blacks in America from the establishment of black slavery in the seventeenth century to the establishment and consolidation of black ghettos in the late nineteenth and throughout the twentieth centuries depended upon systems of white policing. Without such systems whites would have had a difficult time developing and maintaining their ideology of racial superiority. Notwithstanding their increasing relegation from indentured servitude to permanent chattel slavery buttressed by law and custom, the first Africans to be enslaved did not acquiesce in their enslavement. They ran away, set fire to towns and killed whites when necessary to gain their freedom (Aptheker 1943: 79–324). Not unlike other oppressed people throughout history, African slaves in America had to be systematically coerced to accept their abasement. And even then such coercion was never sufficient for maintaining the system of white racial dominance. In order for that system to function as smoothly as possible, the white élites had effectively to police the restive black populations under their control else they disrupt it by either overt or covert sabotage. Therefore, white policing of black populations became an integral component of each stage of white racial dominance of blacks. As we would expect, the stage of slavery necessitated the first system of white policing of black populations. As Europeans set up slave systems throughout the New World, they were forced to design appropriate legal safeguards to 'protect' these systems against black rebellions (Genovese 1979: 118–25; Aptheker 1943: 53–78, 79–324).

These legal safeguards became known as slave codes and black codes; they regulated the behaviour of black slaves in their relationship to the dominant white society. Based on both real and imaginary fears of black rebellions, white planters in England as early as 1667 succeeded in passing an act to regulate 'the Negroes on the British Plantations'. The act referred to the blacks as ' "of a wild, barbarous, and savage nature to be controlled only with strict severity"' (cited in Franklin 1974: 51). The slaves could not leave the plantation without a pass; they could not carry weapons; they could not under any circumstances be away from the plantation on Sundays. Slaves were severely whipped if they hit a Christian (white). If a slave repeated the offence, he, or she, was 'branded on the face with a hot iron' (Franklin 1974: 51). On the other hand, white masters who killed their slaves during 'moderate' correction were immune from legal prosecution (Jordan 1974: 60). Other European countries enacted their own slave codes more at less along the same lines, with the same aim: control blacks by any means necessary (Franklin, 1974: 63–4, 72–3, 76).

In order for these slave codes to be effective, they had to be policed and enforced by all segments of the white community. As early as 1686, a colonial act granted any white person the right to apprehend, chastise and order home any slave who was off his master's plantation without a pass. Four years later, whites could be fined forty shillings if they failed to arrest and chastise a slave for this offence (Henry 1968: 31). By 1755, all whites in the English colonies had the right, indeed the obligation by virtue of their membership in the dominant race, to assist in the policing of the black slave population. As Winthrop Jordan explains: 'All white persons were authorized to apprehend any Negro unable to give a satisfactory account of himself' (1974: 60). This socially-sanctioned granting of large-scale policing rights over blacks obviously reinforced the pathology of white racism as the meanest and most vile white found himself endowed with the power to exercise or abuse his power as he saw fit.

It is important to understand that this policing syndrome of the dominant white population had tremendous influence on future race relations, particularly in the South. As one scholar of the police control of slaves pointed out with some degree of personal bias: 'Almost from the very first the slave population presented the problem of police control that would suit the needs of the community and hold in check this irresponsible and often dangerous part of Southern society' (Henry 1968: 28). This perception of unpoliced blacks would become an obsession of whites for centuries.

The slave patrols constituted the most vital component of the policing of black slaves. Since all slaves had to have written permission to be off their master's plantation, patrols had the responsibility of checking passes to ascertain where the slave was going to or coming from. In 1784, South Carolina passed a law stating that the written pass had to have a destination and that if the slave was on a horse that too had to be stated. Passes also had to include how long the slave could be absent from the plantation. The general rule, therefore, was that no slave could be off his master's plantation without written permission, unless he was with some white person – even a child of ten – who could vouch for him (Henry 1968: 29). Without a system of written passes the slave patrols had little chance of effectively policing the slave population.

One could say, without hyperbole, that the effective policing of slave populations in the South was essential to the mental health of the white populations. As plantation slavery became a way of life and even the majority of slaves attempted to make the best of a very bad situation, plantation masters began allowing their slaves to visit and move about from plantation to plantation so that they could at least carry on some modicum of communal life. This easing of social control also contributed to masters' concerns about happy slaves and high productivity. However, it could lead to an increasing free movement of slaves, to the chagrin of many whites, and complicate the policing functions of the patrols, especially when the law condoned a general pass which allowed the slave free movement over long periods of time. Nervous whites began complaining about such lack of policing. In November 1848 one South Carolina newspaper published a complaint that vividly expressed the obsession of many whites concerning the proper policing of slaves:

> A 'general pass' (as it is called) to enable a slave to go at large, when and where he pleases, is an outrage on the community, illegal in itself and will no longer be recognized. With a proper and specific pass a slave is always safe.
>
> (Henry 1968: 30)

It is clear that by this period of America's inter-racial history, in the white mentality, at least in the South, concern for the necessity of effective policing of slave populations was well established. The free movements of slaves disrupted the white universe of peace and security and had to be policed at all times and in all places. Of course, this caused some inconvenience for those masters who allowed their slaves to go to town for plantation errands. However, the local police generally knew these slaves, who usually could run such plantation errands only during the day and could remain in town after nine only with a pass (Henry 1968: 30–1).

Policing the movements of slaves and free blacks in towns and villages complicated the machinery of white social control. If South Carolina was typical of other southern states facing this dilemma, it appeared that the problems stemmed from the logistics of co-ordinating the functions of rural slave patrols and 'urban' police. Whites feared free blacks in the towns because they suspected them of foul play and conspiracy among the slaves. While few slave patrol regulations applied to free blacks – at least in South Carolina – towns with large numbers of free blacks turned to curfew laws as a form of social control. Charleston had a long history of policing its blacks, both slave and free. As far back as 1744, the Charleston grand jury complained: 'We present as a grievance the great insolence of Negroes (sic) in Charles Town by gaming in the streets and caballing in great numbers through most parts of the Town, especially on the Sabbath day' (Henry 1968: 45). Several decades later, the grand jury echoed its complaint with a greater sense of urgency concerning the problems of effective policing of urban slaves:

> We present that the Negro [*sic*] law is not put into strict execution, and that the slaves of Charles are not under a good regulation, and that they at all times in the night go about the streets rioting, that they do often gather in great on the Sabbath day and make riots where it is not in the power of the small number of watchmen to suppress them, which may without any precaution prove the utmost consequences to this province.
>
> (Henry 1968: 45)

Although whites were prone to hysteria whenever they thought they were losing control and more often than not exaggerated the dangers associated with the free movements of blacks, such movements did pose problems of social control in urban communities. Free blacks in urban areas caused concern among whites throughout the South. In rural areas, the policing of free blacks did not complicate the traditional policing functions of the patrols, since most of them who lived and worked there were only a few notches above slaves, and indeed were still treated as slaves by their bosses. However, the structure, life and economic demands of the urban south differed dramatically from the plantation. Labour demands conflicted with the needs of controlling or effectively policing free blacks. Urban businessmen needed a more skilled and flexible black labour force that would not accept the harsh discipline and social controls so common on the plantations. The problem of effectively policing free blacks in southern cities forced some municipal officials to require various forms of registrations. For example, in 1837 Nashville officials required that all blacks who remained in the city for over forty-eight hours had to register with the mayor. Free blacks had to keep their papers with them at all times and be prepared to show them on demand. They also had to register each year. In 1861 officials in Montgomery ordered blacks to report every time they moved on/moved addresses (Berlin 1974: 318–19).

Much life the pass system for controlling plantation slaves, the registration system for controlling free blacks in urban areas of the South required effective policing. City officials regularly ordered the police to check papers of all free blacks entering the city for the first time. The Petersburg City Council ordered the master of police to make three-monthly checks on all newly-registered black freemen to review their 'good character'. Other cities routinely ordered their police to investigate black freemen who had not registered or did not have jobs. In 1838 the constable of Raleigh was required to check the entire city and its suburbs no less than two Sundays a month and search any suspect house as a preventive measure against strange blacks moving into town. Virtually all southern cities had restrictions on blacks holding night meetings, in addition to curfew laws (Curry 1981: 31).

Notwithstanding these mechanisms of social control, white officials in southern urban areas still had difficulty policing urban blacks (Berlin 1974: 317–20).

After the emancipation of the slaves in the North, whites there found themselves facing similar problems of how to control blacks. Northern cities did not have restive slave populations to control but they did seek to control the movements and activities of free blacks. In 1837 the mayor of Philadelphia issued an order declaring that: 'Every colored person found in the street after (the posting of) watch should be closely supervised by the officers of the night' (Curry 1981: 87). Reduced to poverty by institutional racism, many free blacks in northern cities found themselves struggling to survive in illegal or sub-legal underground economies which led to high arrest rates by white police-officers who tended to arrest blacks more often than they would a white person committing the same crime. It appears that, between 1800 and 1850, northern municipal officials devoted little attention to policing within the black ghetto with a mind towards preserving peace and order among blacks; black-on-black crime did not interest white police. But 'outside of the black residential area, or when in contact with the urban authorities at any location, free blacks could expect to be more frequently arrested than whites in any given set of circumstances' (Curry 1981: 119).

Throughout the antebellum period, controlling blacks by any means necessary occupied most white urbanites in cities where significant numbers of blacks worked and lived. Southern cities developed elaborate policing systems to control both slave and free blacks. After emancipation of northern slaves, northern cities, while not going as far as their southern counterparts, did police their black populations. After the Civil War, southern and northern urbanites worried about the ramifications of the emancipation of 4 million slaves. Many whites believed that slavery had been the most effective form of social control for blacks. Now that so many blacks were free how would white society police them? As thousands of former slaves flocked into the urban areas of the South and North, white municipal officials attempted to continue the pattern of racial dominance by using the police as the first line of defence against black freedom.

WHITE POLICE CONTROL OF NEWLY-URBANIZED BLACK POPULATIONS DURING THE POST-SLAVERY PERIOD

Several years after the emancipation of slaves, the race issue dominated much of the nation's political debate. Two months before the preliminary Emancipation Proclamation was issued in July 1862, the editor of the *Presbyterian Quarterly Review*, predicted that however the war turned out, 'the future condition of the colored race in this country will be the question over-mastering all others for years to come. It has already pushed itself into the foremost place' (Wood 1970: 1). As one racist Congressman of the time said, people 'have got nigger on the brain' (ibid. 2). Such whites preoccupation with race and the future place of freed blacks in a white America raised the age-old question of how to control blacks.

As former slaves moved into northern and southern cities, they found themselves relegated to the worst jobs and housing alongside the red-light districts teeming with crime and vice. As it has at all times and among all oppressed people, relentless poverty and racism broke the spirit of thousands of newly-freed blacks cramped up in hovels and alleys of southern and northern cities. Many fell prey to the hardships of urban life and drifted off into crime and vice. Others turned on themselves, fighting and killing as the only way to vent their frustrations. White urbanites, especially in southern cities, convincingly interpreted such black urban pathology as resulting from the innate character of black people. They blamed the increase in black crime and vice not on conditions that they had created and maintained for centuries but on the lack of control of blacks. In 1873 the Atlanta Constitution expressed the racial views of many white urbanites when it said: 'The truth is that the enfranchisement of the black has worked the enfranchisement of his vices and the liberation of his proclivity to crime' (Rabinowitz 1980: 44). The newspapers also blamed the Republicans and the carpet-baggers for encouraging black crime in the city (ibid.).

Following a long-established pattern of policing and arresting blacks in urban areas before the Civil War, white police-officers after the war, especially in southern cities, arrested blacks in far greater numbers than they did whites. Between 1865 and 1890, black arrests in Atlanta, Montgomery, Nashville, Raleigh and Richmond outnumbered white arrests. Contrary to popular racist beliefs common among southern white urbanites, the higher arrest rates stemmed in large part from law enforcement officials' policy of black control. As stated so well by Rabinowitz:

> the white community and its law enforcement officials were responsible for the great mass of Negro arrests. For them the basic necessity was control, for most whites were convinced that Negroes comprised a criminal class which jeopardized the peace and security of the city.
>
> (1980: 44)

During this period blacks were increasingly being arrested for serious crimes; however the majority of blacks were arrested for such misdemeanours as vagrancy, petty larceny and disorderly conduct. In Richmond, during this period, white police periodically arrested large groups of blacks on general warrants. This was both a method of social control as well as a means for generating extra income, since sergeants and captains of the police-force received fees as county constables. The disproportionately large number of black over white arrests in southern cities led to a higher percentage of black over white convictions and more severe sentences than those given to whites charged with the same crime (Rabinowitz 1980: 47).

As blacks continued to migrate in large numbers to southern and northern cities, police continued to arrest and jail them for the slightest infraction. But it soon became painfully obvious to those white urbanites most obsessed with controlling blacks in the cities that they were fighting a losing battle. By the last quarter of the nineteenth century southern blacks were beginning to trickle into northern cities. During the First World War that trickle swelled into a flood as northern industries opened their factories for the first time to large numbers of southern workers. Suddenly, northern cities found themselves faced with their own 'Negro Problem'. Sharing many of the anti-black racist beliefs of the South concerning the need to control blacks, many officials in northern cities began relying on their own police-force to control and contain the expanding black population.

INTIMIDATION, NON-PROTECTION AND BRUTALITY: ELEMENTS OF SOCIAL CONTROL IN WHITE POLICING OF BLACK POPULATION MOVEMENTS AND LARGE NORTHERN BLACK GHETTOS

As blacks continued to exercise their freedom of movement within the restrictions imposed upon them by white officials, the larger white population grew increasingly nervous. This nervousness was compounded by the increased conflict between white policemen and black slum-dwellers who resented the manner in which the former treated them. One observer in Cleveland during the pre-First World War years remarked that such conflicts had the potential to become inter-racial battlefields not only in Cleveland but in other cities as well (Gerber 1976: 47). The common police practice of arresting blacks for minor infractions such as vagrancy might well have been, as one scholar has suggested, 'conscious or unconscious desire of the police (as well as the courts) to show offensive blacks "their" place' (ibid.: 287). Lower-class blacks resented both the zeal with which white police were arresting them and the rate at which they were convicted and sentenced. Coming from very different cultural backgrounds and sharing a racial history of mistrust, white police and black slum-dwellers in the north had little in common.

One of the most vulnerable areas of conflict between the two groups centred around what Gerber (1976) described as 'their conflicting standards of public behavior', which often led to conflicts on the streets. For example, in 1907 in Cleveland white policemen tried to arrest a group of black men hanging out on the corner. Hanging out on street corners was very common among black males, but the white police considered this cultural practice 'loitering'. When they attempted the mass arrests, fighting broke out. This conflict over interpretations of appropriate public behaviour continued for years (Gerber 1976: 430). However, conflicts between police and blacks in northern cities increased as southern blacks began migrating north in large numbers.

During the First World War, large-scale migration of southern blacks created policing concerns among both southern and northern white élites and public officials. The southern white élites did not want to lose control of their cheap black labour supply and northern élites wanted the same cheap black labour but wanted if safely confined and policed. As thousands of black workers left the south for better-paying jobs in the north, southern officials began using local police-forces to prevent blacks from boarding northbound trains. In Greenville, Mississippi, blacks who had boarded trains were dragged off. In Meridian, Mississippi, the chief of police held up a train loaded with blacks going north on a technical charge. On one occasion in Savannah, one of the largest assembly areas for black migrants in the South, county and city officials combined their forces in an attempt to stop over 2,000 blacks from going north, but their efforts failed. On another occasion, the police were successful. They arrested over 100 blacks going north on bogus charges of loitering and sent them to the police barracks (Scott 1920: 74–8). Such efforts of southern white officials to use the police to control black populations revealed once again the racist mentality of the larger white society that they had the authority and right to control blacks against their wishes.

As we have already seen, northern white police shared this racist mentality. While southern white police attempted to control blacks by preventing them from leaving the South, northern white police attempted to control blacks once they arrived in the North. Most northern white policemen not only believed in the inferiority of blacks but also held the most popular belief that blacks were more criminally inclined by nature than whites. As thousands of southern blacks migrated to northern cities and, as the result of housing segregation, were forced to live in the worst areas in these cities, they encountered white policemen in the worst of all situations. One scholar surveying black housing patterns in northern cities in 1908 reported that 'the distinctively Negro neighbourhood is the same as, or next to, that district which seems, by consent of civil authorities, to be given up to vice' (Kusmer

1976: 49). Not only were blacks forced by housing segregation to live in these 'red-light' areas, they were also deprived of adequate police protection. This policy of non-protection, or minimum protection at best, constituted another form of white social control of blacks.

For decades, white officials in northern cities allowed vice and crime to go unpoliced in black neighbourhoods. This non-protection policy had the effect of controlling the development of the black community by undermining the stability of black family and community life. White stereotypes of blacks during the late nineteenth century portrayed them as having loose morals and inclined to crime. As Kusmer has pointed out, this association of blacks with 'vice amounted to a kind of self-fulfilling prophecy' (1976: 48). Well before southern blacks migrated north in large numbers, white police (condoned by city officials) had established a policy of allowing vice and crime to exist in or near black neighbourhoods more often than in white neighbourhoods. In fact, these mostly white police-forces in northern cities, as Kusmer points out, 'responding to the pressures of white public opinion, often refused to allow red-light districts to develop anywhere except in or near black neighbourhoods' (ibid.).

During the post-war period in Cleveland, white city officials show little interests in cleaning up the major vice and crime section in the black neighbourhood. Police also took their time answering calls in black areas, and when they did finally arrive to make an arrest or to check the area, they engaged in brutal treatment of black citizens. In 1917, one observer reported that since the influx of southern migrants, white police were quick to shoot and kill blacks for minor crime and not concerned about hitting black bystanders (Kusmer 1976: 178).

Blacks faced the same problems of police non-protection and police brutality in other cities as well. In Milwaukee according to Trotter: 'Afro-Americans were both over-policed (meaning police brutality) and underprotected in their lives and property' (1985: 118). Police 'singled out blacks for harsh treatment during the economic retrenchment of 1921–23 (and) arrested several Afro-Americans for vagrancy, who were placed on road work for the county and ordered out of the town at the end of their service' (ibid.). Over four decades later, predominantly white police-forces still 'overpolice and underprotect' black communities. Writing in the mid-1960s, black psychologist Kenneth Clark reported: 'The unstated and sometimes stated acceptance of crime and violence as normal for a ghetto community is associated with a lowering of police vigilance and efficiency when the victims are also lower-status people'. According to Clark, such acceptance 'is another example of the denial of a governmental service – the right of adequate protection – which is endured by the powerless ghetto' (1965: 86).

WHITE POLICE AND URBAN/RACIAL DISORDERS

Urban/racial disorders from the East St Louis riots in July 1917 to the several riots in Miami beginning in 1980 involved many white policemen engaging in both brutal treatment against blacks and supporting white mobs attacking, injuring and, in some cases, killing blacks. Urban disorders in black communities often presented white racist policemen with the excuse they needed to engage in legalized terrorism of urban blacks. Much as the slave patrols were given the responsibility of policing and controlling the slave community, many white policemen saw themselves as controlling 'niggers' in the ghettos.

The East St Louis riots occurred in July 1917. The basic cause of these stemmed from blacks being used as strike-breakers. There had been a series of strikes in the packing industry and in plants of the Aluminium Company of America (Grimshaw 1969: 111–12). In effect, what took place is that whites became incensed because they felt that blacks were going to take their jobs. This caused a city-wide white anger that was vented towards blacks in the city (ibid.). The role of the police in this riot was clear. Testimony of witnesses note that the police failed in their duty to stop the riot. In many cases they fled from the scene of violence. In other situations they actually left the police-station so that they would not be available. This meant that calls of help from blacks throughout the city would go unanswered. The few police-officers who remained on duty actually encouraged white mobs to lynch blacks (Johnson et al. 1918: 69). Fogelson, in reflecting upon the East St Louis riots, points out:

> Angered by employment of black immigrants as strike breakers, white mobs attacked blacks in downtown East St Louis. The rioters dragged their victims out of streetcars, stoning, clubbing, kicking, and afterwards shooting and

lynching them. They also burned houses and, with a deliberation which shocked reporters, shot black residents when they fled the flames. They killed them as they begged for mercy and even refused to allow them to brush away flies as they lay dying. The blacks disarmed by the police and militia after the earlier riot and defenseless in their wooden shanties, offered little resistance. And by the time the East St. Louis massacre was over, the rioters had murdered at least 39 black, wounded hundreds more, and in pursuit of their victims damaged hundreds of buildings and destroyed about a million dollars worth of property.

(1971: 8–9)

It seems that after this riot, blacks started to become more militant in their response to whites in riot situations. In September of 1917 in Houston, a riot took place when the men of 25th Infantry, after a riot with white citizens that left two blacks dead, ceased weapons and killed 27 whites (Upton 1984: 9). Brisbane, in focusing on this riot, notes that:

The troops, mostly Northerners, were avenging an incident which occurred earlier in the day, when a white policeman used force when arresting a Negro woman and then beat up a Negro soldier attempting to intervene. Even before these events, the Negro soldiers nursed a hatred for Houston policemen, who had attempted to enforce streetcar segregation.

(1979: 56–7)

Clearly the best known riot of this period occurred in Chicago in July 1919. Referred to as the 'red summer', this race riot was a culmination of a great deal of hostility held by both blacks and whites in the city of Chicago. The situation evolved into a riot when a few blacks decided that they would attempt to swim at the all-white beach. Whites started throwing stones at four black youths who had built a homemade raft and were innocently floating down the lake from 26th Street towards the white beach at 29th Street. A stone struck one of the boys who had climbed off of the raft and he drowned. His friends then went to the 29th Street Beach and pointed out to the white police-officer on duty the individual who had thrown the stone. The officer refused to arrest the man and would not allow his black colleague to do so. This led to a massive confrontation. Later that day white gangs began roaming the streets killing blacks. In turn, blacks also responded by joining together in large groups and confronting them (Tuttle 1970: 4–13).

The law enforcement during the Chicago riots was next to nonexistent. Many white police did not try to stop the violence and in many cases worked in collusion with white mobs killing blacks. State troops fraternized and laughed with law-breaking whites and in more than one situation were seen helping in the murder of blacks and the burning of their homes (Rudwick 1964: 41–57).

In examining the riots that occurred in the first twenty years of the twentieth century, white police seem to have allowed them to continue and did not try to protect blacks. The police often stood passively by and allowed blacks to be brutalized by white mobs. They appeared to be very concerned about the fact that blacks might have been armed and did all they could do to make sure that this did not occur.

The Harlem riot of 1935 occurred on 19 March. In essence the riot stemmed from five years of the depression which had had a telling effect on Harlem residents because of injustices of discrimination in employment, the aggressions of the police and racial segregation. The spontaneous outbreak that led to the riots stemmed from the rumour of the mistreatment of a black boy by white police. The boy was accused of stealing a knife in a store. The following day after the riot extra police stood guard on the corners in Harlem and mounted police rode through the streets. It was a basic show of white power and control. To the citizens of Harlem these police symbolized the answer of city authorities to their protests of the day before. What the police represented was a demonstration that property would not be destroyed and the destruction of white property was more important than any grievances that Harlem blacks might have (Mayor's Commission 1936: 1–3).

Detroit had two riots during the 1940s in which white police confronted blacks. In 1942 a mob of whites attempted to stop black tenants from moving into a new housing project. The police were called to the scene and began checking the cars of blacks. The white mob was never approached by the police nor were they disarmed by them. This incident set the climate for the one-sided kind of treatment that was taking place in Detroit at the time. In

June of the following year a riot broke out in which such differential treatment was exemplified: in dealing with white mobs the police used persuasion rather than firm action, but when dealing with blacks they used nightsticks, revolvers, riotguns, machine-guns and deer rifles. As a result of this unequal treatment, 25 of the 34 persons killed were black; of the latter, 17 were killed by police (Marshall 1943: 232–3). After the 1943 riot, Judge George Edwards, who became Commissioner of the Detroit Police Department from 1961 to 1963, told riot commission investigators that there was 'open warfare between the Detroit Negroes and the Detroit Police Department' (Kerner 1968: 85).

After the riots of 1943 there was relative calm until the 1960s. The Watts riot of 1965 ushered in a new era of rioting. As the Kerner Commission reported, white police officers played a key role in triggering this disturbance:

> On the evening of August 11, as Los Angeles sweltered in a heat wave, a highway patrolman halted a young Negro driver for speeding. The young man appeared intoxicated, and the patrolman arrested him. As a crowd gathered, law enforcement officers were called to the scene. A highway patrolman mistakenly struck a bystander with a billy-club. A young Negro women, who was accused of spitting on the policeman, was dragged into the middle of the street.
>
> When the police departed the crowd began hurling rocks at passing cars, beating white motorists, and overturning cars and setting them on fire.
>
> (Kerner 1968: 37–8)

Two years before the worst urban riot on American history in Detroit in 1967, Judge Edwards once again commented on the volatile nature of black community–white police relations:

> It is clear that in 1965 no one will make excuses for any city's inability to foresee the possibility of racial trouble.... Although local police forces generally regard themselves as public servants with the responsibility of maintaining law and order, they tend to minimize this attitude when they are patrolling areas that are heavily populated with Negro citizens. There, they tend to view each person on the streets as a potential criminal and enemy, and all too often that attitude is reciprocated. Indeed, hostility between the Negro communities

in our large cities and the police departments is the major problem in law enforcement in this decade. It has been a major cause of all recent race riots.

(Kerner 1968: 85)

A routine raid on a well-known 'blind pig' (after-hours establishment) triggered the 1967 Detroit riot. A black police-officer, who had gained entrance into the club, had established that there was sufficient evidence to make arrests. Twelve police-officers then made the raid. They had anticipated that approximately 35 people would be in the club, but, as it turned out, there were 82. This required additional police-cars. As they were making the arrests, approximately 200 black persons gathered at the scene. As the officers loaded the people into the police-cars, there was a great deal of hostility coming from the crowd. As the last prisoner was loaded, rocks and bottles were thrown at the police-cars. From that point the riot began. (Locke 1969: 26–7).

The Newark riot a month earlier also stemmed from a rather routine arrest. In essence, these riots were precipitated by events that were the outcome of many unresolved grievances – many involving blacks and white police.

The Detroit and Newark riots present some interesting data. These were the only major riots of the 1960s where systematic data are available on the exact circumstances of each death. What emerges from an examination of both of these riots is that the incidence of white police violence against black citizens, leading to civilian deaths, seemed to escalate as the disturbances continued. In addition, the police showed an increasing lack of organizational control. The continuation of the riot, however, did not necessarily entail an escalation in civilian violence towards the police. What this suggests is that in both cities the riot changed into a white police riot (Bergesen 1982: 261–74). These riots seemed to present a licence for police mayhem and a warlike environment where targets of opportunity were chosen and individuals were shot. There was an all-out effort to crush the rioters by any means necessary. A sense of lawlessness was evident on the part of the police; one which was an overreaction to events which seemed to be based on vengeance.

Relative calm prevailed in the 1970s and the next riot of real significance was in Miami in 1980. The precipitating incident in this riot revolved around an individual named Arthur McDuffie, a black insurance man, who was pursued by police as he rode his motorcycle. According to Porter and Dunn (1984: 33–4):

> After only slowing at a red light, according to police, he 'popped a wheelie', a stunt in which the cyclist pulls up his front wheel and takes off, then 'gave the finger' to the police car parked nearby and raced away. McDuffie was soon being pursued by more than a dozen police cars in a chase that lasted eight minutes and at some points exceeded a hundred miles per hour. He finally stopped at the corner of North Miami Avenue and 38th Street as police units swarmed in. The first units to arrive were those of Officers Mark Mier and Charles Veverka. ... Mier drew his service revolver, aimed it at McDuffie, and ordered him to freeze while Veverka approached McDuffie and grabbed him by the shoulder, pulling him off the motorcycle. ... McDuffie managed to fight back in the beginning as Veverka held him in a bearhug; but then he was pulled away from Veverka and was engaged in a milieu. And in three minutes, it was all over: McDuffie lay immobile, his head split open and his brain swelling uncontrollably. He died four days later.

The trial of the officers involved took place a few months later. On 17 May 1980, the officers who had been charged were acquitted. News of this spread and the riots began (Porter and Dunn 1984: 47).

The issue at hand was that the police had murdered a black man and had been acquitted. This inflamed the black community; in essence the verdict said that white police could kill blacks at will and get away with it.

A great deal of the hostility felt by blacks stemmed from the influx of Cubans and other Hispanics into Miami. These individuals were able to garner many of the service-oriented jobs that had been held by blacks. The massive economic expansion that took place in Miami did not include blacks. Unemployment was high for them, yet Cubans and other Hispanics were able to find jobs without any real difficulty. Essentially it was black exclusion from the economic renaissance that took place in Miami through the 1970s. It was within this framework that the riots took place.

In January 1989, Miami experienced another riot; this time it was sparked by the shooting of a fleeing black motorcyclist by a white Hispanic police-officer. This incident again symbolized the insensitivity of Miami's government – of which its police are an extension – towards the black community. Within such an environment, characterized by feelings of complete frustration and impotence on behalf of the black community, an act of police brutality had thus been able to precipitate yet another riot.

BLACK COMMUNITY PROTESTS AND RESPONSES TO WHITE POLICE RACIAL PRACTICES

Over the years the black community has responded in various ways to police brutality. It has always been vigilant and has always challenged the police when it felt that they had been heavy-handed or brutal in their treatment of blacks.

In Detroit in the 1940s the issue of white policemen and their treatment of blacks was a bone of contention. White policemen were not infrequently the source of many of the racial problems in Detroit during the post-war period. Operating much like foreign soldiers occupying colonies, they appeared to many as being concerned only with protecting the rights of the majority against the black minority. In the period between 1943 and 1953, police brutality became a symbol of everything that was wrong with Detroit. Relations were so bad between the black community and the police that during this period the NAACP, along with other groups, spent much of their time processing complaints against the police-department. The black community found itself using the courts to clarify the use of firearms by white policemen in apprehending persons suspected of crime. Unfortunately, the issue was never resolved and continues to the present day.

Much of the racism was the fault of the explicit racial policies, perhaps not on the books, but certainly perpetuated and reinforced by the social mores of the department. Black and white policemen did not walk beats together nor ride together in squad cars. Black policemen did not belong to the motorcycle squad, the arson squad, or the homicide squad. While the white policemen were assigned to black and white districts, black policemen were assigned to predominantly black districts to do a job with blacks. In 1953, out of a department of 4,220, only 101 were black. Out of that number there were four uniformed sergeants and one detective lieutenant.

Another response by the black community to police brutality

has been by PULSE, a group of black ministers organized to improve conditions for black Miami after the 1980 riots. This group has repeatedly accused the Miami police of brutality, as for example, in the following cases, cited by Dugger and Evans (1989:134):

> On July 8, 1988, Officers raided the home of a Baptist minister and his three children. On November 2 a young mother was held at gunpoint while her young children were rounded up. PULSE and the *Miami Times*, a black weekly, strongly denounced the police mistakes.

The actions of the NAACP in Detroit and PULSE in Miami are a few examples of black community protests against policies by the police department that are viewed as being racist and oppressive.

THE IMPACT OF BLACK POLITICAL POWER ON PREVIOUSLY WHITE-DOMINATED POLICE DEPARTMENTS

In a study by the National Urban League they note that black political representation among elected officials was unrelated to either total rates of citizens killed by police in major cities, or rates of blacks killed. The basis of their conclusions stem from an analysis of three different measures of black political power in 54 out of a total of 250,000 cities. Three of the measures were drawn from the Annual Report of the Joint Center for Political Studies on Black Elected Officials and the 1976 census of elected officials: one measure was whether the mayor was black; another was the percentage of city council members who were black; the third was the percentage of blacks in the local judiciary. The analysis by the Urban League showed that none of the measures had a statistically significant correlation with the number of citizens killed, but that the presence of a black mayor was the factor which most closely suggested a degree of correspondence. (Mendez 1983: 114).

Two very important examples of the election of a black mayor being followed by a dramatic reduction in the total number of civilian deaths occurred in the early 1970s in Atlanta and in Detroit which elected black mayors who had campaigned vigorously against police killings of citizens. With their election there was a hasty change that led to more restrictive policies in the area of the use of deadly force (Sherman 1983: 104–5). The Urban League study suggests that it is not only black mayors who were politically sensitive to racial disparities in citizens being killed by police; but as a result of the rising percentage of black voters in big cities, few mayors, no matter what their race, could ignore the issue. Also, this has been true among constitutionally weak mayors who have been successful in campaigning for more restrictive policies that have led to fewer police killings of citizens (Mendez 1983: 115).

Detroit's Mayor Young is a good example of a black mayor having considerable political impact. Detroit's Mayor Young came to office in 1974, partially on the promise to 'reform, reorganize and restrict the police' (Rich 1989: 208). The main target of his campaign was STRESS, a controversial police decoy and surveillance anti-crime programme with a bad reputation among blacks. Set up in 1971, STRESS engaged in close to 'four hundred warrant-less police raids' and killed twenty-two people (the majority of whom were black) during a thirty-month period in the early 1970s. The killings earned Detroit's police-forces the reputation of having 'the highest number of civilian killings per capital of any American police force' (Rich 1989: 208). Three months after Young took office, he disbanded STRESS and began his programme of reforming one of the most racist police departments in the country.

Although Mayor Young had attempted to allay the fears of many whites that if elected he would be soft on crime, those whites who had come to view the predominantly white police department as simply a way to control blacks still feared that a black mayor would turn the police into a black enclave. Not even Young's inauguration speech, in which he told criminals to leave town, was sufficient to quieten the fears of most whites (Rich 1989: 210). However, Mayor Young could not allow white fears to hinder his programme to carry out drastic reforms of the predominantly white police department which had a long history of 'unprotecting and overpolicing' blacks.

Among his most important reform, which radically transformed the historical relationship between the Detroit police department and the black community, were: the aggressive recruitment of black officers, involving such campaigns as having scouts 'cruising the city's black neighborhoods, signing up potential applicants, and encouraging word-to-mouth advertisement', assisted by the Chrysler Corporation, which contributed several vans 'to assist in the police department's Outreach programs'; the setting up of police recruitment offices in inner-city areas 'to encourage inner city youths to consider police work as a career, and to demonstrate its serious intent, the department was coming to them asking for help'; the changing of entrance and promotional exams to reflect less cultural bias; the enforcement of the residency rules – which many police were violating to avoid living in the city; the parallel promotion of black and white police; the appointment of a black police chief; and the appointment of a new board of police commissioners (Rich 1989: 210–11). Of all of these reforms, the Mayor's affirmative action programmes provoked the most conflicts as many white male policemen saw their traditional roles challenged (Rich 1989: 213).

Predictably, the predominantly white police department reacted bitterly to the 'short leash' placed on them by the black mayor. Acting through their union, the Detroit Police Officers' Association (DPOA), white police used various methods to counter Mayor Young's reforms, but to little avail. By 1987 Mayor Young had changed the racial make-up of the police department from one which was only 19 per cent black in 1974, to one which was 47 per cent black (Detroit Police Department 1987). In the process, he demonstrated how black political power could radically change a white-dominated and largely racist police department.

ACKNOWLEDGEMENT

The authors would like to thank Mary Breslin, Fran Fowler, Wen-Hsiung Hsieh, Njeru Murage and Kyungshik Shim for their assistance.

Chapter 4

Black Cops Inc.

Ellis Cashmore

POWER OF PERSUASION

No-one will ever know what thoughts were going through the mind of the arresting officer as he apprehended a 21-year-old black youth who had driven through a red stop light in Los Angeles on the evening of 11 August 1965. Almost certainly, his intention was not to set in motion a sequence of events that was to stretch across subsequent decades. What began as a routine action for a traffic violation spiralled quickly as a gathering crowd witnessed the taking-away of not only the youth, but his mother, brother, an onlooking female who spat at the police-officer and an animated male who, it was alleged, urged the crowd to violence. Half-truths combined with suspicions and rage against the police spread through the district of Watts. Bigger crowds congregated after the circulation of a story that the woman who had spat at the police was pregnant and was being mistreated. The south Los Angeles area contains the largest concentration of Afro-Americans in the city. Its residents were moved to action specifically by the police's action, but also by an accumulation of experience in encounters with the police in the slum environment of south Los Angeles. They rose up and, for the six days till 17 August, the whole area was engulfed in a transforming urban drama that was to become a central symbol in the landscape of American post-war race relations. The events became known as the Watts riot and their motif was 'burn, baby burn.'

In late 1989, another important symbol emerged, this time an individual. Lee P. Brown was a black police-officer appointed to arguably the most influential position in the US police-service, Commissioner of the New York Police Department (NYPD). The department is the nation's largest with over 26,000 uniformed officers. Brown actually inherited the position from another black officer, Benjamin Ward, which made his appointment all-the-more relevant, establishing continuity in the presence of black officers at the fore of the police-service. Brown had previously held positions in Atlanta and Houston, the latter having a 61 per cent white population and a reputation for being a 'redneck' city. Brown's approach was in sharp contrast to the more typically Texan 'kick ass' methods previously favoured by his department. His promotion to head of the NYPD attested to his success or, more accurately, to the public recognition of it.

The two events were separated by almost twenty-five years, yet were connected as if by a historical chain. Linking them were events and episodes which transfigured policing in America, giving the appearance of liberal enlightenment, but perhaps disguising the forces of conservatism that underlay them. The Watts riot served notice of the deep resentment in US ghettos: it precipitated a great, violent upheaval that affected the whole country. Between 1965 and 1968, virtually every big city experienced civil unrest. Detroit and Newark had particularly large-scale disturbances in 1967; both cities housed sizeable black populations. Detroit's disturbances came after a series of tense episodes concerning blacks and an aggressively racist police-force that had resorted to violence too frequently. Newark's black population had also felt the brunt of physical policing up to 1967. Eruptions in these and other cities led directly to changes in police-departments throughout the country.

Uprisings inspired by the effects of racism have quite a tradition in the USA. In the early 1900s, whites initiated attacks on blacks and their meagre property, often because of alleged threats, either to white women or white-controlled jobs. Working-class marauders often invaded black areas, prompting counter-attacks. In a notable incident in 1919, a young black was drowned by whites who had seen him enter 'their' side of a Chicago river. This provided the trigger for prolonged violence in the city. But the Watts episode signalled a distinct break from earlier patterns, in the sense that whites, while instrumental, did not actually initiate collective action. The Watts incident, as elsewhere, was sparked by an encounter featuring white law enforcement officers and black citizens. Blacks then responded to what they regarded as provocation by police. The following contagion ensured that all locals were involved in some way in the action, which was typically spread over four or five days and centred on the destruction of property rather than persons. Police-officers, National Guardsmen and other representatives of state departments were called in to confront the disturbances and many were hurt; though the majority of casualties in all the riots were black civilians.

The unrest of 1965–8 served to focus national attention on two related matters. First was the changing mood of American's black population. Legislation in 1964 and 1965 provided legal protection against outright racial discrimination and guaranteed blacks the right to vote regardless of literacy or any other potentially discriminatory criteria. But expectation of material improvements were rising faster than actual changes and frustrations built. The second matter was white racism, specifically as expressed by police-departments. The police who deal daily with disaffected and, largely, powerless groups were – and probably still are – in the business of control. In the 1960s, this was more obviously so. Robert Blauner, in his 1972 essay *Racial Oppression in America*, argued that a political policy of 'internal colonialism' was being employed, with the police being used to enforce 'the culturally repressive aspects of middle-class American values against the distinctive ethnic orientation of Afro-American and other minority subcultures' (1972: 98). The argument runs that tendencies in the ghettos had been directed at gaining ownership and control of businesses, social services, schools, the police and other 'institutions that exist within or impinge upon their [blacks'] community' (1972: 95). The role of law-enforcement agencies, especially the police, was crucial in repressing those tendencies. As Blauner wrote:

> Police are lay agents in the power equation, they do the dirty work for the larger system by restricting the striking back of black rebels to skirmishes inside the ghetto, thus deflecting energies and attacks from the communities and institutions of the larger power structure.
>
> (1972: 99)

He believed that the uprisings 'dramatized the role of law and the issue of police brutality'. Blauner was careful to point out that it was not a straightforward case of rage being vented at white police-officers. 'Negro police and "responsible" moderate leaders also were objects of the crowd's anger' (1972: 209). The entire institution of law enforcement was under attack; not the personnel who staffed it. Blacks were dramatically assaulting the very basis of law, order and authority and questioning whether it served their best interests. And this fact seemed lost on the Kerner Commission, which later submitted a report on the upheaval based on the testimonies of a team of researchers. The report singled out the police from all of society's 'serving institutions' as the object of most hostility. It recognized that 'beliefs' about physical abuse and outright brutality were influential factors in motivating blacks to rise up; yet without acknowledging an objective rational basis for the beliefs. The research of Kerner *et al.* exposed to a wide readership a 'deep and longstanding schism' between a 'substantial portion' of the Afro-American population and the police (1968). But the report drew short of concluding that any problem of authority existed between many blacks and the police as an institution – as opposed to individual officers. Absent from the report was any disclosure of a total rejection of the rule of law. 'Our society is held together by respect for law', it announced in a memorable, indicative statement of its political position. 'If police authority is destroyed, if their effectiveness is impaired . . . all of society will suffer.' This line of thinking excluded the possibility that, for many blacks, the entire police institution symbolized the controlling forces that maintained their entrapment in ghettos where deprivations seemed self-perpetuating.

The report never faced what Blauner (1972) saw as one of the crucial questions: 'Why poor blacks come to believe that law and authority are not their law and their authority.' This was an influential omission, one which affected the tenor and substance of the commission's recommendations, which were, in turn, responsible for fresh, major developments in American policing. The omission may have been the result of researchers' failing, or maybe a reluctance to expose raw problems that had no clear solution. But the outcome was to create confusion over why battles on the streets of Los Angeles and Newark were being fought in the first place. Instead of producing a conclusion with moral resonances that would span 350 years of black subservience in the Americas, the report suggested that immediate circumstances would be invoked to answer the central question. Widespread unemployment, poor housing, police harassment, or criminal lawlessness: these were cited as underlying conditions for the uprising. They helped make the burning, looting, sniping and fighting understandable; but not rational. They also had solutions, in the long term, at least. Most of the actions that followed were aimed at achieving such solutions. If not, the Kerner Report concluded, there would be more upheaval. 'It warned of potential catastrophe if the nation did not commit more resources to solving the problem of the urban ghettos', wrote William Helmreich (1983: 19–20). Resources had to be directed specifically at the deteriorating inner cities that had been the scenes of violence, much of it perhaps initiated by the police, whose alleged oppression drew calamitous responses.

Public-sector agencies were given a priority: prevent more violence in the ghettos. We might add that the unwritten priority was specifically to prevent *the spread* of violence from the ghetto outwards. The way in which this was to be tackled, according to Kerner *et al.*, was by democratizing the police-force. Further disruption could be avoided, it was thought, by eliminating the possible source of conflict in the inner cities. 'Democratizing' may not be the apposite verb here, for the report dismissed calls for independent review boards and approved of strengthening the authority of existing Boards of Police Commissioners. The new position of Inspector General was advocated; incumbents were to be responsible for investigating civilian complaints. The persons occupying the position were to be answerable not to civilian boards, but to the Chief of Police. While this was supposed to increase police accountability, especially in areas where accusations of police brutality were commonplace, it did not directly address the problem of police–black relations. To this end, the report strongly recommended the creation of community liaison programmes. In other words, police-departments were urged to undertake an internal evaluation: take stock of their own condition and make the necessary adjustments. Any attempt to fix external points of reference for review or complaints procedures was seen as inimical to the 'effectiveness' of law enforcement.

All of these suggestions indicated the Kerner Report's acceptance that police relations with the community were ragged and in need of repair: the issue of the legitimacy of the police as an institution was not addressed. And this led to one further, important recommendation: that police-departments include in their remit the effort to attract more black recruits. Ostensibly, the reason for this was that black youths showed neither desire nor inclination to join the police-force, probably because they saw it as an oppressive institution. They might have had a point, the report concluded; so, if white police were too heavy-handed in the ghettos, maybe black officers could do a better job. Add to this the possibility that white officers would learn some sensitivity from black peers and it seemed a recipe for improved police-black relations.

One immediate option for curbing the uprisings was to use more force. The National Guard had already been called into action and further military control would have achieved a solution of sorts. South African white rulers illustrated after the Soweto riots of 1976 that military force can be effective in suppressing discontent for long periods. But force still comes a poor second to persuasion. Kerner's vision was of a society held together, as he put it, 'by respect for law', but one which might be too slow to realize that respect had to be earned. The liberal argument of the report suggested that blacks had most definitely been short-changed, but had not yet lost confidence in the ability of American institutions genuinely to represent their interests. The Kerner proposals were informed by this; they were aimed at restoring confidence in the social order.

The explicit urging to police-departments to hire and promote more blacks was sound tactical advice. It sanctioned a process of channelling black economic and political activity into existing institutions, most specifically the police, rather than allowing blacks to remain on the outside where they *might eventually* pose a threat to the established order. Implicit in the proposal was the idea that this would effect a change in black working-class ghetto culture from radical, oppositional values based on Afro-consciousness to an acceptance of the dominant, mainstream values of white society. Basic ethnic inequalities would remain, of course, but the illusion of mobility and change would be created. A particularly cynical interpretation of this process would hold that blacks would be attracted into the institutions, then promoted into positions of authority and influence, whereupon their actions would be tantamount to a betrayal. Their loyalties to fellow blacks would be placed under stress and they might act in the interests of the groups they now represented. Slightly more benign perspectives would see it in terms of a co-optation: simply making 'insiders' out of 'outsiders' by electing them to key posts and situating them in environments in which they might absorb the values, ideals, attitudes and objectives of the white middle class.

However one chooses to view the process, the result is basically one of political incorporation and its precondition is the development of an effective 'democratic' pacification in the police-force. Democratizing the police, at least in Kerner's limited sense, was essential to the persuasion he sought: convincing the whole black population of the moral nature of American society. Demonstrating that the racial inequality that persisted long after slavery was a legitimate inequality became a priority. It existed because people *are* unequal, not because blacks have restricted opportunities. Bringing them into the police-force was a perfect way of showing this. Extending participation in the prime agency of law enforcement reminded the whole population that the USA sought commitment to equal opportunities. But it also had the advantage of co-opting significant sections of the black working class – and, later, middle class – into an institution of social control.

ONE FOOT IN THE GHETTO

Many US police departments had what were called 'Negro police-forces' in the 1940s. Black officers were given separate offices to work in, they rode bicycles or walked instead of driving cars and they patrolled only black neighbourhoods. New York City employed Afro-Americans and assigned them specifically to areas such as Harlem, according to Stephen Leinen in his study *Black Police, White Society* (1984: 109–10). The NYPD was slow to abandon this long-standing practice. But, urged on by liberal mayor, John Lindsay, and a favourable fiscal situation, it spent almost $3 million on a recruiting drive targeted at blacks and Hispanics in the mid-1960s. Existing ethnic-minority officers visited college campuses and community centres; advertisements were placed in ethnic minority news media and potential candidates were provided with pre-training for entrance examinations. In 1966, the NYPD instituted a Candidate Review Board to review the case of every rejected applicant. Candidates who had been turned down for 'poor character' or accent, or because of 'cultural factors', were invited to re-apply. The recognition was that interviewers' ethocentric biases may well have distorted the process of recruitment and led to the discarding of potentially sound applicants from ethnic-minority backgrounds. Other police-departments around the country adopted similar procedures designed to minimize the effect of biasing influences in recruitment. One especially caused a stir: NYPD, in 1973, lowered its minimum height requirement to accommodate Hispanic recruits, whose average height tended to be too short by NYPD standards. (Interestingly, in 1989, London's Metropolitan Police Force did exactly the same thing to draw in more South Asian officers.) Another strategy was to divert candidates from the city's Housing and Transit Authority (HTA) police-department to the NYPD: traditionally, HTA attracted more ethnic minorities. Between 1965 and 1973, the number of black and Hispanic NYPD officers doubled to 3,000 plus.

Internal changes resembling these occurred in most US cities. Some struggled with embarrassingly low under-representations of black officers in forces serving genuinely multi-ethnic cities. Newark's black population, for example, amounted to 34 per cent in 1960; yet blacks made up only 7 per cent of its police force. Houston's force was almost 80 per cent white, despite the city as a whole being 61 per cent white: blacks were 28 per cent of the population, less than one per cent of the force. Oakland, from where the Black Panthers originated in the 1960s, saw a virtual exodus due to 'white flight' in the 1970s: this resulted in a 46 per cent black population by 1980. The appointment of Police Chief Charles R. Gain in 1967 was supposed to herald a new dawn in policing, but, in terms of recruitment, his impact was minimal and the force remained over 85 per cent white. In these and other cities where black representation on the force was stubbornly low, purely internal shifts in policy were not enough to boost recruitment. Federal intervention was needed to create something approaching proportional representation.

Rather than let police-departments stumble towards goals, federal courts imposed quotas, actually requiring individual departments to hire black or Hispanic officers. In 1972, for instance, a Cleveland district court judge stipulated that a minimum of 18 per cent of all police recruits in the city had to be black. The Alabama state troopers had not hired a single black officer in the thirty-seven years up till 1972 when a federal court instructed them to employ blacks and whites in equal numbers until blacks represented 25 per cent of the force. A similar ordinance in Philadelphia required the police-department's hiring of at least one black officer to every two whites. Chicago's police-department was directed by court order to introduce a quota system designed to increase black officers to 27 per cent. In 1979 San Francisco was told to bring its level of ethnic-minority recruits up to 50 per cent. Los Angeles, scene of the 1965 uprising, was ordered to reframe its police hiring policies in such a way as to reflect accurately the surrounding population, which comprises about 40 per cent blacks and Hispanics.

Detroit, another city ravaged in the mid-1960s, was at first ordered to make sure that its police-officers lived within the city limits, thus putting indirect pressure on the police-department to employ blacks, as many blacks live in the city and many whites commute to work from outside. The policy was resisted by white officers who preferred living far away from their work. So, in 1975, direct pressure came to bear in the form of a federal court decision which stipulated a quota of 80 per cent of every intake for blacks and women. White males, for long the sole guardians of law enforcement in Detroit, were to constitute just 20 per cent of the total force. Again, the decision was resented. It was fought all the way to the Supreme Court, which, in 1983, declared it unconstitutional. The declaration was made during Ronald Reagan's first term of office as president, when quota systems of all kinds, in housing as well as employment, were under attack. Other cities avoided bitter court wranglings by voluntarily opting for affirmative action programmes or their functional equivalents. These included Tampa, Seattle, Sacramento, Syracuse, Cincinnati, Fort Lauderdale and Ohio State. Virtually every major city engaged in some kind of drive to build up its ethnic-minority personnel profile. Those which did not were vulnerable to the power of the Equal Employment Opportunity Commission (EEOC), which was established in 1972, and charged with the responsibility for investigating discriminatory employment practices and, later, in enforcing compliance with delegated quota systems. NYPD created its own unit for monitoring hiring patterns and reacting to complaints of discrimination.

As the black presence in city police-departments grew, the new officers began to see commonness in their experience. Often despised by their peers for 'selling out', yet frequently spurned by racist colleagues, they shared a peculiar and uncomfortable position, having one foot in the precinct and the other straggling in the ghetto. To defend and advance their interests as police-officers, specifically as black officers, they developed organizations to defend and advance their unique interests. It was not long before reports of outright racial discrimination by white officers began to appear. But, perhaps more significantly, institutional racism in the police-departments became evident. For example, in Bridgeport, Connecticut, a black police group called the Bridgeport Guardians successfully opposed the department's entrance examinations, which, they argued, were structured in such a way as to disadvantage ethnic minorities. Inspired by this, Chicago's Afro-American Patrolman's League, in 1971, challenged not only the police-department's examinations, but its policy of taking 'background' factors, such as family and neighbourhood, into consideration when conducting its selection. The examination was changed and the policy dropped. The Guardians Association engaged in a prolonged legal battle with the NYPD, which, as we have seen, tried to ward off federal imposition by introducing its own affirmative action policy and equal opportunities monitoring agency. But its entrance tests, according to the Guardians, were culturally biased and irrelevant to on-the-job performance. The department fought the action, but, in 1980, were ordered by Federal judge Robert Carter to refrain from using the examinations, which, it was contended, were 'deliberately' discriminatory against minorities. The Guardians Association grew into a influential group in the 1970s, litigating against various police-departments which used entrance examinations or arbitrary qualifications that worked against the admission of blacks and Hispanics. Predictably, whites grumbled that the Guardian Association's pressure would result ultimately in declining standards. But the political climate favoured precisely the kind of reform sought by the Guardians and their colleagues and federal courts typically backed them. The entire ideology of policing was changing and adjustments were made not merely to accommodate more blacks, but to use them as 'effectively' as possible in law enforcement.

INVISIBLE MEN?

A transition from crime control to community service accompanied the active recruitment of black officers. Even prior to the Kerner Report, it was commonly accepted that cleavages between blacks and police were wider and deeper than ever; conflict was occurring sporadically in several cities before Watts set the contagion in motion. One way to put a stopper on this would have been to re-tool police-departments, creating forces along the lines of Denver: heavily-armed and equipped with riot-gear, including visored helmets, for daily duty. This would have been a costly option and probably effective only in the short term, anyway. Employing greater numbers of black police-officers was less expensive, especially as supplementary funds were available for training from the Law Enforcement Education Program (LEEP), which arose from the Kerner recommendations. John Cooper, in his book *The Police and the Ghetto*, recorded that, in the 'holding action': 'Blacks were not to be the catching crooks type of policemen in the traditional American sense of the rugged individualist' (1980: 120). Theirs was a much softer role: 'They were being included to be community relations personnel. They were being used to make police officers more acceptable in the black community' (1980: 120). Blacks in uniform patrolling the ghettos would be a welcome, if unfamiliar, sight, it was reasoned; less obtrusive than whites, whose reputation for violent approaches made 'policing by consent' impossible. The concept of community policing was based loosely on the British bobby model: a foot-patrol officer – usually male – who made himself available as a resource to residents of a particular area, who is accessible for a range of duties, not just crime prevention, and who is actually part of the community rather than an outsider entering for a specific purpose. The image of the police-officer was intended to change from a representative of a de-personalized and possible antagonistic agency to a protector, friend and neighbour. Using whites in the new role might have seemed too much like old wine in new bottles, but black officers were perfect in neighbourhoods where suspicion and mistrust of the police were highest – low-income areas with dense black concentrations.

Controlling such areas by imposed force was to be replaced by a form of self-governance. Mandates were to come from the community; citizens were to support police efforts; police were to be responsive to public demands. Nightstick justice was to be a thing of the past. Many police-departments which had boosted the recruitment of ethnic minorities experimented with community-oriented policing. Amongst them were: Detroit, with its mini-stations exclusively organized for community crime prevention; Santa Ana, with substations that functioned as community group meeting areas as well as locales for disseminating information; and Miami, which adopted new measures, but not until after prolonged rioting in 1980. Over a twenty-year period, most urban police-departments innovated. There was no grand plan, or a coherent strategy, but a variety of formulations designed to involve the community in police activities and vice versa. In virtually all cases, black officers were deployed in the community programmes.

There is no evidence that assigning black officers to predominantly black districts promotes effective community policing. In fact, the very concept of *effective* community policing was never adequately defined by police-departments aiming for it. The assumption that black officers may be better attuned to the 'needs' of ghetto residents rested on racist stereotypes. Why should black officers, perhaps unfamiliar with a new territory, be more capable of dealing with routine problems in a sensitive manner that a white officer with several years of practical experience? If the white officer was heavy-handed, why should the new black officer not be? A black officer is carried to the force by a broadly similar set of motives; in the training process he or she is inculcated with the same range of skills and expertise; on the job, the officer absorbs broadly similar values and attitudes. We will return to this point. For now, note the assumption behind the policy.

Ostensibly, the reason for black assignments is effective police service, but a more compelling explanation derives from the idea that black officers were less invasive and less politically repugnant forms of control. For blacks in the ghetto, the change in policing was, to use Samuel Yette's phrase 'aimed *at* them – not for them' (1971: 20). Stephen Leinen's study of New York suggested that blacks were indeed used to improve effective policing; but effectiveness referred to 'their [black officers] greater ability to cultivate and use informants in their community' (1984: 215). Any form of social control needs intelligence: information of strategic value about the population to be managed must be collected on a systematic basis for the control to remain effective. The police's apparent lack of preparedness and inability to suppress many of the large-scale outbursts in the 1960s indicated that intelligence-gathering was inadequate. This was due to the suspicion and contempt held by black citizens about white police. Black officers were perfect replacements. Their stated mission was to go into the ghettos to patch up tattered relationships and establish harmonious communities. But an unstated aim was to act as conduits for intelligence. At its most benign level, intelligence-gathering might involve developing contacts, observing and listening; it might function to maintain a degree of predictability, to guard against the unexpected. No study of policing has ever denied that police employ this method of control. Occasionally, studies have suggested a more surreptitious and political role for black officers. In his research on the NYPD, Leinen found that the 'goal of promoting good will and rapport between black citizens and the police' in the 1970s was perhaps of secondary importance, as 'minority officers were also needed to counter the threat of some of the more revolutionary groups, particularly those factions espousing illegal, military-type attacks against public property and established authority' (1984: 53).

John Cooper called the officers used for such purposes, 'sacrificial lambs'. He described a complementarity between white officers 'putting down ghetto activism in the most vigilant of manners' and 'the most mercenary of black officers' who were 'being used as undercover agents in the ghetto to infiltrate the [Black] Panthers, the Muslims [Nation of Islam], and other groups that were trying to push off the yolk of oppression' (1980: 120). As well as undermining these radical movements, the undercover officers were responsible for feeding 'the news media discoloring information about the groups', with the result that 'to this day, most white and black Americans do not know the message the Black Panthers were trying to deliver' (1980: 14).

Some might see this as a collision of policing styles: how can you urge community liaison with any credibility, while using black officers as virtual political weapons? Some, like Cooper, would argue that ultimately you cannot: 'Efforts by black policemen to serve as community relations liaisons are doomed to fail' (1980: 123). Cooper likened the black cop to 'The invisible man' because ghetto residents can see straight through him. He is regarded as a 'turncoat', a 'lacky' and an 'establishment tool.'

Sharp as Cooper's vision undoubtedly was, one wonders if he missed, or perhaps just underestimated, the ingenuity of the whole operation, which, in public-relations terms at least, has been epic. Control works most effectively when the controlled are oblivious to the limits placed on their actions. By introducing black officers to the ghettos and handing them a community liaison brief, the police gave the impression that they were actually straining to accommodate black interests and reflect black priorities. At the same time, a fine net was being cast over the inner cities. One has to concede that, in the years following the initiative, there have been no uprisings comparable to those of the 1960s, except for Miami in 1980, where the gathering of forces was around inter-ethnic issues. Even in the period of the publication of Cooper's book, one senses surreptitious concessions designed to display the best of intentions, but with deeper purposes. The appointments of blacks to senior police and mayoral positions have been dramatic examples of the genuine mobility achieved and power wielded by blacks. They have also been testimonies to the continued success of the process of political incorporation touched off by the Kerner proposals.

UPPER INCOME, UPPER STRATA

The appointment of Lee P. Brown to Chief of Police in Houston in 1982 drew an expectedly racist reaction from the population of the Texan city where, as Skolnick and Bayley put it, 'racial feelings are frankly expressed' (1986: 87). At the time, 61 per cent of the city's population was white, 28 per cent black and 18 per cent Hispanic; 8 per cent of the police-force was black. It had one of the nation's most troubled police-departments – 'one with a long history of brutality and poor relations with blacks and Latinos', according to Walter Leavy (1982: 115). Brown was the first black police-chief to be appointed by a white administration, specifically by a white female mayor, Kathy Whitmire, of a predominantly white big city. With the appointment, Brown was elevated to the celestial ranks of a small group of blacks who ran police-departments, though none at that stage as large as Houston's. The majority of the 50 blacks with comparable authority were in charge of small police-forces: only ten headed departments with over 180 officers. Brown was a mould-breaker, who, as we noted at the start of the chapter, eventually moved to the head of America's largest force in New York. Writing at the time of the Houston appointment, Leavy reflected on the other 50 black chiefs: 'Usually Blacks command forces in cities where there is a substantial low-income population and, many times, there are more social and economic ills in those areas' (1982: 118–19). Both Detroit and Newark, centres of uprising in the 1960s, named blacks as chiefs in the mid-1970s. Detroit's Willie Hart was appointed in 1976; Newark made Edward Kerr its Police Director in 1974 and replaced him with Hubert Williams in 1974. All carried with them the reputation of having hard police-forces with little resembling internal discipline. By 1988 the élite group of 50 had been enlarged to 130, an increase of 160 per cent. Six of the ten largest US cities had departments headed by blacks. Interestingly, as Dalton Narine points out: 'Six of the chiefs were appointed by white administrators – city managers in Miami, Pasadena and Greensboro, and the mayors of New York, Houston and Memphis' (1988: 134). Among the most controversial appointments was that of Benjamin Ward to Commissioner of the NYPD in 1984. It was the first time in forty years that a man who was not of Irish background or descent was chosen to head the department. It was also a piece of political opportunism by Mayor Ed Koch, who had been assailed for his slickness in appointing ethnic minorities to key city positions and for his alleged condonation of police violence against blacks and Hispanics.

Results? A general decline in allegations of police brutality; further increase in ethnic-minority recruitment; lower crime all round (as much as 16 per cent in Pasadena under James Robenson, who took office in 1985); and either a continuance of 'softer' community-oriented policing or a change towards it. So, as well as having some symbolic value, black representation at senior levels has had some practical consequences. It is revealing that few have stridently favoured a civilian complaints review board containing no police employees. Lee Brown even went against the New York Mayor's wishes in opposing these (*New York Times*, 15 December 1989: 1). Black chiefs have not significantly affected police accountability. Even those who do favour more accountability are constrained by community, political and organizational influences associated with policing policy.

Black mayors have often pushed for civilian review. They are conventionally thought to wield influence in both appointing police-chiefs and directing policy. Since the Voting Rights Act of 1965, which extended and protected the political franchise of blacks, there has been a steep rise in the number of black elected officials, not only at the municipal level, but also at federal and state levels. This has been in spite of a notoriously low voter registration amongst eligible blacks. (Estimates have been as high as 33 per cent unregistered.) The 'black vote' helped blacks to capture mayoralties in many big cities with large black populations; amongst them East St Louis (95.6 per cent black), Atlanta (66.6 per cent), Detroit (63.1 per cent), Birmingham (55.6 per cent) and Newark (54.9 per cent).

The Chicago mayoral election of 1982 was notable because of the openly racist platform used by the Republican candidate who opposed black Democrat Harold Washington. A Republican had not been elected mayor of the city in the previous fifty-six years, but white working-class reservations about a black male in the city's highest political office manifested in the voting. New York's first black mayor was David Dinkins, elected in 1989, the same year as Seattle and New Haven voted for black mayors. Black mayors reign in 310 US cities, including four of the six largest, in 1990. Many have benefited from a sizeable black working-class vote, though they have also drawn much support from what Adolph Reed, in his critical assessment of Jesse Jackson, describes as 'upper income, upwardly mobile strata in the black community . . . businessmen and other upper status blacks' (1986: 69). Jackson's political success has been based on these strata, according to Reed, and it seems feasible to suggest that an expanding black middle class has been instrumental in electing so many black officials. This might be reflected in policing policies, over which mayors are conventionally thought to have some influence.

A study of 'Black mayors and police policies' by Grace Saltzstein showed that 'police departments might be more likely to respond to the wishes of the black community if that community includes a large number of what are perceived to be stable, responsible citizens (e.g. homeowners)' (1989: 533). An area comprising mostly private property, much of it owned by blacks, might be served by a protective and accountable police, more so than a working-class area, presuming there are black mayors in both. Saltzstein's work casts doubts on the assumption that black mayors make an automatic impression on policing. She notes that black mayors 'are linked to increases in black employment without making changes in personnel procedure' and also to 'the presence of citizen control over the police department' (1989: 539). This has frequently been in spite of resistance from the police themselves – as noted before. But the characteristics of the community in which the mayors serve may have a more decisive influence than the mayors themselves. One might suggest that class characteristics may be significant factors in affecting policy. Saltzstein is not alone in detecting serious limitations on mayoral power in general (cf. Kuo 1973) and specifically on the power of black mayors, whose actual influence on police programmes has been questioned in studies by Nelson and Meranto (1977) and Karnig and Welch (1980).

Naming black police-chiefs and electing black mayors approximates a public-relations exercise. It works as effectively as buying prime-time advertising slots on network television and declaring: 'America's history is exactly *that*. In today's society, blacks can go all the way to the top.' There is a great symbolic value in the drama of blacks hauling their way out of slavery, then marching to Montgomery, before exploding onto the streets of Los Angeles and finally entering the corridors of power. But this colossal symbolic value should not be confused with the minuscule actual value it has had for the majority of America's black population, whose material position has remained largely unaffected by the elevation of specific individuals to powerful positions; or, at least, positions that appear to have power, but whose incumbents usually find their genuine power circumscribed – as the previously cited studies indicate.

But this is a simplification: most blacks may not have been touched by the upswinging fortunes of an élite sector; but the inspirational parts played by these new role models must surely count for something. The betterment of the entire black population may eventually be served: young people might make plans to escape the streets, set their sights on public office and structure their ambitions around the achievements of other blacks, like Messrs. Brown and Dinkins. Yet even this simplifies. Another interpretation of the conspicuous success of some black

public servants in high office would be that it has precipitated a
new set of problems.

Two questions arise: first, how representative are the black
chiefs of an increasingly heterogeneous black population?
Second, will they and the rest of the emergent black élite stay
around the inner cities long enough to serve blacks who are
destined to remain there? We know from an assortment of police
studies that an assimilation process takes place in which the
values, attitudes and perspectives of a 'police subculture' are
gradually absorbed as the new recruit gains more experience in
the ranks. Jerome Skolnick has termed the distinctive police 'way
of looking at the world' the 'working personality' and it has
cognitive and moral dimensions (1975: 42). His work has been
supported by, amongst others, Arthur Niederhoffer, who writes of
'police authoritarianism' which results from 'socialization and
experience in the police social system' (1975: 41). Still others
suggest that the authoritarian personality types are drawn to
police service and are merely reinforced by experience.

Authoritarianism as a concept explains little, but we can
presume that either entering the police-force, or working in it,
involves one with a disposition towards stability and conservatism,
a certain regard for hierarchy and a commitment of some degree
to the morality of law and order. As guardians of the social order,
it seems logical that police-officers would believe in its
preservation. This doesn't necessarily set police-officers apart
from the rest of society as a whole, though their perceptions and
evaluations of what constitutes a threat to order may set them
apart from many blacks. For these blacks, social change of any
kind requires breaking rules; history makes this clear. In other
words, the respect for order, authority and what is often called the
'establishment' held by police-officers is strengthened during
active service. Whatever the ethnic background of the officer, he
or she will probably gravitate towards 'police authoritarianism' in
time and this may widen the gap between them and the black
working-class population. This will be exaggerated for the
ambitious officers who either reach or aspire to senior positions
and secure the financial well-being that they bring (in 1985, the
NYPD Commissioner's position carried an annual salary of
$82,000; in 1989, Brown's appointment was thought to be worth
over $100,000). 'Now that he has a middle-class income, he has

acquired middle-class attitudes', Cooper wrote of the typically mobile black police-officer (1980: 123). This is possibly an overstatement, but one with some truth concealed in it. There most probably is a relationship between financial stability and conservative leanings – a desire not to upset a system that has served your particular interests, if not those of your former peers.

The argument of Cooper, Leinen, Yette and others who have viewed the incursions of blacks into the police-force with scepticism is basically that old perspectives are traded for new ones. Not for them the simplicity of blacks being black and whites being white: progress in the police-force necessarily whitens. Blaming 'whitey' is not an option open to black police-officers. Nor is openly criticizing an 'establishment' that many other blacks regard as based on white priorities. There is ample justification for black police-officers to regard themselves as superior to the majority of the black working-class: not only are their pay, working conditions, job stability, pension rights and overall standard of living better than those of manual workers, but their status, or esteem, too. This is bound to lead to a general acceptance of the dominant values of society and a commitment to its principal institutions.

Personalities, attitudes, political postures and values: these are elements of an assimilation process that may be drawing black police-officers away from the majority of blacks, many of whom remain in the working-class, many more of whom struggle in a developing urban underclass. There is unlikely to be much compatibility in the frames of reference of black police-officers and these groups. The progressive integration of black police-officers into what E. Franklin Frazier (1962) once called the 'black bourgeoisie' is part of a general tendency in contemporary America. More than one-fifth of black families currently earn $60,000 or more. As the professionals have acquired income and status, they have mimicked 'white flight', moving away from the inner cities into the suburbs. With them go their skills, institutions and leadership – the glue that held neighbourhoods together; left behind is a kind of social residue, what some call an underclass. This term has become part of our vocabulary. Douglas Glasgow, in his book *The Black Underclass*, defines it as 'a permanently entrapped population of poor persons, unused and unwanted' (1980: 3). Those comprising the black underclass typically live in highly segregated districts; segregated, that is, not only from whites but also from black professionals, including the police. They will be hard-hit by unemployment: jobless rates of between 50 and 70 per cent are not uncommon in the US inner cities. They may be engaged in habitual criminal activity, usually of a petty nature, and will probably have a record to prove it: one in nine black persons has a criminal record; one in two US prisoners is black.

Hopelessly unreliable as statistics on drug-use are, we have a broad indication that 80 per cent of illegal drug-users in the USA are white. But one of the most debilitating and addictive forms of cocaine, 'crack', is used extensively by inner-city blacks, many of them young mothers who live off welfare payments. There is something of a minor tradition in the attempts to explain this in terms of white interests. Yette's 1971 polemic, *The Choice*, referred to 'pacification programs' and 'plans to "destroy" obsolete people'. His thesis was that blacks had outlived their usefulness in the labour market and were now either to be killed off or sublimated. Drugs served both purposes. They also facilitate a supply of police informants: addicts craving for drugs have little resistance against police interrogation and drug offenders can be easily converted into narks, or supergrasses, for small favours. Yette also entertains the idea that 'the police establishment's heralded concern for drugs is strictly a tactic designed to make the country "legally" into a police state' (1971: 197). These findings, have echoes in Gus van Sant's movie, *Drugstore Cowboy*, where it is predicted that 'in the near future, the government will use the hysteria over narcotics to establish an international police state' (1989).

Whether or not one accepts the connection between the two, one is bound to consider the points independently. The demand for unskilled black labour *is* falling. The police institution *does* have considerably more authority than it did twenty-five years ago. Dismiss the relationship, but take note to the complementarity. An already strong police-force backed by the force of the state has ready answers to the question of why it needs so much power: a large, disenchanted black underclass with chronic unemployment and rampant crime needs a lot of policing. It is unlikely that more blacks in the police-force will make any difference to the material lives of either those locked in the underclass or those striving to escape it. Overt conflict, such as that manifested in the 1960s, has declined in the years since; blacks are now far less threatening than they once appeared to be. The continued growth of citizenship rights such as universal suffrage and political representation means that more blacks have been directly integrated into society. Another trend has been toward heterogeneity in the black population: there are now numerous vertical as well as horizontal divisions that have worked to fragment and atomize blacks. The recruitment of blacks into the police-force and their progression to senior ranks has been part of this process. Its importance spreads far beyond the narrow incorporation of the actual personnel in the force.

Recruiting Afro-Americans into the nation's police-force was an accommodation of sorts. It seemed a direct response to black protests; in fact, it was a response to what Kerner inferred from the uprisings. The recruitment soon lost whatever ethnic aspects it had and became a vehicle for advancing the interests of a very manageable, aspirant middle class. The blacks entering the force and advancing to senior levels had little to do with the mass of working-class blacks. The role models they defined and the positive images they generated had little significance to the material circumstances of the Afro-American majority. Recruiting blacks to the police-force was never a 'black issue': it diverted attention away from black issues while appearing to have stabilizing and integrative effects. In some measure, it did have both of these effects: by opening up an avenue of expression to blacks. But this was an avenue of mobility, not protest; a route taken by would-be poachers seeking to become gamekeepers.

For the blacks who became police-officers, the state's prime control institution was and is a 'way out'. These groups have been incorporated into the system, a system in which they now have a stake. They have taken on the attitudes, absorbed the values and perhaps assumed the typical 'working personality' of police-officers. But what has been the effect on the rest of the black population? It has been to exact compliance, to stifle political activism, to facilitate physical control, to mobilize a co-operative response to the various 'crime problems' while, at the same time, seeming to represent that population.

To some, this may be nothing more than an insidious form of social control and an effective one at that, judging by the evidence: no riots and nearly one in every four young black males either behind bars or on parole (according to the Sentencing Project, Washington DC, 1990). But it *is* more than a form of control. It is a wondrous spectacle enacted over two-and-a-half decades and designed to celebrate a society once caught on the horns of an American dilemma, but now truly directed towards an egalitarian society in which the 'law and authority' Kerner found so vital is stronger than ever. Afro-Americans have the respect they yearned for: many of them have actually worked their ways to positions in which they can dispense respect, not just earn it. It is an example of black Americans being given opportunities and seizing them to assert themselves. It is also an ironic self-assertion.

Chapter 5

Police accountability and black people
Into the 1990s

Eugene McLaughlin

The idea of the democratic control of the police has rarely excited interest in Britain.

(B. Cox, 1975)

We hear a lot nowadays about the much heralded concept of 'democratic community policing' and the need for more involvement by local representatives in the management of police officers.

(J. Anderton, 1981)

Whatever happened to police accountability?

(R. Reiner, 1989b)

Political theorists are agreed that in liberal democracies officials and institutions of governance should be accountable, having a 'continuing obligation to explain and justify their conduct in public' (Day and Klein 1989: 7). Upon such accountability, it is argued, rests the unique legitimacy of the liberal democratic state. However, the institution of the police rests uncomfortably within this particular state form: 'The police more than any institution exhibit an antagonism, both in concept and practice, to some of the basic precepts of a democratic society. In many respects, the phrase "democratic police force" is a contradiction in terms' (Berkeley 1969: 1–2).

The police are empowered to infringe upon the liberties of citizens and are legally entitled to use force and violence to uphold law and order. The police deal in and with conflict and are empowered by the state to do so. In a democracy the key problem is to make sure that there are structures of accountability to ensure that citizens' liberties are not infringed upon in an unjust manner or unnecessarily by the police and that the police do not use undue force and violence in the carrying out of their duties (for a full discussion of definitional issues of policing see Reiner 1989a: 3–4).

During the 1970s and 1980s the issue of whether the police were accountable became an important political issue in Britain. Although the traditional structures of legal, organizational and political accountability looked formally extensive, the substantive reality was very different. The post-war period saw the decline of the political dimension of accountability with the rise to prominence of legal accountability:

> Unlike other institutions, the police apparatus can legitimately justify the absence of a formal political relation – portrayed as partisan – by reference to the legal relation. Within policing ideology the gradual disappearance of the practice of political control is viewed as a progressive reform in the direction of true accountability – the obligation to act according to legal not political direction.
>
> (Brogden 1982: 122)

Such a development would not necessarily have been problematic if the mechanisms of legal accountability had proved to be effective. However, concern began to be expressed that the judiciary was not only unwilling and incapable of calling the police to account but in fact was uncritically sanctioning the constant attempts by the police to extend their powers. In addition it was becoming apparent that the mechanism for pursuing complaints against the police was fundamentally flawed because it was the police who were in charge of investigating themselves.

For civil libertarians the worrying conclusion was reached that the structures of democratic accountability supposedly governing the police had atrophied. The consequences of this breakdown of accountability were most acute in Britain's inner cities, where the phrases 'out of control' and 'out of order' became commonplace to describe the type of policing that black people were being subjected to. This led to renewed demands and policies being formulated which were geared towards strengthening the democratic accountability of the police. Central to those demands and policies was the belief that the political dimension of accountability had to be re-prioritized to bring policing of black people under control. This chapter documents how such demands and policies were neutralized in the course of the 1980s and the implications for policing in the 1990s.

RENEWED CONCERNS ABOUT POLICING

As the 1960s and 1970s progressed policing in Britain was placed back on the political agenda as it became more and more controversial. This was virtually inevitable given the changes that had been effected by the 1964 Police Act, the 1972 Local Government Act and the internal organizational changes that took place in the post-war period. It was specifically because the 1964 Act failed to resolve the problems arising from the lack of police accountability that the issue was destined to resurface. In fact this was virtually inevitable because first, the powers of the police had been expanded, second, the structures of democratic accountability had been legislatively weakened as a consequence of the Police Act and finally the political and economic climate had changed and the public-order role of the police was once more prioritized. Certain sections of the community, most notably black people, were particularly vulnerable to such developments. The empowerment of the police always has drastic implications for the powerless.

The growing concern about the nature of policing in this period covered a diversity of matters (Jefferson and Grimshaw 1984: 1–8; Reiner 1985a: 61–80; Morris 1989: 144–51). First, apprehension was voiced about the increasing gap between the police and the community. Larger, impersonal and professionalized forces and changes in operational philosophy were the corollary of the structural changes that had taken place in the post-war period. These technocratic forces did not feel the need to negotiate their presence in neighbourhoods, to cultivate the consent of the community or to take into account the needs of the community. Policing strategies were decided upon, implemented and changed without consultation. Thus, a 'unit beat' (with panda cars and two-way radios) system was introduced and then replaced by 'fire-brigade' (aggressive response) policing at the professional discretion of the chief constables and under the sponsorship of the Home Office. Such changes had a considerable impact upon the subculture of the lower ranks and the abrasive manner in which they dealt with the public, particularly in the inner cities (Stephens 1988: 9).

Second, there was concern about the growing catalogue of police malpractice in relation to the planting of evidence, instances of extensive police corruption, the policing of public order, the use of specialist troubleshooting units such as the Special Patrol Groups, saturation policing methods, fire-brigade policing methods, anti-subversion and intelligence gathering activities and the application of new control technologies such as computers and surveillance equipment (Jefferson and Grimshaw 1984: 4–8). Allied to this was the seeming incapability of the complaints system to provide an effective means of redress for those on the receiving end of police deviance and malpractice. Third, the words and actions of senior police-officers in the 1970s became more pronounced and controversial (Reiner 1980: 1983). The professional corporate managers of the police-service, both as individuals and through the Association of Chief Police Officers (ACPO), began to assert their professional autonomy. This expressed itself in two key ways. First, they vociferously challenged any possible encroachment upon their powers. And second, through their perfection of the art of political lobbying and utilization of moral panics about rising crime rates and social deviance, they exacted more powers and resources (Hall *et al.* 1978; Hough and Heal 1979; Campbell 1987). When challenged to account for the behaviour of the forces under their command, chief police-officers responded in a manner which attempted to define any questioning of the police as an attempt to subvert the democratic process (Levenson 1981: 43).

However, it was not only chief officers who were intervening in the political process. The Police Federation, as the powerful representative of the junior ranks, became more and more strident in its interventions. In 1975, supported by the Superintendents' Association, the Federation launched a law and order campaign. Between 1977 and 1978 it engaged in a wage dispute with the Labour government which resulted in the recommendation of a 40 per cent pay rise. In 1979 the Federation attempted to intervene in the national electoral process through a national press campaign by asking voters to consider where the candidates stood on law and order. It was in this year also that the Police Federation broke with tradition and appointed as its Parliamentary adviser a government rather than an opposition MP (Reiner 1980; 1983).

The fourth level of concern centred upon the manner in which the main political parties began to focus upon the issue of law and order as a basis upon which to mobilize electoral support. When in opposition in 1977 the Conservatives made an unprecedented intervention by giving full support to the pay claims of the Police Federation. In 1978 the Labour conference saw the party try to wrest the issue of law and order from the Conservatives. As a consequence, in the run-up to the 1979 election both parties tried to outdo each other in their commitment to law and order expenditure and the fight against crime.

As Jefferson and Grimshaw have made clear: 'Crystallizing practically all these controversial causes for concern and providing throughout the most acute and persisting examples for campaigners, has been the issue of police–black relations' (1984: 7). The evidence submitted by the Institute of Race Relations (IRR) to the Royal Commission on Criminal Procedure in 1979 documented two decades of black people's experience of unaccountable racist policing. There were two main groupings of complaint emanating from such policing practices. The first group of complaints related to the overpolicing of black political, social and cultural events. This involved raids on black meeting places and the deployment of specialist troubleshooting police units in black neighbourhoods. The second group related to the failure of the police to protect black neighbourhoods from acts of racial terrorism. In addition to complaining about over- and underpolicing, the IRR also provided evidence concerning the use of police powers on the streets and in the police-stations to harass and unjustly prosecute black people. Such allegations were confirmed by other research carried out into the state of police–black relations on the 'front lines' of Britain's inner cities (Hunte 1966, Humphry 1972; Humphry and John 1972; Pulle 1973; Bethnal Green and Stepney Trades Council 1978; AFFOR 1978; NCCL 1980). It is worth remembering that in the early 1970s Derek Humphry and Gus John argued that the relationship between the police and black men in Handsworth was 'one of war', whilst Margaret Simey was warning that the policing black people were subject to in Liverpool 'could lead to civil war in the city' (Humphry and John 1972: 13–17).

However, when those concerned about the practices and policies of the police demanded accountability from that institution, they were faced with chief officers who had been legally, organizationally and politically empowered during the previous twenty years. They also had to face the consequences of the constant redefining of the role and the position of the police authorities in that period, formally, substantively and ideologically. The 1964 Police Act and 1972 Local Government Act reshaped them in terms of their composition, powers and the size of the forces for which they were supposed to be responsible. As a consequence they had 'passive and quiescent' committees who were both unwilling to call and incapable of calling the chief constables to account (McCabe and Wallington 1988: 135).

RENEWED DEMANDS FOR DEMOCRATIC ACCOUNTABILITY

In the late 1970s the party consensus was broken when the Conservative Party made both law and order and the Labour Party's stance on the matter key electoral issues. Both the Conservatives and the right-wing media, in the run-up to the 1979 election, sought to establish in the eyes of the electorate that the Labour Party was weak on law and order (Phipps 1988). One of the traditional weaknesses of the Labour Party was exaggerated by the support the Conservative Party gave to strong law and order measures during this campaign. The response of the Labour Party was essentially contradictory. As indicated above, in the run-up to the election the party tried to compete with the Conservative Party on the issue of law and order. However, the Left of the Labour Party also attempted to place the interests of those subject to discriminatory policing practices on the political agenda. The resultant campaign for democratic accountability of the police was most intense in London since there was no semblance of substantive accountability.

In November 1979 and March 1980 Labour MP Jack Straw introduced (unsuccessfully) Bills into Parliament proposing amendments to the 1964 Police Act to strengthen the powers of police authorities and to set up a police authority for London (Jefferson and Grimshaw 1984: 150–6; Oliver 1987: 68–70). Between March 1980 and the local government elections of 1981 the issue of police accountability and demands for a police authority for London achieved recognition within the electoral manifesto of the London Labour Party (Bundred 1982). After Labour's victory the Greater London Council set up a non-statutory police committee and support unit as part of its election manifesto promise to campaign for a democratically accountable police-force. Within this initiative administrative and financial support was made available to police monitoring groups to enable them first, to act as the 'eyes and ears' of the police committee, second, to articulate the concerns of the community and third, to link the committee to the community (Walker 1986). Such monitoring groups had their origins in the campaigns around policing issues that had been waged by black communities since the 1960s.

These campaigns concerned racist practices, corruption, deaths in police custody and general policing strategies on the streets. The outcome of some of the campaigns was the development of community-based police monitoring groups. Such groups involved themselves in what Walker (1986: 45) has defined as 'community defence' and 'para-legal defence', i.e., the monitoring of policing practices, providing support and advice for those in difficulties with the police, campaigning for changes in the structure of police accountability and disseminating counter information. Elsewhere in England, after the county council elections of 1981, radicalized Labour administrations were returned to power who were determined, like the Labour Party in London, to have an input into the manner in which policing was carried out in their areas. Most of the Labour parties in the metropolitan areas had manifestos which called for changes in the 1964 Police Act to give police authorities the right to take decisions on matters of policy and in relation to the deployment of police-officers and senior promotions.

The civil disturbances of 1981 added impetus to the demands that the police should be accountable to the elected representatives of local communities. All the simmering issues and concerns of the 1970s took on a new urgency as the inner cities burned:

> The riots of the spring and summer of that year, and the Scarman Report on the Brixton disorders, were a turning point in the increasingly politicized debate about police organization and strategy, and the accountability and constitutional position of the police.
>
> (Reiner, 1985a: 170)

The response of the British state to the disturbance of 1981 and the intense debate about police accountability was formally extensive but geared towards a substantive defence of the status quo. Support was given to the enhancement of the paramilitary response capabilities of the police whilst the 1984 Police and Criminal Evidence Act and 1986 Public Order Act were eventually passed, legislatively empowering the police (Zander 1985; Hillyard and Percy-Smith 1988; Douzinas *et al.* 1988). In addition, the Scarman inquiry addressed the issue of the democratic accountability of the police, particularly the constitutional position of the Metropolitan Police. Although Lord Scarman saw accountability as being important, he rejected demands for a police authority for London and more powers for the existing authorities. Instead he recommended statutory community consultation with the police which did not address the interests, needs and the demands of those sections of the community who had suffered from racist policing practices. The consultation structures were given a specific remit in relation to facilitating community involvement in crime control and prevention. Thus, the interests of those for whom *the police were the problem* were once more defined out by Scarman's recommendations. As Darcus Howe commented, Scarman had failed to 'grasp the nettle' (1988: 67–70).

THE MID-1980s: THE RESOLUTION OF THE STRUGGLES FOR DEMOCRATIC ACCOUNTABILITY

In the bitter struggles for democratic accountability that took place during the first half of the 1980s chief police-officers, most notably in Greater Manchester and Merseyside, asserted their autonomy from the radicalized police authorities. Chief constables refused to account for the manner in which the 1981 civil disturbances were policed. They also refused to allow any discussion of what they defined as operational matters, e.g., the manner in which black communities were policed. In addition, national developments in policy matters were decided upon by the Home Office and senior officers without reference to the police authorities, most notably on issues such as the National Reporting Centre, mutual aid arrangements and the acquisition of riot-equipment, including plastic bullets (McCabe and Wallington

1988). Such was the determination of chief police-officers to make sure that they retained their autonomy from political accountability that James Anderton, the Chief Constable of Greater Manchester, demanded the abolition of the police authorities: 'You cannot police a community by Police Authorities. Unless I am very much mistaken the majority of the public would prefer policing at the discretion of their Chief Constable rather than policing with the consent of the Police Authorities' (Anderton 1985).

In July 1985 the local government bill became law, abolishing the Labour-controlled metropolitan county councils and the Greater London Council as from 1 April 1986. As a result joint boards were established to discharge the duties of the.troublesome police authorities. Strict central government guidelines were laid down concerning the composition and powers of the new boards. The act changed the form of political representation that had previously existed on the police authorities. The joint boards were to consist of councillors nominated directly by the constituent councils reflecting, as far as possible, the party balance of power on the respective councils. The boards were subject to the financial control laid down in the 1984 Rates Act for three years. The Home Secretary was given potential control over the day-to-day running of the Joint Boards through being given a say in decisions concerning staffing and the allocation of resources. In addition, the Home Secretary was allotted the power to restructure Joint Boards through first, allowing district councils to become separate police authorities and second, amalgamating different police areas. Thus, this act gave central government unprecedented formal control over the previously troublesome police authorities. There can be little doubt that the Conservative government, through the passing of the Local Government Act, found a convenient means of putting to an end the unceasing demands for democratic accountability of the police. As Loveday has noted:

> The view of the Home Office is that members and Chief Constables are now working together satisfactorily and that this positive relationship presents a strong contrast with the conflict which characterised the operation of the earlier Metropolitan County Police Committees. It is quite clear that this perception is one that is shared by both Chief Constables

and most members serving the Joint Boards for police in the Metropolitan areas.

(Loveday 1988: 25)

In addition to the neutralization of the police authorities, there were a series of other developments, in relation to the politics of crime and policing, that were to have a significant impact upon the campaign for strengthening the democratic accountability of the police. First, there was the emergence within the Conservative government's law and order project of a concern with crime prevention. Second, there were organizational and policy changes that took place within the police. Finally, there was the impact of left new realist criminology within the overall campaign by the Labour Party to prove itself acceptable to the British electorate. The overall consequence of such developments was the re-emergence of a bipartisan discourse on crime and the community which covered crime prevention, fear of crime and victims of crime (Reiner 1989b).

THE GOVERNMENT, CRIME PREVENTION AND ACTIVE CITIZENSHIP

As in the first years of the 1980s, the government continued to prioritize law and order. There was the substantial allocation of resources to the police; the augmentation of the court system; a substantial prison building programme; and legislation covering all aspects of the criminal justice system (Savage 1989; Pilger 1990). This continuing emphasis on law and order meant that there was no public inquiry into the controversial policing of the 1984–5 coal dispute. In addition, when Handsworth and Broadwater Farm erupted there was no repeat of the Scarman inquiry. Instead at the Conservative Party conference the Home Secretary announced the strengthening of public-order legislation and the upgrading of the riot capabilities of the police.

However, the government did have to face the consequences of its political utilization of the issue of crime. Although spending on law and order had increased in real terms by 31 per cent, it had little effect on the increasing crime rate. As Savage (1989) has noted, the spending had neither prevented crime, deterred criminals, protected people, eradicated fears, helped victims nor reformed offenders. In this context the limitations of the role of the police in fighting crime were becoming apparent. Criticisms of the government's law and order policies were fuelled by the publication of the first national crime survey, which, for the first time, attempted to provide an accurate picture of the extent and the nature of crime in Britain. This survey demonstrated that although crime was much more prevalent than indicated by official statistics, it was of a petty nature. The survey also emphasized that the fear of crime was out of proportion to the risk of being a victim of crime. The survey concluded that more police-officers was not the answer to such fears (Hough and Mayhew 1983: 34). Such conclusions stimulated further debate and studies about the extent, nature and fear of crime, the victims of crime and the effectiveness of the police in controlling crime.

The response of the government was two-fold. First, there was the emergence of the concept of the 'active citizen':

> At the very centre of our ideas on how to control crime should be the energy and initiative of the active citizen. His or her contribution must be mobilised and should be the core of the radical rethinking we need on prevention and control of crime.
> (John Patten, Minister of State, Home Office 1988)

Through the propagation of the notion of active citizenship, the role of the community of active citizens in taking responsibility for the curbing of crime was stressed. The proper role of the community in policing matters was participating actively in consultative arrangements, neighbourhood watch schemes, victim support schemes and the special constabulary to help in the fight against crime (Hope and Shaw 1988; Maguire and Pointing 1988; Mawby 1988; Leon 1989; Walklate 1989). Second, to complement the efforts of the community, a powerful multi-agency approach emerged not only to harness all the criminal justice and related agencies, but also voluntary efforts, central government departments and the media. In April 1986 a ministerial group on crime prevention was set up to co-ordinate the crime prevention strategies of twelve different government departments (*Police Review*, 18 April 1986). All the resultant proposals emphasized the role that statutory authorities should play in co-operating with the police in the fight against crime. Thus, a total community policing strategy was being implemented by the government in relation to crime control. Morgan has also pointed out that this strategy was useful within the government's overall campaign to curb public expenditure (1989: 7–8). Despite public pronouncements to the contrary, community crime control was considerably cheaper than allocating unlimited resources to the police.

THE POLICE AND THE COMMUNITY: TOWARDS A COMMON PURPOSE

The potentially damaging critique of policing that could have developed about increasing crime rates and the manifest failure of the police to control crime failed to materialize. Kenneth Newman, the Commissioner of the Metropolitan Police, the force which was most vulnerable to such a critique, incorporated the criticisms and public debate to neutralize demands for the democratic accountability of his force. The result was the unveiling, from 1983, of a corporatist (multi-agency) community policing strategy aimed at re-establishing the authority and legitimacy of the force. Hence, Newman's strategy and philosophy neatly dovetailed with the government's approach to the problem of crime.

Central to this strategy was mobilizing active community consent in the fight against crime and educating the community about the realistic role of the police in that fight. Newman supported the Scarman consultative arrangements as forums where the consent of community representatives could be mobilized and where the education of the community could take place. Neighbourhood watch, crime prevention schemes, victim support schemes and the special constabulary were designated as the means through which the community could participate with the police in the fight against crime. Community beat officers were given a key role in forging a new relationship between the force and the community. Newman also pressed for corporatist policing strategies to be implemented, under the aegis of the police, to deal with the problems of difficult inner-city areas. In addition Newman embarked upon the attempted internal reorganization of the force. In order to put more bobbies back on the beat civilianization of those tasks not requiring the skills and powers of police-officers took place. Through the implementation of 'policing by objective' programmes there was the prioritization of particular crimes that were of community concern.

Furthermore, the public-order capabilities of the force were enhanced through the acquisition of new equipment, the upgrading of paramilitary training and the re-organization of mobilization procedures to deal with the front lines (symbolic locations) of London's black neighbourhoods. Such a strategy underwent further revision and refinement after the civil disturbances of 1985.

Thus, there was a re-definition of the role of the police in the fight against crime involving the creation of new channels of information and communication with the community and other statutory agencies. As far as Newman was concerned, if the new strategy was successful the effectiveness of the force would be improved in three key areas. First, in dealing with the problem of crime through giving the community and other social agencies the primary responsibility for looking after itself. Second, by building the consent of the community through closer police–community contact through the consultative committees and neighbourhood watch. And third, in the maintenance of public tranquillity through the creation of a more efficient riot-control force, which would have the consent of the community. Central to the latter would be the criminalization of any instance of civil disturbance and targeting this form of crime would be a priority of the Metropolitan Police. Through this strategy, social order in the inner cities would be restored.

THE LABOUR PARTY, THE POLICE AND THE COMMUNITY: PARTNERS AGAINST CRIME

The leadership of the Labour Party began to take the issue of crime seriously because of first, its electoral vulnerability to being labelled anti-police and soft on crime and second, the possibility of scoring electoral points as the crime rates officially soared under a law and order government.

The 'loony left' campaign of the media and Conservative Party during the mid-1980s had a considerable impact upon the Labour Party's law and order stance. The result was the emergence of new realism in the attempt to regain lost electoral support. There was a considerable distancing of the national party leadership from any controversial issues that its political opponents could use against it, most notably during the coal dispute of 1984–5 and in relation to minority issues which were re-defined as fringe issues (Thatchell 1983; Hollingsworth 1986; Wainwright 1987; Negrine 1989).

During this period the Conservatives, the pro-Conservative media and the police pressed Labour on their new-found realism, particularly in relation to law and order. After the 1985 disturbances considerable pressure was exerted upon the party leadership to expel Bernie Grant, Leader of Haringey Council, for his statements after Broadwater Farm erupted. At that year's Conservative Party conference the Prime Minister's key-note speech denounced the Labour Party's anti-police stance. In November 1985 the Police Federation renewed its demands for the Labour Party to deal with those members of the party who were anti-police. In early 1986 the Home Secretary renewed the government's attacks on those anti-police Labour-controlled police authorities who were in conflict with their chief constables.

It was in this period that the leadership of the party began to profess publicly its support for the police, its concern about crime and its apprehension about those members of the party demanding police accountability. Statements by the Labour leadership promised that a future Labour government would give full support to the police and would promote policies to bring about community support for the police in the fight against crime. In May 1986 Neil Kinnock denounced those in his party involved in 'police bashing' and in the same month Sir Kenneth Newman was able to state that the policies of the Labour Party and the Conservative Party on law and order were virtually indistinguishable (Sim *et al.* 1987: 54–6).

Bolstered by the crime surveys and ideological shift of the new realist criminologists (Taylor 1981; Lea and Young 1984; Kinsey 1984; Jones, McLean and Young 1986; Kinsey, Lea and Young 1986) in the run-up to the 1987 election, the party leadership fleetingly confronted the Conservatives on the issue of law and order. Crime prevention was one of the key themes of Labour's 1987 manifesto, which stressed the importance of local authorities and the community, in partnership with the police, spearheading a co-ordinated multi-faceted approach to fight crime. In its critique of the failure of the Conservative government to defeat crime the document harked back to the golden days, before Thatcherism, when the community and the police were at one.

Within this critique and proposals the position of the police was enhanced both in relation to the community and other government and voluntary agencies.

As a consequence, the issue of police accountability was downplayed to a commitment to first, give more (unspecified) powers to police authorities, second, abolish magistrate representation and third, create community police councils whose functions were to be similar to the existing consultation committees. As a consequence, during the 1987 election on the issue of police accountability 'inter-party conflict was muted by a 'new realism' which seemed to infect all parties' (Reiner 1989b: 5). That the conflict was muted was an indication of how far the Labour Party had reconstructed its policies to accept once more the dominant ideologies concerning law and order in Britain (Bridges 1986: 80).

THE VICTIMS OF CRIME

For the government, the police and the Labour Party, the aim of active community participation in crime prevention and multi-agency policing was to make it more difficult to become a victim of crime. As the 1980s progressed, and as a result of the various crime studies, concern with the victim became 'a powerful motif' within the criminal justice system (Rock 1988: 172). In 1987 the Home Office allocated £1.5 million to support previously underfunded victim support schemes and Home Office circular 20/1988 called for the criminal justice agencies to improve the manner in which they dealt with victims. Within this prioritization of victims certain sections of the community came to the fore. The concerns of feminist groups and the police monitoring groups concerned about racial attacks became part of a formal political agenda on crime victims. As a consequence the anxieties of women and Asians in relation to crime became a key concern for all agencies and institutions.

Home Office circular 69/1986 to chief constables offered advice on how the police should treat victims of rape and domestic violence. The police responded by developing specialist training for police-officers, recruiting women doctors for forensic examinations, establishing specialist police units, producing publicity on women's safety and setting up rape examination suites.

Within these professionalized and medicalized structures there was no necessary place for groups such as 'Rape Crisis', 'Taboo' and 'Women's Aid' (Scott and Dickens 1989).

After the Home Office reports on the subject of racial attacks in 1981 and 1985 formally acknowledged the nature of the problem the police began to take the issue seriously. In January 1987 Sir Kenneth Newman announced that the Metropolitan Police would be launching a concerted campaign against the 'moral and social evil' of racially-motivated attacks. It was no coincidence that this campaign specifically focused on Newham and Ealing where the local police monitoring groups had been vociferous in their criticisms of the police response to racist attacks. Since then the Metropolitan Police in particular has continued to make highly public statements concerning its commitment to responding to those who have been racially attacked. In February 1989 a £400,000 publicity campaign was launched to encourage the reporting of racial attacks and harassment. However, the monitoring groups still point to the discrepancies between the publicity campaigns and the continuing tendency for the police to de-racialize such incidents. As a consequence there is no correspondence between the police's conceptualization of the problem and that of the police monitoring groups (Newham Monitoring Project 1989; Rose 1989).

The manner in which these issues have been prioritized has had considerable implications for those radical women's groups involved with the issue of male violence against women and those police monitoring groups involved with the issue of racial terrorism. As a consequence of their response the police have been able to reclaim groups of victims and in doing so have been able to marginalize radical feminist analyses which are premised upon the idea of women being the survivors of male violence not the victims of violence and radical black analyses which are premised upon the notion of racial terrorism not racial harassment. In addition to neutralizing the opponents of the police, the dominant conceptualization of the problem has both legitimized and facilitated corporatist policing strategies.

The overall impact of the emergence of the discourse on community and crime was three-fold for those campaigning for police accountability within the Labour Party. First, it made them vulnerable to the accusation of being anti-police by their political opponents. The practical implications for local authorities who were at the forefront of campaigning for police accountability and fundamentally opposed to such corporatist community policing approaches to crime prevention were serious. Non-co-operation was ideologically and financially damaging, particularly in a climate when local authorities were under constant attack from central government.

Second, it made them vulnerable to those sections of the Labour Party, both locally and nationally, who alleged that an anti-police stance was an electoral liability. Third, they had to confront the issues of crime prevention, the fear of crime and the mobilization of the community to participate actively in a co-ordinated fight against crime. As a consequence, considerable pressure was brought to bear on Labour-controlled local author-ities to participate directly in multi-agency crime prevention projects. This pressure resulted in local authorities, such as Manchester, distancing themselves from the controversial police monitoring initiatives. Instead of monitoring the actions of the police, Labour local authorities began to concern themselves with community safety. As a consequence, the concerns of those sections of the community for whom the police were a problem were once more excluded from the political agenda.

POLICE ACCOUNTABILITY INTO THE 1990s

Towards a national police-force?

A series of developments in relation to the overall organizational structure of the police had serious consequences for the issue of democratic accountability. A succession of important statements and recommendations were made by senior officers and politicians that provided an indication as to how British policing should develop in the 1990s. The statements and recom-mendations indicated a final move towards a fundamentally restructured nationalized police-force in some form or another.

In autumn 1988 the Chief Constable of Sussex, Roger Birch, suggested that serious attention should be given to the idea of a regionally differentiated *de facto* national force. Both Sir Peter Imbert and Sir John Wheeler, the chairman of the all party House of Commons' Home Affairs Committee, added their support to the idea of existing police functions coming under more nationalized or regionalized control. Wheeler stated that such rationalization would facilitate easier consultation for the Home Secretary. In terms of accountability he suggested that a regional board of directors could be appointed, made up of a financial director from outside the police-service together with appointed community representatives. Although the then Home Secretary, David Waddington, effectively rejected the suggestions relating to full nationalization, he supported the idea of further intra-force co-operation through ACPO co-ordination and further rational-ization of the police function. In September 1989 the Home Secretary announced his support for Imbert's idea of a national criminal intelligence unit. Further support for the idea came at the Superintendent's Association conference in October when a call was made for the separation of local and national policing functions. After much debate in July 1990, chief police-officers finally agreed in principle to the establishment of a *de facto* national detective force which would be supported by a criminal intelligence network at an estimated cost of at least £60 million.

The impetus for such radical developments stemmed primarily from first, a trenchant fiscal critique of the effectiveness and effici-ency of the present policing system and second, the policing implications of the commencement of a single European market in 1992.

Fiscal accountability

The police-service, through the unquestioning support of the Conservative government, effectively negotiated demands for democratic accountability. However, this dependency upon central government patronage has had a negative side for the police. In the latter half of the 1980s the government's Financial Management Incentive attempted to increase the financial accountability and performance of the public-service sector. Such Treasury attempts to control public expenditure resulted in close attention being paid to the effectiveness and efficiency of the police (Horton and Smith 1988: Morgan 1989).

Furthermore, the House of Commons' Home Affairs Committee, which was also concerned with the monitoring of public expenditure, also confronted the issue of the effectiveness and efficiency of the present policing system. In July 1989 the Chairman of the Committee, Sir John Wheeler, stated that he supported the idea of a drastically reformed policing system. He argued that the police-forces in England and Wales should be merged to create between 5 and 10 regional forces because as they stood they were 'insufficiently business like'. The report of this committee reiterated Wheeler's criticisms. It was asserted that it was necessary to create some form of national police-force if the 'glaring deficiencies, incompetent use of resources and blinding incompetence' of the management of the present system were to be overcome (*The Independent* 26 July 1990).

The possibility of stricter financial accountability came as a shock to a service which has had access to considerable financial resources since the 1979 election. In late 1989 the representative bodies of the police service set up an 'Operational Policing Review' to counter the possibility of a possible 'slow down' on expenditure on the police. This review body was highly critical of the government's efficiency drive and objected to the police-service being subjected to market-place economic criteria. Sir Peter Imbert, Commissioner of the Metropolitan Police, in a manner reminiscent of other public-sector leaders, stated that a 'non-profit making, caring public service could not be judged by economic criteria used by ICI and Marks and Spencers' (*The Independent*, 5 March 1990).

The struggles in 1989–90 over resourcing resulted in the Home Secretary being accused of betrayal during the 1990 Police Federation conference. The threat was made that if the government did not respond to the needs of the service the Police Federation would be forced into considering its non-trade-union status. It was within this context of the possibility of relatively strict financial restraints being imposed on the police by the Conservative government that the issue of 1992 began to take on central importance.

1992: the single European market

Whilst fiscal rationalization was dominant in the explanations for such moves, an over-arching justification was given as the supra-national consequences of 1992. Bilateral and multilateral agreements which facilitate cross-border police co-operation are already operational. In December 1989 the Home Secretary signed an agreement, within the forum of the Trevi group, to facilitate closer co-ordination between European police forces in the areas of narcotic controls and counter-terrorism. In addition to these specific concerns, the agreement aimed to bring about increasing co-operation on training, science and technology as well as supporting the idea of establishing a European criminal data base. The only thing that Britain was not party to, at the time, was the agreement between France, Germany, Belgium, the Netherlands and Luxembourg allowing communal opening of borders in 'hot pursuit' operations after 1991. In May 1990 Britain signed an accord with Italy enabling their respective police-forces to confiscate the profits of serious crime.

In addition the meetings of the highly influential Trevi working groups, since their inception in the early 1970s, have tried to harmonize policies on terrorism, drugs, frontier checks, extradition, organized crime and, since 1986, immigration controls. Such moves would be all the more effective if, as is suspected, Britain is pushing for the Prevention of Terrorism Act to be the basis for a European Internal Security Act. Effectively this would mean that the tightly-controlled border regulations that have been built up in Britain since 1974 could become the basis for policing the boundaries of Fortress Europe. The aim is to create what official jargon refers to as a 'security surplus', as opposed to a 'security deficit'. This involves constructing a strict external frontier and creating a co-ordinated internal law enforcement and intelligence gathering organization.

The policing implications of the realization of a single European market in 1992 have provided opportunities for the British police to break out of the financial constraints being imposed by the Conservative government. The implications of 1992 have provided an extra lever to counter government criticism whilst also providing the police with access to supra-national funding arrangements. It has been estimated, for example, that a capital outlay of one billion pounds and a significant increase in personnel will be needed to bring about the initial harmonization of the various European policing systems (Weeks 1990).

The Metropolitan Police: the professional police-force for the 1990s

The ramifications of 1992 and the move towards official

acceptance of the idea of some form of national force has had significant implications for one force in particular, the Metropolitan Police. One can make sense of the reforms taking place within the Met only through understanding that in any shake-up of policing in Britain this force will take the lead role. As a consequence of the internal debate stimulated by the 1988 Wolff Olins report, *A Force for Change*, the *Plus Programme* was launched in April 1989. According to Imbert, this programme is intended to be 'the hallmark' of professional policing in the 1990s. Internally there was to be both strong management but more flexible and responsive management through the streamlining of the command hierarchies. In addition considerable emphasis was placed on open management and meaningful consultation with all ranks of officers. Imbert's intention was, unlike previous commissioners, to carry the force with him in the implementation of the reforms. Externally a new relationship was to be forged with the community. The *Plus Programme* stressed the idea of providing a professional public service. The Commissioner stated that the police had behaved in an unaccountable manner in the past and emphasized that the force would have to respond to community determination of needs and law and order priorities. Imbert elaborated upon the ideas as the basis of the approach at the 1989 International Police Exhibition and Conference. He stressed that if the Metropolitan Police was to achieve its force goals, the confidence of the community was essential. This could be achieved only by a commitment to openness and a commitment to sharing power and responsibilities with the community.

At the same time as Imbert's professional policing strategy was being unveiled, a series of other statements relating to the future professionalization of the British police was made. In October 1989 the Audit Commission, in an efficiency study into general force training, was highly critical of existing arrangements and put forward the idea of creating centres of excellence. In the same period the above-mentioned House of Commons' Home Affairs Committee was also highly critical of first, the training and career development programmes for senior officers and second, the appointments procedure. The Home Office responded immediately by announcing measures for the further professionalization of the top officers through the upgrading of the Senior Command Course and the introduction of a central monitoring training structure. However, a more startling response came in the form of a suggestion by the Home Affairs Committee, and subsequently supported by the Prime Minister, that senior police-officers should be in a professionally managed career structure equivalent to that which operates in the military. The idea of a military-style cadre of senior officers sparked off another internal debate similar to one precipitated by the Trenchard reforms in the 1930s.

Implications for police accountability

What is significant in the debates that have taken place about the future of policing in Britain is the lack of discussion of police accountability. To whom will this restructured police-force with supra-national functions be accountable to? From what can be gleaned from the various statements there seems to be little possibility of the structures of local accountability being enhanced. Sir John Wheeler in his discussions with representatives of the Association of County Councils and the Association of Metropolitan Associations during 1989 and 1990 stated bluntly that as far as he was concerned local control of policing 'must go'. He advocated the setting up of regional boards of directors which would be made up of a financial director from outside of the police service and community representatives. These boards of directors would be accountable to the Home Secretary. In addition he suggested that a national police policy committee be set up which would consist of the regional chief constables and representatives of the Home Office. When James Sharples, the Chief Constable of Merseyside, was asked about the implications of such moves for police accountability he tersely stated that chief police-officers were fully aware of the problematic issue of accountability. However, he would not be drawn on what type of accountability senior officers would favour.

For those groups who are subject to the attention of the police the ramifications of the seeming lack of concern about police accountability for their substantive rights of citizenship are staggering. It should not be forgotten that whilst the debates about the future of British policing were taking place, there were at least 41 official inquiries taking place into controversial incidents involving the police. Central to many of these cases were the experiences of black as well as Irish communities.

Many of the 55 people who made formal complaints against the disbanded West Midlands Serious Crimes Squad were black. The Commission for Racial Equality pressed the Police Complaints Authority to investigate allegations of racial discrimination by members of this squad. The policing of the 'front lines' is still causing controversy in terms of the inadequacy of the means of redress against discriminatory policing. In 1986 the Police Complaints Authority initiated an investigation into the policing of Notting Hill, after a series of acquittals of those who had been charged during 1984-5 with possession of drugs and/or assaulting police-officers. All the complainants claimed that the drugs had been planted and that they had been assaulted by police-officers, known as the 'Black Watch'. The result of this investigation, announced in 1990, was that the eighteen complainants were told that there would be no criminal or disciplinary proceedings against any officer. The outcome of the investigation confirmed the worst suspicions of those in the black communities who are cynical about getting justice through the official complaints procedure. Figures released during 1988-9 confirmed the growing trend of those with complaints against the police initiating private prosecutions rather than utilizing the cumbersome and ineffective official procedure. An indication of this shift was demonstrated by the fact that between 1987 and 1989 the total damages awarded against the Metropolitan Police rose from £11,000 to £250,000, with out of court settlements by the force increasing from £82,000 to £266,000.

The allegations about police malpractice in Notting Hill were strengthened further by a series of controversies in 1989. In June 1989 Frank Critchlow of the Mangrove Club was acquitted of drug charges despite 66 officers testifying against him during the five-week trial. In December 1989 the Metropolitan Police had £100,000 awarded against them for planting cannabis upon a black man and subjecting him to racial abuse in Notting Hill. In the same month the key prosecution witness in the conviction of Alban Turner for a murder at the 1987 Notting Hill Carnival admitted that he had lied and that the police had paid him to give evidence.

Such complaints and scandals confirmed the allegations and suspicions of those who, since the early 1980s, had campaigned for new structures to be implemented to strengthen the democratic accountability of the police. However, given that such demands had been defined out by the mid-1980s, what was notable about the above-mentioned incidents in the late 1980s was the absence of political debate or concern. This is not to say that there was not a political context or political implications. But the debate that did take place was located firmly *within* the legal and organizational context of police accountability. Those participating in the debate were the same senior police-officers, the respective police organizations, Home Office officials and senior government figures who were also at the forefront of the debates about the future of the British police.

There seemed to be a concerted attempt by senior police-officers and members of the judiciary to minimize the impact of such scandals and to persuade the public that the very fact that such investigations were taking place was proof that the police were capable of rooting out the rotten apples. More liberal members of the judiciary indicated that the overturning of the Guildford and Winchester convictions was proof that British justice was the finest in the world. Sir Peter Imbert, who was the intelligence officer of the bomb squad responsible for assessing the information in the Guildford case, issued a warning to those who might demand that the police-officers involved be held to account for perpetrating such a miscarriage of justice.

> let's not fall into the trap which it seems police are accused of falling into at the end of 1974 of having convinced themselves that those people were guilty of that particular crime. I see a very clear similarity between the atmosphere now and then, let's be careful that we don't make another mistake now.
>
> (*Guardian*, 24 October 1989)

The Chief Inspector of Constabulary in his annual report for 1989 also defended the police as an institution from being held to account over such incidents when he stated that: 'It would be quite wrong to condemn all policing practice on the strength of a few, albeit significant incidents, even though they may have had tragic consequences' (Her Majesty's Inspectorate 1989). Whilst it was emphasized by all concerned that they had every confidence the internal inquiries would get to the truth of the matter, the judiciary and the police were setting clear limits to any investigations into the miscarriages of justice.

Given this context, it is little wonder that civil libertarians expressed concern about the implications of 1992 for those communities susceptible to non-accountable policing. They have argued that the advent of a single European market will detrimentally affect those groups already disadvantaged and discriminated against in the present system, that is, third world migrants, political refugees and asylum seekers and established black communities (see Joint Council for the Welfare of Immigrants 1989; Arnott 1990; *Spare Rib* 1990). The supra-national Eurocops will have the key role of policing Fortress Europe and certain groups are, if past experience is anything to go by, vulnerable to their attentions. As Sivanandan (1988: 9) has argued:

> Citizenship may open Europe's borders to blacks and allow them free movement, but racism which cannot tell one black from another, a citizen from an immigrant, an immigrant from a refugee – and classes all immigrants and refugees as terrorists and drug dealers is going to make such movement fraught and fancy.

It is because of this context that the issue of the democratic accountability of the police must once more be placed on the political agenda in the 1990s.

Chapter 6

The policing of black women
Ruth Chigwada

It is an undeniable fact that black people, women as well as men, are over-represented in Britain's prisons. Black people make up 4.7 per cent of the population in England and Wales yet the prison statistics released in September 1989 showed that they constituted 16 per cent of the total prison population. However, most academic research which focuses on black people and the agencies of the criminal justice system has tended to concentrate on males, with the end result that black women's experience has been marginalized.

The same is true of research on policing. Robert Reiner (1989a: 6) has argued that 'the police are by far the most researched group in the criminal justice system in the context of race relations'. However, there is very little information available on black women's experience of the police (see Benn 1985; Institute of Race Relations 1987; Dunhill 1989). There are no statistics available, for example, to show the frequency of black women being stopped by the police.

The omission of studies of black women's experiences is surprising when one considers the fact that the number of black women sentenced to prison has increased over the years and, according to 1989 statistics, black women now make up 25 per cent of the total female prison population. A need now exists for research in this area, in order to ascertain the role of police practices in accounting for this over-representation of black women.

There is evidence that police practices and the disposal of the courts towards black people leads to their disproportionate representation in penal institutions. A report by the Greater London Council (GLC), for example, states that:

The police, the courts and the press have combined in the criminalization of the black community. . . . Policing strategy and practice which equates black people with criminals and targets the black community for attention while supported by the racist press results in black people being more likely to arrive in court, to be charged with more serious offences, and thus to have longer criminal records.

(1985: 4)

Research has shown that the number of black people arrested increases with police operations. A study carried out by the Home Office Research Unit at two London police-stations found that young black males aged between sixteen and twenty-four were stopped frequently – approximately ten times above the average (Willis 1983). Before its repeal they were also more likely to be arrested, under the 'sus' law, for suspicious behaviour (Demuth 1978). The Policy Studies Institute (PSI) study of the police in London found that West Indians were not only one-and-a-half times as likely as white people to be stopped and searched, but that the average number of stops was nearly three times as high, since West Indians who were stopped tended to be stopped repeatedly and they were more likely to be arrested for offences of assault and robbery. The Home Office breakdown of the Metropolitan Police's criminal statistics in 1989 showed that 18 per cent of those arrested were black out of a population proportion of approximately 5 per cent. For certain offences the racial differences were even more striking with blacks accounting for over 60 per cent of those arrested for street robbery and theft from the person.

How do we account for these disparities? Although it is difficult to make causal connections, the existing literature does document considerable racial prejudice and stereotyping within the police (see Reiner 1985a; Brogden *et al.* 1988). Although the PSI researchers found that racial prejudice had less effect on policing behaviour than they expected, they warned that the level of prejudice was such that it should give cause for serious concern. They found that: 'racialist language and racial prejudice were prominent and pervasive and that many individual officers and also whole groups were preoccupied with ethnic differences' (1983: 109).

A recent book by Roger Graef (1989) found widespread racism

amongst the officers he interviewed. The book shows that many police-officers were socialized into a culture 'actively hostile to all minority groups' (1989: 124). This culture despised blacks, mocking, harassing, abusing and insulting them through the use of crude jokes and offensive nicknames. In an attempt to reassure the interviewer about their prejudices one officer stated: 'Policemen are insulting about everyone. Its not specially the coons. You hear remarks about poofs, Pakis, lesbos, women, students, the Irish – you name it. We hate everybody' (ibid.). A glaring example of the racist stereotyping and assumptions made about black people by the police is provided by the case won by the Commission for Racial Equality in 1988 against the Staffordshire Police. This force distributed a leaflet around neighbourhoods, asking residents to look out for cars being driven by blacks and to record their numbers as a crime prevention measure (*Birmingham Post*, 23 June 1988).

With the kind of racially discriminatory policing practices and racial prejudice to which black people are subjected it is not surprising that research has found that blacks are hostile to the police. The PSI study found that young blacks were considerably more likely to accept that the police fabricated evidence, used excessive force and abused their powers. The researchers concluded that 'the lack of confidence in the police among young West Indians can be described as disastrous' (1983: 326). Gaskell (1986), in a study comparing the attitudes of black and white young males towards the police, found evidence to suggest that although young blacks have more negative attitudes to the police than young whites, they are not anti-police merely because the police are seen as symbols of an oppressive white society. Nor are they more hostile solely as a result of higher unemployment levels among blacks. It was concluded that past policing strategies themselves have contributed to young blacks' hostile attitudes towards the police.

Given the above context, it is not surprising that the level of complaints against the police has been found to be higher amongst ethnic minorities. However, because of the deficiencies of the official complaints system, black people have increasingly resorted to using the civil courts to seek redress against police malpractice. Of the £500,000 that the Metropolitan Police paid out to wronged citizens in 1989, over half of the figure went to black people (*The Voice*, 6 March 1990). Many courts have awarded damages to black defendants for being framed or for having drugs planted on them by the police. In the case of Mrs Clementine George, who alleged that the police hit her, causing extensive bruising, the judge accused the police of 'concocting evidence' to cover up their outrageous behaviour (*South London Press*, 6 April 1984). In 1985 Mr Eugene Wilson was arrested during a raid on a club in Notting Hill, in London, accused of assaulting police-officers and possessing drugs with intent to supply. He was later acquitted after successfully arguing that the drugs had been planted on him by the police (*Kensington News Post*, 20 March 1986). In another case, Mr Rupert Taylor was awarded £100,000 in damages against the Metropolitan Police in 1989 after the High Court found that he had been wrongly arrested, stripped and searched, and accused of possessing cannabis (*The Voice*, 12 December 1989).

Although no academic study has focused specifically on black women's experience of the police it is the contention of this chapter that it is likely that they too are subject to the discrimin-ation and prejudice documented above. This chapter will present mainly anecdotal evidence concerning black women's experience of the police. Black women are more likely to come into contact with the police than white women for several reasons. Firstly, black women are seen as suspects as they are perceived as being more likely to commit criminal acts. Secondly, the fact that many are single parents tends to bring them into greater contact with the police who search their homes looking for youth suspects. Thirdly, black women are seen as immigrants by virtue of their colour and are therefore more likely to be stopped by police-officers carrying out passport checks. Finally, black women come into contact with the police who target them as suffering from mental disorder under Section 136 of the 1983 Mental Health Act. Each of these points will be discussed in detail below.

BLACK WOMEN AS SUSPECTS

Cultural assumptions made about black women are likely to affect police attitudes towards them. Common stereotypes attributed to black women include the over-aggressive African woman and the strong, dominant Afro-Caribbean woman who is the head of the household. Asian women are seen as 'passive' or 'hysterical' or subject to oppressive practices within the family. Such stereotyping has deterred police from taking action or prosecuting in cases of domestic violence involving black women as they are viewed as 'macho' and therefore able to look after themselves.

The police regard black women as suspects in part because of the media's portrayal of their lifestyle. Views of black women presented in the media also affect police treatment of black women upon arrest and are likely to influence whether the police exercise their discretion to caution or prosecute black women. Black women are labelled 'deviant' because they are powerless to conform to what British society conceives of as 'correct behaviour'. The following press report exemplifies the stereotyping of black women by the media:

> Young black men commit a disproportionately high number of violent crimes in London because most black mothers, when they are young girls, have children out of wedlock and are not supported by the fathers. There appears to be less stigma attached to single parenthood in the black community. The only hope is that somehow the West Indian marriage can be encouraged and supported.
>
> (*London Evening Standard*, 12 December 1987)

The implication of this report is that black women, as single parents, deviate from the norm and in doing so are to blame for the criminality of their offspring. As far back as 1973 the *Hornsey Journal* reported that the Broadwater Farm Estate in north London was occupied by: 'Problem families and the sight of unmarried West Indian mothers walking about the estate aggravated racial tensions' (11 May 1973). Such reports only serve to criminalize and pathologize black women and contribute to their image as suspects and the likelihood of their receiving custodial sentences for relatively minor offences.

Visher's research indicated that lenient or harsh treatment by law-enforcement agencies at any stage of the process depended on the degree to which a woman's behaviour was in accordance or at variance with the female role. This research concluded that chivalrous treatment at the stage of arrest depended upon a larger set of gender expectations that exist between men and women in their encounters with police-officers and that 'those female suspects who violate typical middle-class standards of traditional female characteristics and behaviour (i.e. white, older and submissive) are not afforded any chivalrous treatment in deciding arrest decisions' (1983: 22–3). Swigert and Farrell make a similar point, arguing that 'the processual consequences of stereotypes not only shape public attitudes and behaviour towards deviants, but guide the very choice of individuals who are to be so defined and processed' (1977: 17). The problem of stereotyping explains in part why the police are less likely to 'caution' black women and thus why black women are over-represented in prison. Because black women are labelled as deviant they may be seen to deserve harsher treatment.

Player's research on women and crime found that differential patterns of policing were meted out to women of different races. The black women in her study had been stopped and arrested more frequently than the white women. The police-officers she interviewed indicated that 'they would be more likely to arrest a woman who behaved aggressively or who was verbally abusive or obstructive than a woman who was trying to be helpful or appeared to regret what she had done' (1989: 124).

It is in this context that the police-officer's views of black and white women are important. The officers interviewed thought that black women were 'far more heavily involved in crime and knowledgeable about criminal matters', unco-operative and disruptive. In addition they were seen as being 'frequently hostile and difficult to handle and tended to attribute these difficulties to innate racial characteristics. Blacks were seen to be highly volatile, aggressive, and as having a 'chip on their shoulder' (1989: 123).

By contrast, white women were described as being 'innately less aggressive and thus less of an intractable problem', more likely than black women to express regret and remorse and to be more sensitive to the social stigma of arrest. It is within this overall context that police assumptions concerning black culture foster a view of black women as suspects and as being more likely than their white counterparts of committing a criminal offence. It is interesting to note that on the issue of social stigma the views of the police are at variance with what happens within the black community. Black women who have been in trouble with the police or who are ex-prisoners tend to be ostracized by their community and run the very real risk of being deserted by their family. In order to counter such stigma, organizations such as the Black Women's Prison Scheme have taken on the task of educating the black community to be more supportive towards black women ex-offenders.

With the kind of views expressed above, it is not surprising that the black women in Player's study were found to be more hostile towards the police than the white women:

> Without exception, all the black women in the study held staunchly anti-police feelings and accused the police of racial prejudice and corruption. Claims were made that officers had lied in court; and had used an unnecessary degree of force and intimidation during their investigations.
>
> (1989: 122)

This hostility can only be compounded when some specific examples of black women's experience of the police are considered. In the early 1980s a furore was created when, for the first time, a black woman spoke out publicly about sexual assaults by police on black women. Mrs Esme Baker was arrested when she went to investigate the arrest of her son. During her arrest and on the way to the police-station she was physically and sexually abused by police-officers. Both Mrs Baker and her son were later acquitted of charges of threatening behaviour and assaulting the police (James 1985).

Heaven and Mars (1989) have noted that some black women who claim that they have been sexually assaulted by police-officers feel unable to report the offence. The following cases provide an indication of why black women may hesitate about making official complaints. On 19 April 1984 Jacqueline Berkeley and three other young black women were arrested after an alleged street disturbance and taken to Moss Side police-station, Manchester. Jacki Berkeley later alleged that she had been stripped, racially abused and raped by two policemen whilst two policewomen held her down. She was subsequently found guilty of obstruction, assaulting three police-officers and wasting police time by making a false complaint of rape and received suspended prison-sentences of various lengths (John 1985). In 1989 a police-officer from Surrey who raped a young black woman in the front seat of his patrol-car was sentenced to seven years' imprisonment. A Court of Appeal subsequently overturned this conviction on the ground that the judge in charge of the original trial had failed to direct the jury properly on the previous good character of the police-officer. The quashing of this sentence brought an angry response from many women's organizations and requests for the sacking of the judges involved. 'Black Women for Wages for Housework' and 'Women Against Rape', for example, stated that the police-officer's successful appeal 'does not reinstate police credibility. Rather it further tarnishes the credibility of the courts' (*The Independent*, 10 July 1990). This decision will not encourage black women, or indeed any woman, to report cases of rape and sexual assault by police-officers and to have confidence in the courts. As one protest group spokeswoman noted: 'How can any woman have any confidence at all in the courts after such a decision, which gives the go-ahead to rape? (*Police Review*, 13 July 1990).

The above cases have illustrated the racial and sexual discrimination that are present in policing practices. In this sense they are examples of what Ruth Hall describes as 'racist sexual violence' (Hall 1985: 48). The issue of the class position of black women is also important. The police always fall heavily on the powerless and poor people. It is a fact that many black women are unemployed, single parents and their lifestyle does not match middle-class expectations. Therefore, they are vulnerable to being picked upon and treated harshly by the police.

BLACK WOMEN AS PARENTS AND THE POLICE

The fact that many black women are single parents has meant that they are often harassed by the police who enter their homes to look for or arrest their sons. Thus, while black men are harassed on the streets, black women feel the violent force of targeting on the home. In one case Ms Linda Williams lodged an official complaint after the police arrived at her home in Peckham, South London and demanded to see her son. Ms Williams said that when she asked to see their search warrants she was dragged downstairs by her hair and was repeatedly kicked in the back, while a police-officer stood on her legs. She was pregnant at the time (*West Indian World*, 8 February 1984).

The following two cases describe the maltreatment of black women by the police in the process of booking or arresting their sons. They are doubly significant in that aggressive – and fruitless – police searches of black homes in Brixton and Tottenham are thought, in part, to have triggered the riots in 1985. In each case the suspect's mother was on the receiving end.

With regard to the Brixton riots, the case involves a black woman who as a consequence of a police operation was left paralysed for life. On 28 September 1985 a team of armed officers went to the home of Mrs Cherry Groce in Brixton to arrest her son, who was wanted for armed robbery. In fact the son no longer lived at the address. The officers smashed down the door with a sledgehammer and then an inspector rushed in shouting 'armed police'. Mrs Groce said the officer suddenly rushed at her, pointing a gun. She tried to run back but he shot her (*The Times*, 16 January 1987).

The riots in Broadwater Farm in Tottenham were sparked by the death of a black woman at the hands of the police. On 5 October 1985 Floyd Jarrett was stopped by police and arrested for suspected theft of the vehicle he was driving. The police, who had no grounds for suspecting Mr Jarrett, then proceeded to search his family home for stolen goods. The search of the house was carried out by four officers, with a District Support Unit held in reserve. The officers, without warning, let themselves into the house with the keys taken from Mr Jarrett while he was at the police-station. During the search an officer brushed past Mrs Jarrett, pushing her out of the way. She fell, breaking a small table. The police continued their search while the daughter called for an ambulance. When the officers realized Mrs Jarrett was seriously ill, one of the officers gave her mouth-to-mouth resuscitation. However, she was dead on arrival at hospital. Lord Gifford called this raid: 'a shocking violation of the privacy of the Jarrett's house' (*The Broadwater Farm Inquiry* 1986). At the inquest of Cynthia Jarrett a verdict of accidental death was returned thus vindicating her family's case that the police search contributed directly to the heart attack which killed her. As Melissa Benn and Ken Warpole have pointed out:

> What these . . . very recent cases confirm is an ominous trend with regard to deaths in police custody – which we have been studying for the past two years – and that is that the site of such deaths has now reached into people's homes.

(1985)

No disciplinary action was taken against any of the police-officers involved. After the Brixton and Broadwater Farm riots black women lived in fear of the reality of being separated from their children, either if they, themselves, were arrested, with the likelihood that their young children would be left alone, or if their older children were arrested (The Women of Broadwater Farm 1989). The police, in many instances armed, 'visited' the 1,063 homes on the Broadwater Farm Estate after the riots and an indication of the fear that such visits caused is provided by the testimony of one black mother:

> They [the police] said that he [her son] had been picked up for the murder of the policeman, and it would be better for him if I told them everything I knew about what he was doing on the night of the riot. When I said my son didn't know anything about the murder they called me a 'stupid bitch' and refused to let me see him. I never had any quarrel with the police, but now I lie awake at night worrying in case the boys have been picked up again.
>
> (Quoted in Platt 1986: 7)

POLICING OF BLACK 'IMMIGRANT' WOMEN

Black women's experiences of policing are often bound up with Britain's immigration and nationality laws. These racially discriminatory laws have undergone considerable refinement and expansion in the post-war period. Paul Gordon has argued that such laws have not just been concerned with controlling who has right of entry to Britain: 'Immigration control has increasingly entailed the growth of controls and surveillance of those [black people] already here. To this end, the police and the immigration services have been given ever-increasing resources, both in terms of personnel and technology' (1985: 95).

Such powers and resources have resulted in the police stopping and questioning black people about their nationality as well as conducting controversial passport raids on black communities (Institute of Race Relations 1979: 13–17). In 1989 the *Observer* (15 October) reported that junior police-officers in London were being accused of having found a new ploy through which to harass black people over their nationality status. Alison Stanley of the Joint Council for the Welfare of Immigrants stated that:

It is the experience of many lawyers, advisors and community groups that in certain areas of London (worst beat areas include Hackney, Southwark and Lambeth) a new Sus law is effectively being operated, in which black people are regularly stopped on the pretext of minor road traffic infringements and then asked to produce passports.

She added that it was extremely worrying if policing priorities were being decided not by senior officers but by junior officers. One chief superintendent, who asked not to be named, told the *Observer*:

> I was unaware that this kind of targeting was going on until I overheard a Sergeant on the phone referring to a BSB! Out of curiosity, I asked him what he was talking about, and with a red face he explained that an immigration case was one for the Big Silver Bird [being put on a plane and deported].

The enforcement of nationality and immigration laws which, as the Joint Council for the Welfare of Immigrants (1989) has pointed out, are both racist and sexist, pose particular problems for black women. Jalna Hanmer has pointed to the problems that the laws cause for Asian women. She notes that in certain police districts 'the first response officers make to Asian calls for assistance, whether complaints of violence in the home or racist assaults, is to investigate the status and rights of the complainant to be in the country' (1989: 104).

The problem of the police's use and abuse of such powers in relation to black women is highlighted dramatically by the following cases. In 1978 the magazine *Campaign Against Racism and Fascism* (no. 7) reported a case in Goodmayes, Essex, where an East African woman who stopped to ask a policewoman for directions was held at the police-station until her passport could be produced. Some police-officers seemingly go to great lengths to take advantage of black women who are seen as suspect illegal immigrants. In one case a police-officer from Stoke Newington in north London called at the home of a Nigerian woman, under the ruse of checking her immigration status, which was in fact legal. He threatened her with deportation and demanded sexual favours as an assurance against this. Eventually the woman was awarded £8,000 in damages with the judge stating that the police-officer had 'acted behind the shadow of the Warrant Card and the strength of the law for his own squalid purposes' (*The Times*, 1 August 1989).

In another case a black woman was taken to the police-station by police-officers who had come to her flat to look for her partner. After the police had searched the residence and found nothing, they took the woman with them to the station 'to answer questions about a forged passport'. When she pointed out that the picture on the forged passport bore no resemblance to her the officers said: 'we know you black people, you disguise yourselves'. The police used family responsibilities to force a confession out of her. She was told that if she signed a statement admitting her marriage was 'for convenience' she would be released to be her eighteen-month old daughter. In fact this was a trick. After signing the statement they took her to Holloway Prison and the statement was used against her in court proceedings. She was further victimized in that she was not told of her rights and was not seen by a solicitor. On the second day of the hearing the passport charge was dropped (Chigwada 1989: 102).

THE RELEVANCE OF SECTION 136 OF THE 1983 MENTAL HEALTH ACT TO THE POLICING OF BLACK WOMEN

Section 136 of the 1983 Mental Health Act is intended to cover those situations 'where a person's normal behaviour is causing nuisance or offence'. Incidents leading to the employment of this section are usually reported to the police by members of the general public and routinely involve minor offences (Faulkner 1989: 216):

> If a constable finds in a public place to which the public have access a person who appears to him to be suffering from mental disorder and to be in immediate need of care or control, the constable may, if he thinks it necessary to do so in the interests of that person or for the protection of other persons, remove that person to a place of safety.

Any person removed under this section can be detained at the 'place of safety' for a period not exceeding seventy-two hours. The intention behind these provisions is to ensure that the 'mentally disordered' person is examined by a registered medical practitioner and interviewed by an approved social worker in order to make arrangements for his/her care.

This section of the act has become controversial for two reasons. First, it is the only provision in the act which allows one person alone (the constable), acting without medical evidence, to deprive a person of his/her liberty. The appropriateness of police involvement in medical diagnoses and the use of police-vans instead of ambulances has been questioned by organizations such as the National Association for Mental Health (MIND). Second, the official definition of a 'place of safety' includes the police-station. Given the history of black deaths in police custody, the designation of the police-station as a 'place of safety' for black people would seem ironic to say the least. Alison Faulkner has argued that

> Section 136 of the Mental Health Act is essentially a way of dealing with situations that cannot be dealt with by direct recourse to the mental health social services. As such, it is a necessary inclusion in the Act. However, the procedure followed in London [where the section is most frequently used] gives the police greater power with which to detain and refer people, as a result of which both men and women tend to be admitted to hospital for three days following police detention, and are rarely assessed by social workers.
>
> (1989: 216)

An excess of compulsory and police-referred psychiatric admissions from the Afro-Caribbean population has been reported by various studies (Ineichen *et al.* 1984; Dunn and Fahy 1987; McGovern and Cope 1987). As a consequence, police admissions to psychiatric hospitals have been a focus of attention for those who advocate a social control hypothesis in relation to psychiatry (Miller and Rose 1986). The possibility that high rates of police admissions may be partly affected by conscious or unconscious racist attitudes has also been a cause of concern among some psychiatrists. Writing about his clinical experience in the East End of London, Littlewood (1986) stated that it was 'certainly true' that the police could be behaving in an overtly racist manner in, as an alternative to arrest, selectively picking out mentally healthy black people and taking them to psychiatric hospitals under Section 136.

The study by Dunn and Fahy (1990) is important in that it aimed to compare black and white emergency police referrals to an urban psychiatric hospital based in a catchment area with a large Afro-Caribbean population and included black and white women. They attempted to establish whether rates of referral of blacks were different from those of whites; to ascertain the ability of the police to identify mental disorder among different ethnic groups; and to examine the reasons for referral and the outcome of admission among ethnic groups.

There were 268 referrals during the period of their study. Amongst this number 165 (61 per cent) were white and 88 (33 per cent) were black. The majority of the patients had a previous psychiatric history: 73 per cent of white men and 67 per cent of black men had a history of psychiatric admission, in comparison with 87 per cent of white women and 92 per cent of black women. The proportions admitted on Section 136 previously were 40 per cent for white men, 24 per cent for black men, 24 per cent for white women and 32 per cent for black women. Schizophrenia was the commonest diagnoses in all groups, but was made twice as often in blacks as whites. Personality disorder and alcohol and drug-abuse were more commonly diagnosed in white patients and drug-induced psychosis was more frequently diagnosed in black men.

The study also found that black people were more likely to receive psychotropic medications, especially neuroleptics: 90 per cent of black men as opposed to 63 per cent of white men, and 83 per cent of black women as opposed to 80 per cent of white women. Furthermore, 88 per cent of the black men were kept in hospital after the Section 136 order had lapsed as opposed to 74 per cent of white men, and 81 per cent of black women as opposed to 73 per cent of white women. Black men (48 per cent) were also more likely to be offered follow-up treatment than white men (25 per cent), as were black women (71 per cent) when compared with white women (58 per cent).

It is also clear from the above study that more black women than white women are referred by the police to mental hospitals under Section 136. These findings support the Police Monitoring and Research Group research which found that many more black women than white women were detained in police-stations or taken to mental hospitals under this section (1987, no. 26).

Because black women tend to speak loudly and are from a different cultural background their behaviour tends to be misinterpreted and this results in black women being seen as in need of psychiatric help and being taken to a 'place of safety'. MIND found that in a minority of cases the police breached the conditions of Section 136 by removing people, mainly women, from their own or other people's homes. Black women could be particularly vulnerable to such breaches. In neighbourhood disputes police tend to take a black woman to the police-station or another 'place of safety' if the other neighbourhood is white. If the neighbours are both black the police tend to take no action. Furthermore:

> Strong protests from women who are distressed as a result of male violence and appear hysterical or apathetic may be labelled 'madness' and judged by a police officer to be sufficiently threatening to warrant sanctioning – removal to a place of safety.
>
> (Police Monitoring and Research Group 1987, no. 26)

This has also been found to be the case in prison (Chigwada 1989) and it applies to offences committed by blacks against white people where the black defendant is seen to deserve serious punishment (Zimring 1976). This partly explains the increase in the number of black women referred to a place of safety and the high number of black women, compared to white women, who have a previous psychiatric history and who have been referred to a 'place of safety' on several occasions.

There are serious ramifications in being sent to a psychiatric hospital under Section 136. The period of detention can be indefinite. The patient is under constant observation and good behaviour can actually mean patient's submitting their rights to the ward staff. If a patient tries to assert his/her rights he/she may be labelled as 'disturbed' and this may further prolong the stay. Doctors and nurses have the right to give drugs to a patient against his/her will and the effects of some of the psychotropic drugs which are given in high doses to blacks (e.g. Haloperidol and Hargactil) have serious side effects. Once taken to a 'place of safety' psychiatrists tend to diagnose black women and working-class women as suffering from 'psychosis', rather than neurosis, which is the preferred diagnosis for white middle-class women (Sashidharan 1988). Such labelling in police records may adversely affect a woman's future involvement with the police as well as negatively impacting upon other aspects of her life.

MIND found that a large number of black women sanctioned by police action were later diagnosed 'not mentally ill' at the hospital. Since more women are detained under Section 136 than for criminal charges their rights are limited. Under Section 136 one has no right to see a solicitor and one's children may be taken into care. If employed one's job may also be jeopardized. Another problem under this section is that if a woman is not diagnosed as in need of hospital treatment, but released after the seventy-two hours allotted by the act, she has no redress in the law, unless she can prove that the police acted 'in bad faith or without reasonable care'.

CONCLUSION

This chapter has shown the multiple ways in which black women are victimized by the police: because of their colour (as suspected illegal immigrants); as single parents; due to the over-use of Section 136 of the 1983 Mental Health Act and as a result of racist stereotyping of black women by the media. The cultural assumptions made about black women beforehand target them as potential criminals and suspects, thus resulting in a disproportionate number of arrests. Black women who commit minor offences are unlikely to be merely cautioned. Such presumptions also contribute to the high number of black women referred by the police under Section 136 and subsequently diagnosed as in need of psychiatric help. Predictably the process of criminalization which begins in the streets with the police ends in prison and other custodial institutions.

Black women are not only criminalized but are also maltreated by the police. The repercussions of such maltreatment have become increasingly serious. As the review panel into the 1985 disturbances in the Handsworth/Lozells area of Birmingham has noted:

> We were told repeatedly that the 'trigger' events from which the initial eruptions arose involved a street confrontation between a Black woman and the police. . . . This brutal encounter between police and a Black woman is an important

link between the events in Handsworth and the disorders in
Brixton and Tottenham.

(1986: 66)

The police must be educated to understand other cultures and
must stop all racist and sexist behaviour towards black women if
we are to see a decrease in the number of black women arrested
and sentenced to prisons and mental institutions. It is also
necessary if the 'trigger' incidents of 1985 are not to be repeated.

Chapter 7

Back to school?
The police, the education system and the black community

Trevor Carter and Jean Coussins

This chapter concentrates on the relationship between the police, race relations and schools, drawing in particular on the experience of inner London during the 1970s and early 1980s, when the issue of police presence in schools became so controversial that some schools and teachers' groups had policies to exclude the police altogether from their institutions. In this context the Inner London Education Authority (abolished at the end of March 1990) conducted a wide community consultation exercise to review and revise policy in this area (ILEA 1986). The role of the police in schools was also the subject of a number of working parties and committees of senior police-officers, education officials, government departments and the Commission for Racial Equality.

We intend to examine the influences which brought the role of the police in schools into the limelight, often very dramatically, during this period. By the end of the 1980s, however, the issue had all but faded completely from the educational agenda as the political climate shifted and in the face of the far more wide-ranging and radical impact of the 1988 Education Reform Act (ERA). The 1986 Education Act had prescribed by law, for the first time, that schools have a duty to take account of police views on curricular matters and to report annually on contact between schools and the police. A few years earlier, this might have been capable of triggering off another inner-city rebellion, but has in fact attracted very little opposition or attention .

But although the subject of police-school relations is no longer high on the *educational* agenda at present, it is still an important item on the *black* agenda. The National Black Caucus, a loosely organized campaigning body representing Asian, African and

Afro-Caribbean interests, for example, remains opposed to any police presence in schools, for any reason, 'until genuine dialogue and tangible progress can be seen to be taking place, both in the police force and in the courts to eliminate racism and discrimination'.

We would argue that the profile of the police in schools issue does need to be considered again across the board, given the potential disasters as well as potential benefits which co-exist for black children under the Education Reform Act. A strategy must be forged to achieve the 'tangible progress' required by black leaders, and quickly. But the vision must then be extended so that the ultimate focus is on finding positive ways to *include* the police, within an agreed and properly controlled framework, rather than on simply prescribing the limitations of their access to and involvement in the education process. The possibilities for polarization, socially and economically, and therefore racially, which the ERA and other fundamental reforms in areas of social policy present, could easily prevent the gap between the police and the black community being bridged by dialogue and changed practices based on understanding common goals. Alternatively, the black community could, as before in education, take the lead and achieve a decisive shift in thinking and practice on the police in schools issue which would act as a catalyst for change in police–community relations more generally. The route from resistance to participation involves finding the right issue and the right time to switch from an oppositional emphasis to a constructive emphasis. The police for their part cannot afford not to be receptive to any proposition for dialogue with the black community, if for no other reason than because their capacity to recruit significant numbers of black and ethnic-minority officers will diminish even further if they do not accept the need to rethink attitudes and operational matters in a much more rigorous way than hitherto.

To understand why police presence in schools became such an explosive 'race' issue in the 1970s and 1980s, it is important to appreciate the attitudes of the majority of post-war immigrants towards the police. These people were to be the parents of the children in schools when the crisis of racism in education, alongside the role of the police, grew into the major challenge it did. We draw here mainly on the experience of families who came from the Caribbean to London, although, as we shall see below, the experiences of young people from the Asian communities at the hands of the police became equally decisive in developing a deep consensus of community opinion about the police and their priorities over the next decades.

In the West Indies, policing had been colonial, paramilitary and so, by nature, repressive. The adult immigrants of the 1950s, therefore, had been brought up with a particular attitude towards the police and authority generally. The image of the British bobby, friendly and parochial, was sold to them as part of the whole 'Mother Country' package which brought them here in large numbers from 1948 onwards in search of secure employment and the best education in the world, as they thought. Racism was not anticipated, least of all from the British bobby, and it came as a shock to be on the receiving end of the police's hostility towards black ownership of cars, for example, or the late night parties which were held largely because pubs and clubs closed their doors to all black faces.

What took time to develop in the black community was the understanding of racism as something systematic or institutional, as opposed to personal irritation which needed to be survived and coped with. For the stronger pull at first was still the motivation to do well in what was regarded by minds trained by a colonial society and a colonialist education system as a superior society. Knee-jerk respect for and belief in white figures of authority was difficult to dislodge. So it was that in the 1960s and 1970s, when the children of the West Indian immigrants began encountering racism in their schools, parental understanding and support was not always easy for them to find. This dislocation between adults' assumptions and childrens' experiences provided the subject of some of the interviews we conducted for *Shattering Illusions: West Indians in British Politics* (1986: 83–4).

To begin with, we – the parents – were baffled. Our children were not succeeding as we expected, but our lack of knowledge about the education system and our defensive unwillingness to believe that racism was to blame, tempted us to think that something might indeed be wrong with us or our children. I remember reacting with amusement when my own children came home from school deeply upset because the teachers had told them to go home to the jungle. I just couldn't believe that a teacher would say that sort of thing except as an innocent joke. The children would also say how their teachers found it difficult to engage in any conversation with them. I and my contemporaries, however, were still labouring under the illusion that these schools and these teachers were good for our children. When the children told the truth about their sufferings from racism, we simply could not see it. It even took time for us to develop respect for the few black teachers we came across. At first, it was the white teachers we sought out to discuss our 'problem' children with. We assumed they knew best. Only when it became clear that they were, on the whole, on a completely different wavelength from us did we turn to the black teachers and begin to understand that we were in the same sinking boat and that we needed to form an alliance to save ourselves and our children.

The experience of the young at school began to be mirrored on the streets. Parents' initial inclination to assume that their children must be misbehaving soon turned into support for the younger generation and an open criticism of the police, once the impact of 'sus', stop and search and racism generally was seen to be widespread and systematic. Despite actual crime rates for the black community being below average for the white population, black people, particularly the young, were virtually assumed to be criminal or potentially criminal by the police on the streets. The 'sus' charge, as it was known, derived from Section 4 of the 1824 Vagrancy Act and was used effectively to clear the streets of young people whom the police suspected of loitering with intent to commit an arrestable offence. Those accused had no right to be tried by jury. Black people accounted for a disproportionately higher percentage of those arrested on 'sus' compared to their numbers in the population as a whole. One study indicated that, in London, blacks were fifteen times more likely to be arrested under 'sus' than whites (Carr-Hill and Drew 1988: 43). As John La Rose, owner of the New Beacon bookshop in Finsbury Park, London, said in 1970, revealing the dominant fear within the community: 'No black people are free from police brutality. If you haven't been arrested, it merely means you haven't been arrested yet' (Carter 1986: 126). The early 1970s also saw high-profile racist campaign against 'mugging', a term imported by the media from the United States, with no legal meaning in Britain. The

National Front took up the campaign, as did Enoch Powell, and their definition of mugging as a black crime was widely covered in the media (Hall *et al*. 1978).

That 'stop and search' actively constituted unwarranted harassment is suggested clearly by the low figures for subsequent arrests. In 1972, for example, out of 41,980 people stopped and searched, only 3,142 were arrested. In 1975, out of 18,907 stop and searches in Greater London, 14,000 were in Lambeth and Lewisham alone, over a two-month period. This assault on two of London's biggest black communities resulted in just 403 arrests.

The consequences and implications of such practices are discussed elsewhere in this book. Our point here is to make the link between what was happening on the streets and what was developing in schools. There was a growing and deepening community feeling across the generations about police racism. The campaigns centred around families and communities to support the young people involved in collective trials such as the Stockwell 3, the Cricklewood 12, the Bradford 12, the Newham 7, the Newham 8, the Islington 18, and so on, finally dispelled the older generation's confidence in British justice.

The other strand in the backdrop to the police in schools controversy concerns the links between developments in educational theory and practice, the rise of the National Front and the later response of the Anti-Nazi League and similar anti-fascist groupings. The 1960s and the 1970s were years of great experimentation and innovation in the state education system in Britain, with the move towards comprehensive education at the heart of change. A child-centred approach combined with teachers seeing themselves carrying a wider, more caring role within the community, not just within the school building. People began to analyse ways in which the institution of 'school' and the professionals who ran it were alienated by means of race and class from the community, and to assert that more representative structures, such as the governing body, the teaching profession and the educational administration, would assist the achievement of all children in school. Curriculum developments mirrored these new approaches. In addition there was a new politicization in teacher trade unionism.

It was natural, therefore, that teachers played a significant role in the organizational response to the activities of the National

Front. 'Paki-bashing' of kids on the street affected what went on, and who learned what, in their classrooms. The racism, authoritarianism and militaristic bigotry of the young National Front members was in direct opposition to the more open, participative and inclusive philosophy which informed their new professional ideas and practices. Schools were seen by some as a microcosm of the society outside with all its prejudice and discrimination naturally reflected. Others saw school as a potential haven from the brutality of the streets, somewhere where black children in particular could be protected from the kind of harassment they faced on the way to and from school. A serious tension built up between schools in certain areas and the police. On the one hand, it was official and longstanding practice to invite police-officers to participate in various ways in the educational process, ranging from talking to young children about road safety to discussions with older pupils about law and order and citizenship (Schaffer 1980). However it is worth noting that until the late 1960s police participation in the educational process was viewed as being sensitive precisely because there were 'doubts about the propriety of using the police for such a function' (Boss 1967: 71).

Increasingly, during the 1970s the presence of the police in schools became problematic and in certain instances provocative. Police involvement in schools was a central part of the multi-agency community policing initiatives that arose out of the Cranfield Institute's 'The Police and Social Collaboration' conference in 1975 and the 1977 Ditchley conference (MacDonald 1976: 50; Pope 1985: 111–14). Paul Gordon has noted that police access to schools was regarded by the Scottish Office, for example, as 'the cornerstone of the community involvement branch's interests and concerns because the education system provides a ready-made structure in which the police contribution can be accommodated and through which they have comprehensive access to young people' (1987: 125).

Given the official statements being made on police involvement in schools, it is hardly surprising that educational conventions seemed to be abandoned by some police-officers who clearly began to identify schools as legitimate targets for invasion rather than dialogue. One school in north London was taken completely by surprise when several police-officers landed, totally unannounced, in the playground in a helicopter. Another incident, which we described in *Shattering Illusions* (1986), occurred in an east London school in 1979 when a black teacher was on playground duty. In full view of 200 boys, five or six policemen climbed over the school as the teacher was engaged in conversation with other officers. When the teacher asked what they were doing the response was a 'one finger salute from one of the Guardians of the Peace'. The teacher finally got through to a sergeant who said that a woman had made a complaint that one of the lads had exposed himself. Why then, the teacher asked, were police-officers in the process of searching two boys, one black and the other white, and having them empty their pockets – 'the sergeant got the point'. There was a sting in the tail for the police over this whole episode. The school complained and discovered the support of one witness they had not known had observed the entire charade: the local beat policeman. He too complained to his seniors that in fifteen minutes those five or six officers had undone about eighteen months of painstaking work he had done trying to build bridges with the school's staff and pupils.

If the police had trouble exercising their crime-solving role in a manner suitable for the occasion, some were also having trouble in contributing appropriately to the curriculum, as these extracts from *Shattering Illusions* illustrate:

As a teacher of social studies, I had to deal with the topic of 'law and order'. In 1972, the school's policy was to invite police officers in to speak to the third year pupils about their jobs. Four policemen came into the school. During the discussion, one black boy began to describe his recent experience of being arrested. He had been standing at a bus stop and witnessed some other lads breaking a shop window and running away. Together with an elderly white woman at the bus stop he went over to look at the damage. Within minutes the police arrived and, without asking any questions, held the boy, taking no notice of his protestations of innocence, despite the support of the old lady. . . . In my classroom that afternoon, the boy challenged the police. Did they think it was right, he asked, that he should have been dealt with so unjustly? To a man, they disputed the story. They quizzed him as if he were under arrest again, but he stuck to his guns. When they realised they were not going to catch him out, they changed tack and said that while the police were right in most cases, there had obviously been some mistake here. All this was said without one iota of sympathy for the boy or his family. Their behaviour took no account whatsoever of their school surroundings or the purpose of their visit: they just carried on like a bunch of officers in their interrogation room. I pointed this out and said I thought they were achieving the exact opposite of what was intended by the session. . . . I knew I would never forget the sight of a third-year black kid holding forth against four police-men at his articulate best. Neither would I forget the looks of incredulity on the faces of the rest of the class. I knew I had to pick up the pieces. I would certainly need to find a different approach to 'law and order'.

(Carter 1986: 102–3)

The milestone which led to a more organized and high-profile stand against the police presence in schools was the tragic death of Blair Peach during an anti-National Front demonstration in Southall on 23 April 1979. Blair Peach was a teacher and he exemplified the links between the anti-racist struggles within education and those against the racism of the police on the streets. After a baton charge by police officers, including members of the Special Patrol Group, Blair Peach had to be taken to hospital with head injuries. Despite surgery he later died, the cause of death being a single blow to the head. The report of the Unofficial Committee of Inquiry into events in Southall reached the conclusion that:

There is no reason to believe that Blair Peach was killed by an SPG officer, and no evidence to suggest that he was killed by anyone else. It is a matter for astonishment that the police investigation into his death has resulted in no criminal or disciplinary proceedings.

(Dummett *et al.* 1980: 177)

No police-officer was ever brought to account for this death because the Director of Public Prosecutions concluded that there was insufficient evidence to warrant judicial proceedings. Blair Peach's death was part of a picture which was being more fully appreciated by the public year by year. It was a picture in which police operations over and over again appeared to give protection to racists and fascists, but harassment and aggravation to their opponents. Horses and riot-shields, for example, were used against anti-fascist demonstrators in Lewisham in August 1977. On 11 June 1978, 150 National Front members rampaged through Brick Lane in London's East End. The police failed to appear, although two Asians were subsequently charged with threatening behaviour for defending themselves and their bail conditions included a 7 a.m. to 7 p.m. curfew every Sunday.

It was also a picture in which there was a blatant resistance by the police to define racial attacks and harassment as such: in December 1977 the Moonshot Club in Lewisham was burnt down amid National Front threats, but the police refused to classify the incident as a racial attack. In January 1981 thirteen black youngsters were killed and twenty-seven suffered serious injuries in the New Cross fire, Deptford, London but no satisfactory explanation has ever been found. And 1985 was a year peppered with racial attacks of the most vicious and extreme kind imaginable across East London (see Gordon 1986). These are just a few examples of what was a relentless daily pattern of life for vast numbers of black families and individuals.

Throughout the decade the picture on the streets of Britain's inner cities was also characterized by police tactics which, from a black point of view, criminalized whole communities. This is not surprising when the most senior police-officer in London, Sir Kenneth Newman, held the view, for example, that: 'In the Jamaicans you have people who are constitutionally disorderly. . . . It's simply in their make-up. They are constitutionally disposed to be anti-authority'. This opinion was expressed in an interview for an American policing magazine on Newman's appointment as Commissioner of the Metropolitan Police in October 1981 (see *Policing London* 1982, no. 2).

Since many of the young black people being harassed on the streets in the evenings and at weekends were the same young people attending schools during the day, schools became a focus for their and their parents' expression of anger and frustration at police behaviour. Teachers like Blair Peach saw it as their duty to respond not just as individuals to the racism which offended them personally and politically, but to respond also as organized professionals. Thus the emergence of several groupings such as Teachers Against Racism and the All London Teachers Against

Racism and Fascism. Pressures from them, alongside the pressure from the black communities, led to a major challenge to the education authorities and the police to justify and reappraise the role of the police in schools. The Hackney Teachers' Association, the National Union of Teachers branch in Hackney, where Blair Peach had taught, called in 1979 for a total ban on police in schools. This policy was reaffirmed after the 1981 uprisings when Hackney Teachers' Association stated that it would be 'impossible for us to retain the confidence of black parents and pupils if we are seen to be allowing police access to our schools and classrooms'. The Socialist Education Association produced guidelines on *Schools and the Police Force* (1983) which questioned the involvement of a democratically unaccountable organization in the educational process. The guidelines stated that there should be limited access and that the police would have to learn to negotiate the degree of their presence in schools. In addition the guidelines stressed that the police should have to recognize school policies such as anti-racist and anti-sexist teaching approaches.

It is during this period that the issue of police and schools began to figure on the formal political agenda. There was a proliferation of official statements, documents and initiatives specifically addressing the issue. The influential Scarman Report hoped that teachers and parents would 'welcome and encourage' police involvement in schools. Lord Scarman stressed that:

> Police assistance in the education of children in the fundamentals of an ordered society can, however, be of great value. Indeed, as the pressures on our society grow in intensity, the need for programmes of instruction for all children in the way government works, in the law, and in the duties, as well as the rights, of citizenship, increases.

> (1981: 166)

After collecting information from thirty-seven forces HMI produced a report, *Police Liaison with the Education Service* (1983). The objectives of police/education liaison were stated as being the promotion of (a) good citizenship and social responsibility, (b) crime prevention, (c) the role of the police and other criminal justice agencies and (d) safety guidance for children. A follow-up seminar took place in June 1984 between Chief Education Officers, Chief Officers of Police, Her Majesty's Inspectorates of

Constabulary and Schools, DES, DHSS and the Home Office. This seminar 'recorded a consensus in favour of further discussion designed to reach agreement on practical measures for improvement'. A joint Association of Chief Police Officers/Society of Education Officers working party was set up and eventually produced a discussion document, *Liaison between Police and Schools*, in April 1986. Throughout this period a series of initiatives was introduced by different police-forces to facilitate more systematic police involvement in schools. Sir Peter Imbert, as Chief Constable of Thames Valley, justified his force's involvement on the grounds that 'we should not allow children's attitudes to be formed without an introduction to a scenario of a well-ordered, law-abiding society' (see *Policing London*, no. 2).

In 1986 the Inner London Education Authority issued centrally a detailed discussion paper for consultation on the subject. There were three generally accepted ways in which the police might be involved in ILEA schools, each of which was described and analysed. They were first, in pursuit of their duties in respect of the maintenance of law and order; secondly, within their general practice of community relations; and thirdly, in the process of education.

An example of the first type of involvement might be a police-officer being called in to deal with an intruder. The police may also enter a school if they are in immediate pursuit of a suspect, if they are responding to an emergency call, or (and this last possibility is meant to be exceptional and must have the headteacher's consent) if they need to interview a pupil; in connection with a criminal investigation. Codes of practice under the 1984 Police and Criminal Evidence Act provide that pupils should not actually be arrested on school premises unless this is unavoidable.

'Community policing' is not easily defined, although in London during the 1980s it was particularly cynically regarded in the light of the absence of any structure for local democratic accountability for the police and because of the police practice of defining who the 'community' and its leaders were. Nevertheless, as we have shown in the previous extract from *Shattering Illusions*, some individual community police-officers or home beat officers can be much closer to the concerns and perspectives of their community than their superiors. Such officers, however, tend to be undervalued in the police culture, where macho behaviour and hi-tech methods are more favoured, as the Policy Studies Institute study on the Metropolitan Police disclosed in 1983.

It is, however, the third area of traditionally accepted police involvement in schools – as part of the educational process – which has posed the sharpest contradictions and controversy. It is also the area for which school governors are now statutorily responsible. The national working party of chief police-officers and chief education-officers, referred to previously, defined four specific aims of educational visits by the police to schools:

1 to inform schools and pupils about the role of the police;
2 to inform about the law and the rights and duties of citizens;
3 to make young people aware of dangers; and
4 to help in fostering crime prevention (see ACPO/SEO 1986).

The problem is that although these educational objectives are perfectly valid ones, with which no parents or teacher would disagree, their delivery by the police (rather than teachers or possibly other professionals), who are within the black community so clearly and widely associated with racism, may seem to be putting the cart before the horse. Thus NUT guidelines released in April 1986 emphasized that the carrying out of these educational objectives needed to be prepared and controlled very carefully, both in the light of local circumstances and on the basis of a clear understanding on the part of the police and teachers about each other's role and the demarcation lines between them.

The NUT was also concerned that police-officers involved in education should receive proper training (see NUT 1986). The study of the Schools Involvement Programme in Hillingdon in 1984 concluded that national assessment of such programmes was urgently needed. In Hillingdon, even though it was thought that liaison between the education authority and the police was better developed than elsewhere, there was no clear statement to be found of the programme's objectives and the exercise on the whole was felt to have had a greater influence on pupils' attitudes than their levels of knowledge. It was noted that, as a result of police teaching, pupils' attitudes shifted towards the view that the law should be harsher, sentencing stricter and the penal system more punitive. The researchers stated that the 'social control' function of the police programme should be more freely acknowledged, so that schools can ensure that a correct balance is maintained in the curriculum (Vorhaus 1984). Hackney Teachers' Association also forcefully reiterated their critique of school/police liaison guidelines:

> The guidelines are a public-relations exercise. Young people here don't see the police as their friends. We do not want to be associated with them. We don't ask vets to teach biology, so why should police have right of admission? Until they make fundamental changes in their behaviour, which we consider to be racist, I don't see our policy changing.
>
> (*The Independent*, 17 October 1988)

One of the problems raised by the unresolved racism within the police-force, which impedes proper educational co-operation, is the risk of the baby being thrown out with the bath-water. There are some situations in which the same people who are opposed to police racism might want to see a higher police profile rather than their withdrawal. In the ILEA, an example of this contradiction was over a video film made in conjunction with the Metropolitan Police called *Have Fun, Take Care*, designed to raise children's awareness of the danger of contact with strangers and the possibilities of abduction or sexual offences. Some schools and sections of inner London's NUT criticized the ILEA for working with the police on this issue and accused the authority of collaboration with racism.

Newer organizations, notably the National Black Caucus, do not share the policies of a blanket no contact with the police, as held by the Hackney NUT in the 1980s. National Black Caucus members, for example, are willing to participate in police training programmes, precisely because they do subscribe to the view that the only viable long-term vision for the police-force in Britain is for them to achieve a representativeness appropriate to a multi-racial society, with operational criteria and priorities to match. Participation in police training by black community leaders, therefore, is considered to be a worthwhile exercise which can be justified in the present circumstances, although the practice was once regarded by many in the black communities as a 'sell out'. Groups like the National Black Caucus, although willing to participate in police training, will presumably not condone the kind of behaviour displayed by police-officers who humiliated the black boy in the social studies class described in the extract above, and they are not prepared to risk exposing more black children to such treatment until there is a clear chance of classes involving both teachers and police-officers including more black people, in either or both professional roles. The role of school governors (amongst whom there also needs to be a larger black contingent) will be instrumental in carving out the ground for a more fruitful relationship between schools and the police in the future.

Apart from the provisions of the education legislation which could help either to make or break police/school relations, there are also implications for progress in the right direction from the government's Interdepartmental Racial Attacks Group report (the RAG report) published in 1989. This is the first official document unreservedly to embrace what has become known as the multi-agency (by which we mean the multi-disciplinary co-operation of a number of organizations/institutions on an equal basis) approach to racial attacks and harassment. The scope of the RAG report covers not only the police, but also the education and youth services, housing and social services departments and the voluntary sector, ascribing to each 'agency' a vital and interdependent role in the prevention of and procedures for dealing with racial attacks. The report was widely welcomed by black groups, the Commission for Racial Equality and others who have called for co-operation between relevant agencies for some time, and who saw the report as a breakthrough in official – particularly police – thinking.

Rather like parts of the Education Reform Act, however, the officially-endorsed multi-agency approach has either the capacity to make a genuine difference for the better, or alternatively the potential for stagnation and buck-passing. It is essential that the opportunities be seized to achieve the former. Each professional grouping involved would benefit from the cross-fertilization of ideas and practices in pursuit of the common goal to eliminate racial attacks and harassment. It is arguable that the police stand to gain the most from working professionally with other groups. The wider benefits of this would include a clearer acceptance within the ranks of the need for the police to operate as a community service and to work for the benefit of all sections of the community. Once this basic change in self-perception has taken root, the doors are more likely to be open for a different type of person to join the police, which will naturally include those from black and ethnic-minority communities.

Just as schools, particularly those in the multi-racial, inner-city areas, have in the past decade undergone an often painful process of evaluating their function in the community and tried to find ways of becoming a resource for the whole community, so the police too must assess their role and the nature of their institutional practices and philosophies. The time may not be right for uniformed police to be regularly present again in schools in any of the three traditionally accepted ways. But that does not mean that the police and schools have not a great deal to learn from working alongside each other, so that, ultimately, both agencies may strengthen each other and help to safeguard the processes by which young people learn to participate in – and which perpetuate – democracy.

Chapter 8

Discrimination, disadvantage and police-work

Tony Jefferson

INTRODUCTION

Within ten years Britain will have solved its 'black problem' –
that is the message of the White Paper – but 'solved' in the sense
of having diverted revolutionary aspiration into nationalist
achievement, reduced militancy to rhetoric, put protest to
profit and, above all, kept a black under-class from bringing to
the struggles of the white workers political dimensions peculiar
to its own historic against capital. All these have been achieved
in some considerable measure in the past decade and a half –
through immigration control and social control – and the
process has already thrown up the class of collaborators so
essential to a solution of the next stage of the problem: the
political control of a rebellious 'second generation'. And it is to
this exercise that the White Paper addresses itself.

(Sivanandan 1976: 347)

The best contribution criminology can make to socialist politics
is to concern itself with specific analyses of crime and crime
policies.

(Hogg 1988: 47)

Rereading Sivanandan's uncompromising mid-1970s account of
'The black experience in Britain' is salutary, since it reminds us,
forcibly and with considerable rhetorical skill, of the absolute
importance of the political economy of immigration for a proper
understanding of the story. But, from the vantage-points of the
late 1980s, a decade of radical Conservative administrations and
the new 'left realism' this has evoked, it is now equally revealing
for its neglect of another level of analysis, namely, anything to do

with 'crime and crime policies'. Moreover, since analytical accounts at either level do not necessarily ring true at the level of experience, we need also to understand how the relevant social processes are understood and experienced by those subject to them. In other words, if we wish to produce an understanding of 'race and police-work' which is faithful to all the complexities of the reality covered by that phrase – my object in what follows – we shall need to explore what we know at all these levels. Hopefully, this will prove to be a critical but cumulative journey.

In order to do this I intend, first, to take a historical look at the political economy of police-work in order to identify the organic (or structural) features of the relationship between police and ethnic minorities. Second, I propose to take a closer look at the present in order to identify the particular, contemporary processes which, in conjunction with the organic features, are determining police-black relations. Then I shall look at the debate about race and crime. And, finally, I will examine what we know of the attitudes, perceptions and experiences of ethnic minorities. Though I do not expect to be able to resolve all the problems posed en route, I do hope this stock-taking will leave us better placed to do so.

Two caveats, finally: because space is at a premium, race and ethnicity are used interchangeably throughout, Cohen's valuable strictures to the contrary notwithstanding (Cohen 1988: 24); secondly, and also for reasons of space, I shall confine myself to a discussion of British data and materials, which means, broadly speaking, to the experiences of Afro-Caribbeans (Blacks) and Asians (from the Indian subcontinent).

POLICING THE 'ROUGHS'/POLICING RACE: A POLITICAL ECONOMY OF POLICE-WORK

Up until relatively recently a conservative, evolutionary picture of the emergence and development of modern police-work dominated accounts with the idea of the restrained use of force as a central feature. From this perspective, the widespread cross-class hostility to the very idea of a permanent, paid police-force in the late eighteenth and early nineteenth centuries ensured that the resulting force was unarmed, without special powers and charged to use the minimum force necessary. This restrained approach quickly won over the middle classes, and eventually the working classes, once the benefits of a more orderly and less crime-prone society became evident, and the fears (of intrusion, surveillance, loss of liberty, etc.) proved relatively groundless. With increased acceptance went a reduction in the sort of hostility and violence (from both sides) characteristic of early police–public contacts. This new 'maturity' in police–public relations inaugurated a 'golden age of policing', which in turn provided further vindication of the restrained approach. A key problem for this conservative perspective is how to explain interruptions to this evolutionary progress – the continuation of conflict or any remaining police-public hostility (both of which characterize police-black relations currently) – without invoking exceptional or pathological explanations.

Such accounts have been challenged by radical alternative accounts which start with the function of the new police. Whether the object of policing was crime, disorder, culture or morals, the function remained broadly the same, namely, the coercive imposition of a 'new civility' on the swelling labouring classes of the growing towns and cities of Victorian England. This coercive, class-based 'civilizing' function at the heart of the police role – captured neatly in Storch's notion of the early police as 'domestic missionaries' (1976) – not only accounts for the initial hostility and violence of police–public contacts, but also its continuation in working-class communities. 'Restraint' may characterize the police handling of the middle classes, but not the disorderly and criminal activities of the working classes. The 'golden age of policing' is thus a convenient myth. If the touchstone for evaluating policing is the experience of working-class communities and not an undifferentiated 'public', conflict and hostility, not acceptance, is the enduring legacy. A key problem for this approach is the inverse of the former, namely, how to explain the general legitimacy police have acquired for much of the time with significant majorities of the population, including working-class communities (for fuller treatment of both sorts of account, see Brogden *et al.* 1988: 49–100; Reiner 1985a: 9–82).

The resolution to this dilemma of whether police-work is best conceived primarily in terms of 'acceptance' or conflict can be found in a third approach, which is based on a recognition that both – acceptance and conflict – are *contingent* not inevitable features of police–public relations. The idea that consent is always conditional derives from Gramsci, for whom the question of consent was crucial. If traditional marxism had emphasized the centrality of understanding the role of conflict between the classes for political or social analysis, Gramsci was one of the first to recognize the importance of consent for understanding how advanced capitalist democracies worked. He recognized that the strength of 'civil society' in such societies rendered an 'old-style' revolutionary seizure of state power redundant. He also recognized that a well-developed civil society made coercion a strategy of last resort; what happened when the ideological struggle to produce consent failed. Both the 'ruling bloc' (the ruling class and its allies from other classes) and its opponents were constantly struggling to widen their sphere of influence by winning over allies to their vision of the world. To the extent that a ruling bloc was successful in such a struggle, its dominance could be said to be 'hegemonic'. To the extent that it failed to do so, it was appropriate to talk of a 'crisis of authority'. Such moments of instability might have many outcomes, including, if the alliance of radical forces failed to produce a successful counter-hegemony (and as Gramsci knew to his personal cost), the horrors of fascism and other 'exceptional' modes of capitalist rule.

The idea of politics as the outcome of the balance of forces at particular moments, and of this balance being constantly in flux as each side enjoins the ideological struggle in order to 'win friends and influence people' (and disturb their opponents' similar attempts), renders a very different historical framework to those of the two previously looked at. Rather than the conservative idea of history as progress, or the radical one of history as constant conflict, what we have here is the idea of history as a series of moments or 'conjunctures', each more or less stable, each more or less hegemonic (or consensual). Whilst long-term 'organic' trends determined by the mode of production set certain limits, within these limits political outcomes are the product of (or *contingent* upon) the successful (or unsuccessful) management of the political field. And crucial to such management is the 'battle of ideas'. (For an elaboration of Gramsci's key ideas, see Gramsci 1971.)

Phil Cohen's article (1979) on the changing nature of the policing of Islington before and after the First World War is an excellent example of this 'contingent' approach applied to the history of police-work. The basic argument runs something like this. Like the radical approach outlined above, the starting-point is the idea of the new police having a 'civilizing' mission ultimately motivated by economic considerations which was fiercely resisted by the city slum-dwellers who bore its brunt. However, and here the importance of ideology and consent becomes crucial, this mission embodies a *contradictory* function. On the one hand, the relentless pursuit of the mission – the enforcement of 'statutory norms of public order' (ibid: 120) in working-class neighbour-hoods where strong countervailing norms operated – could not help but overstretch limited resources and feel oppressive to the community on the receiving end. Hence the fierce community resistance. On the other hand, anything less than full enforcement threatened the very idea which gave the new police-force its general legitimacy, namely, impartial law enforcement. The result was to confront 'the force . . . with the impossible choice of enforcing law *or* order' (ibid: 130).

In terms of 'consent', the problem was one of competing ideologies: the old ideology of what was acceptable public behaviour in working-class neighbourhoods – the *popular* notion of public order espoused by the new urban proletariat; and the new 'juridical ideology of crime' (ibid: 128) – the unpopular bourgeois legal order 'in which the bourgeoisie has enshrined its version of the rights of capital and the obligations of labour' (ibid). In other words, 'proletarian order' versus 'bourgeois law.' The solution to the 'impossible choice' was, eventually, compromise: a change from the 'outright physical confrontation' characteristic of policing in Islington before the First World War to 'an unwritten system of tacit negotiation' (ibid: 123) in the post-war period. In practice this meant 'turning half a blind eye to the rule book' and 'turning the other half of the blind eye to a good deal of minor infringement' (ibid: 130).

This change – from confrontation to negotiation – was not just attributable to the new ideological function of the police. A whole host of changes, especially structural changes in the labour market, assisted. Critical to the latter was the growing divide between the declining 'informal' casual labour market and the developing formal economy, with its 'labour aristocracy' at the apex and gradations of other skilled, semi- and unskilled workers beneath. Whilst those in the casual, informal economy – led by the costermongers (barrow traders) – remained committed to the traditional street culture with its associated popular institutions and mores, those in the regular economy, led by the 'labour aristocrats', like the 'skilled print and railway workers' (ibid: 124), were establishing and participating in a whole range of new institutions – political, cultural and social – and developing a new morality to match. This new morality Cohen has termed 'public propriety' (ibid). In short, a structurally-based divide was beginning to open up between those workers with a stake in the new urban order (the 'respectables') and those without (the 'roughs'). This division, and the associated development of the notion of 'public propriety', provided the material basis for the change from confrontation to negotiation, namely, 'an alliance between the spokesmen of proletarian patriarchy [the 'respectables'] and the enforcers of bourgeois law and order [the police]' (ibid: 132).

However the willingness to allow certain notions of community 'order' to prevail over juridical notions of bourgeois 'law' does not eliminate the ideological importance of the latter. In other words, the contradictory choice of law or order remains. The organizational solution has been to institutionalize this contradiction in the form of an internal division of labour. Within this, some officers, like local beat coppers, have the task of 'maintaining negotiated order'; others, 'like the Special Patrol Group and Regional Crime Squads' are charged with restoring 'statutory order without regard for any of the factors constraining the operations of the local force' (ibid: 134). The consequence is the constant undermining of each other's work:

> The more resources allocated to increasing the efficiency of repressive policing, the more manpower has to be poured into 'community relations' to restablize the public image of the force. The more technologically sophisticated, and hence impersonal, the systems of surveillance, the more home-beat coppers are needed on the ground.
>
> (ibid: 133)

Finally, the fragility of negotiated settlements is emphasized, and the connection between class and race is made. Because of the way in which the labour force under capitalism is constantly being recomposed and relocated, any negotiations made with existing communities will need to be constantly renegotiated with any new group of workers (or 'non-workers') generated by these changes in the division of labour. To illustrate, Cohen particularly mentions changes in the juvenile labour market and the arrival after the Second World War of 'immigrant workers'. The temptation for the police with such 'new social forces' is to take the easy way by 'falling back on the more or less brutal reimposition of statutory public order when policing these groups' (ibid: 132). Thus it is that the idea of 'negotiated' consent is necessarily contingent; new contingencies constantly threaten the 'unstable equilibria' of existing accommodations.

The advantages of this kind of approach over the others is, hopefully, obvious: it requires neither exceptional nor pathological explanations for the re-emergence of hostility and violence, yet it can also explain why much public-order policing is relatively peaceful, and why there is strong support for the police amongst the working class. In short, neither consensus nor coercion are seen as inevitable features of police–public relations; rather each is regarded as contingent. And Cohen offers an account of the relevant contingencies operating at a crucial transitional moment in the 'policing of the working class city', and points – with his references to the arrival of 'immigrant groups' and the simultaneous developments of community relations and Special Patrol Group type policing – to their contemporary relevance.

Within this approach, then, 'immigrant workers' become heirs to the coster tradition – the new 'roughs' who understand only the 'brutal reimposition of statutory public order' – and the explanation of why race has become such a significant modality of police–public conflict is given a firm, structural basis.

The strengths of such an account lie in the way processes of marginalization and criminalization are connected to broad shifts in the political economy, and in emphasizing the importance of law and the legal mandate (the contradictions between law and order), as well as ideology ('public propriety'), in mediating such shifts. But there are limitations too: an overemphasis on proactive crimes (crimes which come to light through police-initiated activity and which are sometimes regarded as 'victimless', e.g. offences related to prostitution, drunkenness, drugs, gambling, etc.) and a comparative lack of attention to reactive ones (crimes to which police react indirectly, upon citizen request, and which collectively constitute the broad range of conventionally perceived 'normal' crimes, e.g. burglary, thefts, frauds, assaults, etc.). this has the effect of playing down intra-group crime. Moreover, lumping different ethnic groups together as 'immigrant workers', as Cohen does, obscures the possibility of differences between racial groups.

CRISIS, THE NEW RIGHT AND PARAMILITARISM: RACE, RIOTS AND POLICING IN THE PRESENT CONJUNCTURE

For our purposes, the inner-city riots of the 1980s offer, in condensed form, the most pertinent comment on police–black relations in the present conjuncture. But, to fully understand these, the nature of the conjuncture needs briefly to be established.

In broad terms, the present moment is framed, first, by a general crisis of hegemony and, second, by the particular response of the radical right. Loosely speaking the 1960s witnessed a breakdown in the consensual hegemony that had characterized the 1950s and ushered in the more coercive, less hegemonic 1970s and 1980s. Of course, 1968 was pivotal here, as was Mr Heath, who made the first attempt in the early 1970s at a radical right solution to Britain's economic ills, only to be brought down by working-class solidarity and union resistance across a broad front. Jim Callaghan's subsequent attempts to revive social democracy's flagging fortunes via a new 'social contract' with the unions proved, in the event, to be both ill-fated and temporary. Consequently Thatcherism, hatching in the opposition wings since the mid-1970s, was able to take up the reins of office and, in the new highly divided climate, complete the attempted Heathian revolution.

This has involved a triple-pronged attack: economic, ideological and political. In the economic field it has entailed putting the fight against inflation and uncompetitiveness above the evils of recession, a strategy which resulted in huge losses to Britain's industrial manufacturing base, a massive rise in unemployment, cuts in the social wage and a growing divide between the 'haves' and the 'have-nots'. In short, the economics of Thatcherism have meant a relative worsening of the position of the most disadvantaged groups in society – amongst which the young, and especially black youth, have been particularly prominent.

Ideologically, it has entailed a combination of transforming diffuse social anxieties into a series of moral panics through the process of scapegoating deviant and dissenting groups; reducing all dissensual voices to manifestations of a single, undifferentiated 'threat' – 'the enemy within' (e.g. striking miners); and then denying dissent any political meaning by labelling it 'criminal', or, where the label 'violent' could be attached, any meaning whatsoever (e.g. striking miners, inner-city 'rioters', Irish republicans). The overall achievement of this set of changes has been the installation of an ideological repertoire capable of reading all dissent as part of a violent conspiracy against 'our' way of life requiring legal constraint and firmer control. Once again black youth – first through the early 1970s mugging scare, then through the more general mid-1970s equation of blacks and crime, finally as 1980s' 'rioter' – have figured prominently in all this.

If dissent is part of a conspiracy, then 'legal constraint and firmer control' is justified. And there is no doubt that greater coercion has been at the heart of the political attack. This increase in coercion has entailed an extraordinary 'mobilisation of legal instruments against labour, political dissent and alternative lifestyles' (Hall *et al.* 1978: 284), starting in the early 1970s, and the gradual institutionalization of a paramilitarized policing response to strikes, protest and inner-city crime. The sorry history of police-black youth relations through the 1970s and 1980s bears witness to the role black youth have played in this moving up of coercive gear. (For a fuller account of this crisis of hegemony, see Hall *et al.* 1978: 218–323).

Casting our minds back to Phil Cohen's historical account of policing in Islington can now assist our understanding of this conjunctural coincidence, namely, a breakdown of hegemony and the simultaneous emergence of a more coercive, paramilitarized policing response. The essential features of the current breakdown of hegemony have been, to simplify, an economic crisis in which the accompanying recomposition and relocation of the labour force has entailed a massive (and, for some, seemingly permanent) shake-out of labour, and the creation of what might crudely be called 'the new lumpen' or, as some see it, a new 'underclass' (cf. Auletta 1982); a political crisis characterized by a tough 'law and order' response to increasing numbers of belligerent dissidents of all persuasions; and an ideological crisis in which a repertoire of negative evaluations is constantly applied to all forms of dissent, and which in turn is constantly being challenged. The essential feature of the paramilitary response has been a rough and uncompromising 'no nonsense' approach to the swift re-imposition of (an essentially police-defined sense of) 'order'.

Applying Cohen's terminology, the paramilitary response represents the option of last resort – the 'falling back on the more or less brutal reimposition of statutory public order' (1979: 132) with those groups (in this case 'the new lumpen', in which sections of male, especially black, youth figure prominently, and militant dissidents of all kinds – pickets, demonstrators, etc.) with whom the (preferred) negotiated approach – the 'unwritten system of tacit negotiation' (ibid: 123) – has never been properly established or has broken down. This breakdown may be fairly temporary, in the case of say a particular industrial dispute, or, in the case of some highly alienated groups, Afro-Caribbean youth for example, apparently irrevocable.

The irony of this, as Cohen points out, is that the straight-forward repressive legal approach constantly threatens to undermine the order it is designed to uphold (witness the way the repressive Swamp'81 contributed to the first Brixton riots), a dilemma Cohen refers to as the police's 'impossible choice of enforcing law or order' (ibid: 130). The result is that 'the more resources allocated to increasing the efficiency of repressive policing, the more manpower has to be poured into 'community relations' to restabilize the public image of the force' (ibid: 133). And that is precisely what has happened. The growth of paramilitarism has been accompanied by a parallel growth in community-relations policing (i.e. all forms of policing variously concerned with the question of 'negotiated' rather than strictly 'legal' order). Moreover, and in line with this logic, such initiatives are largely aimed at those groups furthest removed from the existing 'tacit negotiations', such as youngsters in Northern Ireland (in the form of police-run blue-lamp discos), and the black communities (to whom community-relations departments owe their very existence: cf. Judge 1974: 201).

If paramilitarism belongs broadly to the moment of hegemonic breakdown, certain features of the Thatcherite years have exacerbated the situation. In the first place, the multiple crises – economic, political and ideological – signalling the breakdown of hegemony have continued to worsen, and hence to stimulate further paramilitary developments. Secondly, these developments are increasingly technologically sophisticated, which not only makes them more dangerous, most obviously in the case of the new weaponry, but which also makes them prey to 'technological drift': the internal technological dynamic whereby the technologically feasible constantly threatens to pre-empt the politically desirable. Thirdly, the present Conservative government is *committed* to the tough political response, unlike say the social democratic government of the Callaghan years which also presided over paramilitary developments, but less willingly. Within this political climate paramilitarism is not only a 'necessary evil', but is seen as a positive weapon to enforce key changes (witness the absolutely central role of the police in breaking the miners' strike of 1984/5: McCabe and Wallington 1988: 130). Finally, and most depressingly, there is the crisis of alternatives, evidenced by the surprising degree of support the government managed to maintain even while implementing a highly divisive strategy. Though there is a debate about the relative strength of the New Right's ideological hold which is beyond the scope of this chapter (which from the vantage-point of 1990 is clearly weakening), I subscribe to Hall's idea that, generally speaking, these have been years characterized by 'authoritarian populism' (but see Hall 1988a and 1988b; Jessop *et al.* 1984). Jointly these features – the intensity of the conflicts to be policed, the technological capacity of police, the willingness of the government to sanction 'tough' methods, the relative support for these and the absence of ideas about alternatives – provide the essential conjunctural backcloth to an adequate understanding of the riots. But, before we turn to consider them briefly, one final point about paramilitary policing (given policing's importance to the 'riots' story) seems worth making, namely, its inherent tendency to amplify the very problems of disorder it is designed to quell. As I have argued at greater length elsewhere (Jefferson 1987b: 47–53; and 1990), this tendency stems from the very nature of the paramilitary approach: the use of specially trained, usually male, officers in large numbers and their deployment in groups offering each other unconditional support; the anticipation of trouble; the provision of equipment and lethal weaponry to deal with it, violently if necessary; and the employment of pre-emptive and offensive tactics, simply to exert control or as a means of dispersal.

Benyon's review of 'interpretations of civil disorder' (Benyon 1987: 23–41) makes it evident that understanding this backcloth – the downside of Thatcherism – is a prerequisite for understanding the riots. Having looked at the range of interpretations, he lists five 'characteristics . . . common to the areas where rioting . . . occurred in the 1980s' (ibid: 33), namely:

(1) *Racial disadvantage and discrimination are major afflictions.* A significant proportion of the population in each area in which rioting occurred is Afro-Caribbean of Asian . . .
(2) *Unemployment is high*, and particularly affects youth, and especially young black (i.e. Afro-Caribbean people . . .
(3) *Deprivation is widespread*: environmental decay, poor educational and social service provision, inadequate recreational facilities and crime are problems . . .
(4) *Political exclusion and powerlessness are evident*, in that there are few institutions, opportunities and resources for articulating grievances and bringing pressure to bear on those with political power . . .
(5) *Mistrust of, and hostility to, the police is widespread* among certain sections, particularly the young. There is disquiet about police tactics, such as stop-and-search, and allegations are frequently made about harassment, abuse and assault . . .

(ibid: 33–5; emphases in original)

Though 'opinions varied as to which of the . . . five factors were the most significant' (ibid: 35), 'the immediate precipitants or trigger events in each case involved police officers and black people' (ibid: 33; emphases in original).

This brief conjunctural analysis confirms, then, the historical evidence of the previous section, namely, that the basic problem stems from the 'ongoing' police mission of policing the poor and powerless – a process which affects blacks particularly adversely, not only because of their concentration amongst the disadvantaged and unemployed, but also because of the evils of racial disadvantage and discrimination. Its strengths lie in pointing towards the relationship between economic crisis and ideological signification in the criminalization process (the scapegoating of black youths), and in showing how a repressive response (legal coercion and paramilitary policing) can itself become part of the problem (i.e. result in outbreaks of disorder). However, once again the approach tends to downplay the relationship between disadvantage and 'normal' crime and, perhaps in consequence, the relationship between policing developments and normal crime. Possible differences *between* races, for example, Asians and Afro-Caribbeans, also tend to be obscured.

RACE AND CRIME STATISTICS

If, so far, the question of 'ordinary crime' has been relatively sidelined in considering the relation between police and ethnic minorities, it seems fairly obvious that any consideration of police-work that neglects their 'bread and butter' work is insufficient. And ordinary crime is, of course, a genuine concern of victims, as the recent upsurge of victimization studies has revealed – though whether 'fear of crime' outstrips the level of crime remains contentious (cf. Walklate 1989: 25–51). However, the difficulties of drawing conclusions from any published criminal statistics, because of the series of decisions about whether to report and to record that lie behind their construction, are now well documented. So caution is necessary. Where race is also an issue, this is even more the case – as the fairly contentious debate about race and crime statistics has shown (cf. Bridges, 1983a, 1983b; Gilroy 1982, 1983; Gutzmore 1983; Lea and Young 1984). With these strictures in mind, let us briefly review what is presently known.

The broad picture looks something like this. So far as stops are concerned, the evidence we have – gleaned either from police records or from surveys of the general public and mostly relating to London – suggest that black males, particularly young black males, have a higher chance of being stopped by the police than white males (cf. Willis 1983: 14). However, a survey in Manchester conducted by Tuck and Southgate (1981), the one study that compared 'black and white groups *living in the same areas*, found no difference between the rates at which they were stopped by the police' (Walker 1987: 49; my emphasis). What this suggests, as

Walker points out, is that the decisive factor in determining who gets stopped may be less race than (broadly speaking) 'class' – a possibility supported by the Policy Studies Institute (PSI) findings that the stop rate was higher for the unemployed than those in work, and, for vehicle stops, for unskilled manual workers than professional and managerial workers (Smith 1983).

This interpretation finds further support in our own recent Leeds-based study (Walker *et al.* 1989). Our findings based on police records which were *not* 'within area' comparisons support the general conclusion mentioned above of disproportionate stopping of black males. However, when we made 'within area' comparisons (our attempt to hold social class constant) a more complex picture emerged, for disproportionate stopping of black males was confirmed to areas with less than 10 per cent non-whites. In the areas with more than 10 per cent non-whites – the relatively disadvantaged areas – it was only the *white* arrests rate which was disproportionate (Walker *et al.* 1989: 7). Asians, by contrast, both in London and Leeds, had a comparatively low stop-rate, regardless of area (Smith 1983: 96, 98; Walker *et al.* 1989:9).

When it comes to arrests, similar points can be made, though it should be noted that we have data only for London and Leeds. The London data (see, for example, Home Office 1989) revealed black over-representation in all offence groups, though when age was controlled for in the earlier analysis (Stevens and Willis 1979) – necessary because 'known offenders tend to be young, and . . . the black population tends to be younger than the white' (Walker 1987: 40) – this was particularly accounted for by four offence categories, namely, assault, robbery, 'other violent theft' and 'other indictable offences'. However, social class, also critical to arrest rates, given the established relationship between low social class and known offenders, was not controlled for.

In Leeds we also found that black males – in two age-groups (11–21) and (22–35) – were disproportionately arrested, when arrest rates were considered simply in relation to the city of Leeds as a whole (Walker *et al.* 1989: 7). But, once again, when 'within area' comparisons were made, a pattern identical to the one we found for stops emerged. So the 'area effect' – area being some sort of rough control for class – seemed to be consistent. Whilst we would need to know more about any differences in policing between these areas, as well as whether race affected public reporting and police recording practices (something our study was not designed to uncover), before we are in a position to explain this pattern, it does at least suggest that area of residence/social class is an influential factor that should not be ignored in analysing race and crime statistics. (For a fuller discussion, see Jefferson *et al.* 1990.)

Asians, under-represented in the overall arrest rate in London and Leeds (Stevens and Willis 1979; Walker *et al.* 1989), present, once again, a markedly different picture.

Though there have been some studies of police cautioning of juveniles (e.g. Batta *et al.* 1978; Landau 1981; Farrington and Bennett 1981; Landau and Nathan 1983), and one looking at police decisions to prosecute (Cain and Sadigh 1982), these have proved difficult to interpret for various reasons and hence, for brevity's sake, will not be dealt with here.

Given the above findings, the question of interpretation remains. Is the black over-representation in the police statistics a consequence of their involvement rate in crime, or has it more to do with police discrimination? It may be worth reminding ourselves, first, of the proactive/reactive distinction – the former referring to police-initiated, the latter to citizen-initiated, acts. Stops clearly come under the heading proactive – as do certain offences, most notoriously the now abolished 'sus' offences (for which the black arrest rate in London far exceeded the white rate in its 1970s heyday (Demuth 1978: 40–1), a factor which was certainly influential in its eventual abolition). Moreover, certain offences – such as 'robbery' and 'other violent theft' (two of the four categories, it should be remembered, for which Stevens and Willis (1979) found a disproportionate black arrest rate in London once age was controlled for) – are highly subjective categories for recording purposes (cf. Stevens and Willis 1979: 41; Blom-Cooper and Drabble 1982). And then there is the question of the importance of 'demeanour' in determining who gets stopped and arrested, with 'disrespect' more often being rewarded with arrest for 'contempt of cop' (cf. Piliavin and Briar 1964) – a fate to which the more hostile black youths are perhaps particularly prone (cf. Jefferson 1988: 528).

But, when all is said and done, most commentators conclude that at least part of the explanation for higher black arrests has to be the result of higher offending behaviour (cf. Stevens and Willis

1979; Smith 1983; Reiner 1985b; Benyon 1986; Lea and Young 1984). Monica Walker's graphic calculations that 'black people must have four and a half times the chance of being arrested for burglary (compared to white people) . . . [and] 14 times . . . more often . . . for a robbery if the offender rates were the same' (1987: 40) would seem to make 'implausible' the idea that all of the black over-representation can be accounted for simply by discrimination – though Walker does point out that her calculations are based on 'arrests and not convictions' (ibid.).

If black over-offending constitutes at least part of the explanation for their high arrest rates, then it puts back squarely on the agenda the question of disadvantage and crime. For, if blacks are disproportionately involved in known offending behaviour, they also have much higher rates of social disadvantage, being more likely to live in poorer housing in deprived areas, attend worse-off schools and, in the job market, to find manual (rather than non-manual) jobs or be unemployed (cf. Brown 1984). Since known offenders are disproportionately drawn from the ranks of manual workers, the unemployed and the socially deprived, the higher black arrest and offender rates should not particularly surprise.

But, finally, we must confront the question of Asians, who are also subject to disproportionate levels of disadvantage (cf. Brown 1984: 315–18), including, we might add, an even greater likelihood (than blacks) of being victims of racist attacks (Home Office 1981). However, their arrest rates, as we have seen, do not match their levels of disadvantage. Though I have no space to explore this properly – and, in truth, little research exists to help here – it seems clear that we will need to look towards certain cultural factors (probably those to do with family and community structure and religion) for an explanation (cf. Bains 1988). Whatever the answer, it certainly suggests that the link between deprivation and offending is not unmediated – a point I shall return to briefly in the following section.

What the race and crime debate has done – its strength – has been to put the issue of ordinary (i.e. largely 'reactive') crime back on the agenda and, in so doing, to have refocused on the offender. It has at least indirectly, reaffirmed the traditional link between disadvantage and crime (to complement that between disadvantage and crime control which we saw in the first section above). But it has also revealed that race needs to be conceptualized in the plural, given the differences in stop and arrest rates found between blacks and Asians.

The limitations of the approach, if taken on its own, are that the comparative statistical approach – the typical methodological tool – serves to obscure the more general point about the police focus on deprived areas. This, in turn, effectively severs any link with political economy and effectively removes from the agenda any sense of the broader ideological role of discussions about crime.

ATTITUDES, PERCEPTIONS, AND EXPERIENCES: ETHNIC VIEWS 'FROM BELOW'

> At the end of the summer term, 1984, a crowd of between 30 and 40 schoolchildren aged 14 to 16 from Stockwell Park School, South London, were celebrating the end of term, shouting and throwing bags of flour at each other (an end-of-term tradition) outside the school gate. Three police transit vans pulled up and the children were confronted by 15 police officers who, the children say, bashed their heads against the pavement and the side of the van. Five children were arrested and charged with assaulting the police. The charges against them were later dropped.
>
> (Institute of Race Relations 1987: 34)

Whatever the comparative statistical reality and its meaning, there is no doubt that the experiential meaning of policing for black people, especially for black youth, over the past twenty years or so, has been one of a hostile and alien force – one which has subjected their communities to aggressive, harassing and intimidatory 'overpolicing', yet has been only indifferent or half-hearted in the face of black and Asian victims of racist attacks. The evidence for this conclusion comes from the many deplorable case-studies assiduously collected in many forms by the communities themselves, and the various surveys of attitudes, perceptions and experiences.

One of the most persistent collators of cases has been the Institute of Race Relations. Its evidence submitted to the Royal Commission on Criminal Procedure and published in 1979 under the title *Police Against Black People* is a horrifying catalogue of general harassment, neglect and misconduct – none of which is regarded as exceptional.

In 1987 this 68-page pamphlet was reprinted as an Appendix to a new Institute publication, *Policing Against Black People*. The only changes between the two publication dates have been for the worse: hence the catalogue of abuses, at ninety-three pages, was longer, and the title had been changed – to signify, in Sivanandan's introductory words, the 'more systematic police surveillance and special policing of whole communities' now 'required' by the growth of unemployment, social deprivation and racism (Institute of Race Relations 1987: viii). If all this is unfamiliar, *Policing Against Black People* should be compulsory reading; or you could try the recent Independent Committee of Inquiry Report (1989) into the death of Colin Roach published as *Policing in Hackney 1945–1984*; or the recent report of racism in Liverpool, *Loosen the Shackles*, by Tony Gifford and colleagues (1989). It does not matter where you turn, the experiences are depressingly similar.

The survey evidence broadly mirrors this black antipathy to police, though the Policy Studies Institute (PSI) survey of Londoners reminds us that the hostile views of West Indians in London 'by no means amount to a complete rejection of the present policing system' (Smith and Gray 1983: 332). Age is especially critical: 'there is a dangerous lack of confidence in the police among substantial numbers of young white people and a disastrous lack of confidence among young people of West Indian Origin' (ibid.). In conformity with the cases cited by the Institute of Race Relations, black youth were much more likely to believe that the police abuse their power, use excessive force and fabricate evidence.

Our own survey in Leeds supports such findings. When it came to attitudes to the police, blacks had the highest (of all racial groups) overall 'disapproval' score, and they were less likely (when asked what they would do on witnessing various crimes) to co-operate with the police. About one half of blacks thought that the police were guilty of various malpractices – that they used threats, employed unnecessary violence, took inaccurate records and fabricated evidence – and thought police discriminated against non-whites. The figures for whites (who lived in the same areas it should be added) were similar, unlike in London, where all areas were included (Walker *et al.* 1989: 96–8).

Asian attitudes and perceptions, echoing the situation we found with stops and arrests, were different. In London the PSI found Asians to be less critical than West Indians (except with regard to racial attacks), though more so than whites (Reiner 1985b: 173). In Leeds we found that Asians held significantly less critical attitudes than both blacks and whites (Walker *et al.* 1989: 16).

One obvious way of explaining any differences between blacks, whites and Asians would be in terms of differences in experiences. Does the fact that Asians have fewer arrests and stops account for their more positive attitudes? The short answer is 'no'. What Smith found from his PSI data was that although there was 'a strong relationship between people's hostility towards the police and their perceptions of their personal experience of contact with police officers' (1987: 70), this was not a total explanation because he also found that 'people of West Indian origin who report *no* personal adversarial contact with the police are still more hostile to the police than white people, who have not had contact with the police of this kind' (ibid: 71; emphasis in original).

Our own Leeds study endorses this: 'Although all the measures of attitude to the police were related to stops etc, and Asians were stopped less and Whites more than Blacks, differences between races on attitude were consistent regardless of the number of stops' (Walker *et al.* 1989: 18).

Smith's explanation of this – what he calls 'the extra element in the formation of the views of West Indian people' (1978: 72) which accounts for this greater hostility – is in terms of 'a sense of solidarity with all other people belonging to the same ethnic group', a 'collective consciousness' which in its developed form becomes 'some kind of political ideology' (ibid.). By this Smith means 'a coherent view within the collective consciousness about what is to be done in response to what is perceived as being police oppression and also oppression by wider forces in society' (ibid.). In other words, the *collective* experience of racial discrimination appears to have produced both a collective consciousness and a political ideology to match which is over and above the particular experiences of prejudice and discrimination suffered by *individuals* within the group. The political implications of this distinction are important and I shall return to them in the conclusion.

If a 'collective consciousness' beyond that of the experiences of individuals explains some of the black hostility to police, it may be that a different 'collective consciousness' is informing the markedly more conforming behaviour and attitudes of Asians. It can only be speculative to proceed further at this stage, but one point seems worth making. If, as I have argued elsewhere, the consequence of the mutual hostility between blacks and police is a 'self-fulfilling prophecy' which can produce a 'deadly dynamic of mutual distrust, tension, hostility, and, eventually, hatred' (Jefferson 1988: 537), it may well be that more positive and conforming Asian attitudes are 'rewarded' with more positive police attitudes, one consequence of which is the more favourable Asian stop and arrest figures that we have seen. In other words, what we are witnessing in police–Asian relations is a self–fulfilling prophecy of a more positive kind. One small piece of evidence from our Leeds study lends this notion some support; we found Asian juveniles significantly more likely to be cautioned and adults to have 'no further action' taken after arrest. On the other hand, there is also evidence of conflictual relations between police and some sections of Asian youth in places like Southall (e.g. April 1979 – see NCCL 1980) and Bradford (most recently in connection with Salman Rushdie). But, as Bains' (1988) thoughtful insider view of youth politics in Southall reveals, the picture is fraught with complications such that generalizations in this area are very hazardous.

The strengths of these accounts of experiences and attitudes are that they act as a reminder of what policing feels like for those groups routinely on the receiving end, i.e. from below. In that sense it provided the human stories to complement Cohen's political economy of police-work outlined in our first section above. It also reminds us of the limits of the quantitative approach: comparative statistics deal in outcomes, not the quality of interactions preceding these. So far as black people are concerned, these interactions have clearly been found wanting. The surveys also show that the relationship between attitudes and experiences is complex, not simple. Though black and Asian experiences of discrimination and disadvantage – when measured by certain objective indices (such as earnings or level of unemployment) – are similar, their subjective perceptions and attitudes are not identical.

What is missing most from these accounts is any strong sense of ordinary crime and of justified policing of it. Moreover, though these accounts are compatible with the political economy outlined in our first section above, they do not themselves deliver one.

SUMMARY AND CONCLUSIONS

What our broad historical overview established is the importance of situating crime and its control within a broad structural framework constituted by the economic, political and ideological changes to which societies are constantly subject. From this perspective, law, ideology and the process of criminalization are as problematic as the 'crime' they seek to control. Proceeding from this starting-point, we found that 'policing race' is but a contemporary manifestation of the traditional police role of 'policing the powerless'.

One conclusion from this establishment of a historical link between policing and social disadvantage is that of the need to address questions of social disadvantage as well as of policing. Lord Scarman made the point after the 1981 Brixton riots; 'urgent action is required if the social conditions which underlay the disorders in Brixton and elsewhere are to be corrected' (Scarman 1981: 6.42).

But, if anything, the situation is getting worse, as Benyon and Solomos (1987: 192) gloomily conclude in their review of 'the roots of urban unrest': 'Unemployment is higher, housing is worse, incomes have fallen, crime is higher, and black people continue to suffer from racism and exclusion.' Downes and Ward (1986: 61) make a similar point in the conclusion to their review of the debate about police accountability: social justice, not policing, is the key to social order.

> Rather than place policing at the centre of a socialist response to crime, we would emphasis the cardinal importance of social justice as the only legitimate basis of order, and the need for a range of social and environmental measures to improve the quality of life, as well as preventing some kinds of crime, in those neighbourhoods most afflicted by crime and insecurity.

Questions of police accountability bring us to our conjunctural analysis. Here a closer look at these same structural processes in operation currently showed how a worsening (for the already disadvantaged) economic situation coupled with a tougher political response and ideological attacks on all forms of dissent has made a repressive, paramilitary policing response a central feature – and how the 'riots' are symptomatic of the resulting complete breakdown of relations between police and sections of the powerless.

One conclusion from this is that so long as paramilitarism is seen as part of the solution and not part of the problem (cf. Waddington 1987; Jefferson 1990), and as long as questions of police discretion and accountability are not tackled (cf. Jefferson and Grimshaw 1984), policing has itself now become part of the social disadvantages experienced by the powerless, perhaps even its cutting edge.

The debate about race and crime statistics also reminded us of the importance of 'social disadvantage', but from the 'other' side. Here, the narrow focus on ordinary crime (not the processes of criminalization) and (primarily) the offender re-emphasized the link between disadvantage and crime – even if the issue of disadvantage (ironically) has been obscured by the focus on the race of offenders. At the same time, in identifying the differences between blacks and Asians it *also* rendered the link, between crime and disadvantage, problematic.

Three conclusions follow from this. First, failing to take crime seriously in its own terms means not seeing that a common response to disadvantage is a diffuse, apolitical and sometimes amoral frustration that is highly negative in its consequences (cf. Rook 1979). Second, such failure also entails ignoring the fact that victims of crime are invariably similarly disadvantaged. Thirdly, the apparently different response of Asians to similar levels of disadvantage places the need to take cultural as well as structural factors seriously firmly on the agenda.

When we turn, finally, to what all this feels like 'from below', we find that those having most negative contacts with police – young blacks – have the most hostile attitudes, and that these are often very critical indeed. But we also saw that there is no simple one to one equation between experiences and attitudes; and that, in the case of Asians, high levels of disadvantage and discrimination can be associated with positive attitudes to the police.

Two general conclusions flow from this, if we intend to 'take racism seriously'. The first is the need to see racism in the plural;

the second is that 'success' in this area, ultimately, is a subjective category. The perceptions and attitudes of the system's most disadvantaged groups, not so-called objective dimensions of discrimination and disadvantage, will, and do, determine the level of social tranquillity (though, of course, the former are profoundly influenced by the latter). What all this points towards, generally, is the deep-rooted complexity of the issues involved – a point only underlined by the ethnic conflicts that accompanied the democratic explosions of 1989 around Eastern Europe. For better or for worse we had better get used to that fact, and attempt to respond – both intellectually and politically – in ways which do it justice.

Chapter 9

'Policing a perplexed society?'
No-go areas and the mystification of police–black conflict

Michael Keith

It is a clichéd but important commonplace to suggest that it is only through examination of the manner in which the conflict between police and black communities was realized in long local histories, catalogues of antagonism, that anything approaching an accurate picture of the inter-relationship of policing, 'race' and civil disorder can be drawn. Such locations in themselves tell the histories of racial injustice in microcosm, injustice that stretches throughout the institutionally racist configurations of British society in general but was commonly articulated most visibly through the offices of the British police-force in particular (Gilroy 1987; Gilroy and Sim 1987; Keith 1987, 1989; Solomos 1986, 1988).

But these places have both a public and a private face. In this chapter I want to suggest that alongside the privately lived experiences of local history there exists a public reconstitution of these same places, an imaginative geography in which the nature of black community life is represented in a series of powerful discourses in a manner which legitimizes the particular policing practices that are maintained there, naturalized by a set of debates that reshapes social history in the tainted vocabulary of *'social problems'* (Keith 1989).

I have suggested elsewhere that the 1980s uprisings represented dramatizations of conflicts deeply rooted in particular places (Keith 1987, 1989). Moreover, police responses to rioting confirmed the notion of a power struggle based on specific, officially recognized *'symbolic locations'*, though did not do so intentionally. In these locations a repertoire of policies has evolved that are tied explicitly to the categorization of these places as potential sites of disorder.

By the late 1980s the deployment of special patrols, dogs, surveillance operations, various forms of rapid response units, and official monitoring and contingency planning all lent an official seal to a notion of certain officially designated *symbolic locations* that were constructed as potential centres of disorder, officially delineated *heartlands* of the enemy within.

In this context it has also become a commonplace to suggest that black communities have for a long time been policed in a way that is qualitatively different from the rest of society (e.g. IRR 1979, 1988; HCRC 1983). The broad contours of these differences are well documented, from the post-war overt racism so typical of white society generally, most horrifically evinced in the 'nigger-hunting' expeditions of the 1960s, through to the paranoid suppression of anything that was construed as akin to the US Black Power movements in the 1960s, the mugging moral panics of the 1970s and the insidious, gendered and racist representation of rebellious black youth, the folk devil as 1980s' rioter.

As a putative centre for sedition, as an alleged hotbed of criminality, or even as offence to the delicate sensibilities of 'British culture', the black community has for so long been cast not simply as an 'alien wedge' but more profoundly as the incarnation of a threatening *other* that could always serve as both a frightening cautionary tale of urban decline and convenient scapegoat for the ills of society (cf. Said 1979).

The theme that links such images together is the representation of black communities as criminal and the origins, salience and policy relevance of such an imagery can be understood only in terms of the broad societal context of British racism (cf. Gilroy 1987; Solomos 1988). But for the purposes of this chapter I want to look at one particular section of this broad social context. This conflict is now seen as normal within the daily routine of police-work and this is in part because of a set of debates that served as a way of making sense of this violence and came to stand as a rationalization if some of the most profound changes in policing witnessed in post-war Britain, changes that embody the institutionalization of racial subordination that has become perfidiously mundane in practice and invidiously powerful in its effects in criminalizing large sections of the British black community. In short I want to talk about the manner in which particular understandings of the nature of collective disorder came to serve as euphemisms that justified the selective oppression of one section of British society.

REPRESENTATIONS OF VIOLENT CONFLICT

On a broader canvas the events of 1981 were to provide the focus for a series of issues from accountability to minority rights that coalesced in a crisis of confidence in British policing. Not only was the long-running, if mostly hidden, story of police/black conflict briefly allowed to surface in informed media discussion, but also all the other groups who had been voicing discontent with the nature of policing were able to seize on a specific issue in order to raise once again the more general question of police legitimacy.

Consequently, the early 1980s witnessed a period of history in which 'policing' emerged as a major political issue, particularly on the Left and among those who tried to harness the power of the new social movements of collective consumption which had emerged in the 1960s and 1970s. The municipal socialism exemplified by Ken Livingstone's ascendancy at the Greater London Council from 1981 to 1985 tried to unite a coalition of the oppressed; by the characteristic challenges to the established social order that these movements embodied, 'policing' was an issue of common concern and a political reference point around which such a coalition could be moulded. However, following successive general election defeats, the political climate has changed and the Labour party appear set to replace the issue of 'policing' with the issue of 'crime' on their own political agenda.

It is too early to say whether or not this will come to be seen as the beginning of a return to a popular, if not universal, consensus over issues of policing or whether renewed crises will spring up from the further revelations of police corruption and the parade of dubiously achieved 'terrorist' convictions.

Yet it is worth noting that such a return was anticipated by the Metropolitan Police's internally produced Force Appraisal for 1986 which stated that 'one thing is clear, the Labour Party is determined to shake off its anti-police reputation and wrest the law and order issue from the Conservatives' (Metropolitan Police 1986: 81, section 7.1.14). It is also worth noting that such swings in public opinion do not occur randomly or without preparation. Instead I want to suggest that a great deal of groundwork in preparation for this change can be traced to the manner in which violent conflict in British society is now popularly understood. This production of a new 'common sense' was deeply rooted in the production of academic social-science 'knowledges' that sought to provide an objective account of these developments.

It is here that the interaction between 'researcher' and practitioner is so important, that the tension between theory and practice is so problematic, the responsibility of the one echoing in the culpability of the other.

There is a social basis to the conflict between black communities and the police. It is a conflict rooted in the material causes of institutionalized racial injustice, realized in particular historical and geographical contexts. However, it is the manner in which received wisdom or common-sense understandings mirror this situation that structures popular and official reactions to this conflict. Here again is the perennial tension between perception and 'the real world'. This process is a function of the 'social construction of reality', the images of disorder on the streets refracted through a glass darkly, which have shaped the reproduction of conflict between police and black communities at all levels, from the heights of institutional police-making right down to the rationalizations of the individual psyche.

What is of concern here is the relationship between 'writing' about policing and the social context in which that writing is set. It is essential to analyse the way in which particular accounts of processes and events are proffered, heard, authenticated and, most importantly, remembered or forgotten.

In a book that was written in 1972 expressly for a police audience, Professor Michael Banton boldly states that: 'Police training is too important a matter to be left to policemen (*sic*) alone' (1972: 9). The book that follows, which takes as a central objective the task of 'informing the police what they should know about community relations', is replete with stereotypical generalization, although only a few examples need be listed:

> West Indian immigrants bring with them many ideas about family life which are better suited to their old environment than to life in a British city.
>
> (1972: 130)

Youngsters of West Indian descent are therefore in greater

conflict with the British, and at the same time often in dispute with their own first generation, whom they accuse of submitting to white arrogance instead of fighting back. Many of them react against their parents' strict ideas of family discipline and leave home, putting themselves into the sort of position in which they are more tempted to theft as a means of making ends meet.

(1972: 40)

Children also

suffer more from being brought up in a society which looks down upon a black skin colour. This too helps increase the generation gap in the West Indian family in Britain. It makes young black children turn more to their agemates for psychological support and in some districts often leads them into hustling and other forms of petty crime.... Police officers cannot do much to prevent delinquency among black youth but it can help them to understand how a situation of psychological conflict, of normal aspirations to a worthwhile life, but of only restricted economic opportunity, can produce this sort of reaction.

(1972: 131)

In a list of problems faced by police in multi-racial areas that is not without value (for instance Banton points to the fallacy of the existence of 'community leaders') there is also the serious suggestion that 'West Indians are sometimes regarded as more difficult to deal with, being disputatious and very ready to register complaints against the police. They are also regarded as more violent than English men' (1972: 118).

Such notions are racist and dangerous but they are derived from an ostensibly benign academic social science. Most significantly, the content explicitly transforms the status of migrant communities themselves into special problems. It would be fair to suggest that such notions are now widely discredited in academic fields. It would be fair to acknowledge that the insidious deployment of the pathologies reinforced by such description does not reflect the liberal intent that informed the writing. Yet the logical extension of such statements is that such accounts provide the raw material both for the rationalization of 'black youth' as a social problem category (Solomos 1988) and for an explanation of police/black clashes in terms of cultural deprivation. Reproduction of conflict between police and black communities becomes naturalized through the vocabulary of cultural difference.

In this context it can be of no surprise that at a conference in September 1974, the papers of which were published in order to give a wider public the chance to hear police 'thinking aloud', the head of the Metropolitan Police Community Relations Branch, Peter Marshall, echoed Banton's words almost to the letter in conjuring up a vision of West Indian cultural impoverishment, family collapse and ethnic deprivation. These were together embodied in common criminality which inevitably provoked confrontation with the police:

> West Indian immigrants, lacking common cultural identity, have tended to become more socially fragmented. Problems of adjustment are most clearly revealed among young West Indians. . . . Homelessness, unemployment and alienation provide the major ingredients of a formula whose end result is often an involvement in street crime. The police clearly should respond to the immediate manifestations of the problem and give priority to the suppression of street robberies and thefts; but our involvement with the symptoms does not preclude us from trying to identify and understand underlying causes.
>
> (Marshall 1975: 17)

The pernicious notion of a cultural disposition to crime is made explicit through the *objective* realm of academic description. Similarly, it is hardly surprising if the Commissioner of the Metropolitan Police between 1982 and 1987 echoes such received wisdom when analysing in public the difficulties of 'Policing and Social Policy in Multi-Ethnic Areas in Europe' (Newman 1983a).

The reason for drawing attention to this sort of work is not to malign Banton or Marshall, only to draw out the connections between theory and practice. Through the respectability and status of 'objective' academic accounts an *authoritative* explanation is derived. Logically, clashes between police and black communities have focused attention (and policy reaction) on *the problem* of migrant communities, in situations that are exacerbated by the occasional incidence of rotten apple racism. Such clashes are *to be expected* in situations where mutual cultural misunderstanding is paired with economic deprivation. In this vein, Robert Mark suggested that: 'The police have no influence on employment, housing and education. The problem of alienated black youth is dumped on their lap without any means to resolve it' (1978: 286).

It is not that such generalizations are *true* or *false* in any straightforward sense of these terms. An academic gloss is painted over the major problems of (good or bad) policing in a racist society and the deviant nature of the social problem category 'Black youth' is legitimated.

'RIOTS'

There is a common vision of the uprisings or riots of 1980s' Britain that attributes them at root to the injustices and dislocations of a society that in transforming itself will inevitably exclude some from the benefits of change, victimize some through the combined deprivations of poverty, unemployment, ill health and no wealth. It is a vision whose provenance draws on the long and respectable history of liberal-minded benevolence and the sociologies of alienation. It produces an account of 'rioting' that embraces the spectrum of the old consensus politics that was wheeled out in Parliament by personifications of this tradition that crossed the parliamentary divide, from Roy Hattersley to William Whitelaw. Crucially, it is a vision of violent conflict which links deprivation to disorder, represents the causes of rebellion as an exercise in blame allocation, with the endemic forms of poverty taking the lion's share of culpability. The link is crucial. Its importance derives from the historical diagnosis, policy ramifications and theoretical prognosis that stem from such conceptions of violent disorder. For again it was to this sort of liberal social science, not to the explicitly racist ideologies of the new right, that the police most often looked for the explanations of the violence of the 1980s.

Memory is important. It is important because the way in which events were remembered becomes the stuff of folklore, informing common-sense understandings of 'riots', how they occur and how they should be prevented. Here again, like Keynes' famed businessman labouring under the influence of the economist of yesteryear, the police themselves often echo the axioms and generalizations of past sociologists. When coupled with the notion of causality as blame allocation, 'social theory', in the loosest sense of the term, becomes one of many arenas in which institutions are not only vindicated or condemned but also are defined in terms of legitimacy, neutrality and vague, but significant, measures of social utility.

In such circumstances there was, after 1981, a clearly felt need in some police quarters to reassess the role of the police, most readily evinced in the many statements and essays, including a high-profile submission to Lord Scarman, of John Alderson, an individual at various times Commandant of Bramshill Police College, Chief Constable of Devon and Cornwall and criminologist academic. It is not possible to do justice to the scope and significance of Alderson's many interventions on the political stage in the early 1980s. Nevertheless, it is significant that whilst often decried at the time, the Alderson line epitomized a conception of technological, sociologically informed policing that was in large part to become 1980s orthodox thinking in London under the aegis of one of his successors at Bramshill, Kenneth Newman. It was Alderson, in his submission to Scarman, who focused on the need to create a new 'social contract' between police and public and it was Alderson who was repeatedly to situate the riots of 1981 as a social problem, not divorced from policing practice but beyond police control: 'Not only were the traditional social controls of family, school, religion and culture weakened in the affected areas but the idea that the problem of social disorder could be cured by the police was a gross error' (1984: 41).

The contingent nature of social description here is crucial. The attempt to draw in a wider social context is laudable, as is the refusal throughout Alderson's work to duck the issues of policing, but it is worth noting that in such analysis lay the potential for the shift of attention away from the police-force, a powerful political tool.

The events of 1981 raised questions about police legitimacy and liberal social science provided the resources through which these questions could be answered. In the 1980s similar diagnoses were increasingly to be found in the journals which attempt, at various levels of sophistication, to address the nature of the policing function. In periodicals such as *Police Journal*, *Police Review*, *Police* and, latterly, *Policing* this shift of focus could be completed by the mobilization of academic models of crowd psychology (Brindley 1982; Trevizias 1983), or the credentialist expertise of sociology (Waddington 1984).

Though not always the case, this too was a task not irreconcilable with sympathetic visions of city life (Wells 1987). At one level such an approach may appear unexceptionable:

> Senior police officers have a difficult path to tread in being sensitive to a variety of differing and conflictual pressures upon them. They have to exercise their professional judgement and make decisions which have to finely balance these conflicting pressures. It would appear that as our society is becoming more socially divided and ideologically divided the policing job will become more difficult not merely in terms of physical violence which the police will have to face but also in making decisions that strike a balance that can help to continue the tradition of policing by consent.
>
> (Vick 1982: 277)

Yet even here the contrast between police professionalism and political ideology renders the two mutually exclusive. The politics of policing become an exercise in common-sense diplomacy rather than the problematic routine enforcement of a contentious social order, a process hidden by appeal to a tradition of policing by consent (cf. Brogden 1982; Reiner 1985a).

Moreover, compiling a historical record of the events of 1981 was at times recognized as more than an exercise in cataloguing and comprehension. This can be seen in Thackrah's study of 'reactions to terrorism and riots' (1985). Here the tension between theory and practice is particularly marked and the relationship between academic discourse and public policy of particular concern as the author writes as a lecturer at Bramshill Police College. Thackrah does not advance an explanation of the rioting as such, yet the assumptions he makes about the disorders throws light on a conception of the phenomenon that may structure policy oriented reactions to it.

The policing problem is two-fold. There is a question of public order: 'In the 1981 riots unprovoked attacks with firebombs resulted in the police needing to take a fresh look at their capability to cope with lawlessness on such a scale' (Thackrah 1985: 150). There is also a problem of public image: 'Police intelligence has to work against the Left trying to link the question of policing to what is seen as the underlying causes of recent rioting' (ibid: 153).

The rioters are unquestioningly seen as an irrational and cohesive 'crowd' that must be subdued, policing *per se* is to be removed from the political agenda as the attacks on police are classified as unprovoked, and the focus is returned to British society as a whole. The transformation from violence as politics to violence as crime assumes the status and incontrovertibility of received wisdom.

Notwithstanding the significance of such examples, any generalizations about the dominant modes of explanation of civil unrest necessarily take on the veneer of simplicity when constrained by the amount of space available here. Struggles between memories and counter memories permeate civil society at all levels from the grand institutions right down to the individual. Here it is intended to note only three points.

1 The importance of memory. It is how uprisings or riots are remembered rather than how they actually occurred that dictates policy reaction and future popular mobilization. It is not reality alone which structures the political agenda of today and tomorrow (cf. Edelman 1971, 1985). Though realization of the importance of remembering is far from novel, the significance of this discovery has not always been taken on board by empirical research. When Marx said that 'the tradition of all the dead generations weighs like a nightmare on the brain of the living' (quoted in Miles 1987: 170), he did no more than echo Voltaire's comment that 'history is a trick that we play on the dead'. Sometimes unintentionally, it is those who write about events of the recent past that perpetrate such acts of deceit.

2 It is possible to define the existence of policing conceptions of rioting which were sufficiently broad to cover the range of opinion from James Anderton, reactionary former Chief Constable of Greater Manchester, to John Alderson, darling of the liberal establishment, yet simultaneously remain firmly within a police perspective on the nature of social disorder. These conceptions were not necessarily conscious exercises in self-excuse. The single uniting theme was an implicit equivalence between 'cause' and 'blame', no more than an

acceptance of 'common-sense' notions of causality, often incorporating mainstream social science in the production of accounts which in varying degrees exculpated police in allocation of 'responsibility' for civil disorder.

3 It has been demonstrated elsewhere that a major theme that differentiated 1985 from 1981 in the foremost spheres of public discussion was the removal of the problem of policing from the public agenda (Solomos 1986, 1988). Such a change has to be related to a changing perception of policing in an unjust society. These perceptions are themselves tied to a cultural construction of the policing function in the writings of police discourse. This does not mean that the study of policing should relate exclusively to the nature of civil (dis)order. There is no call here to resort to a reversal of the process of blame allocation or, necessarily, a demand for the privileged recognition of counter memories of uprisings. It is important to realize only that in the arena in which explanations of 'riots' competed against each other for recognition, like a collection of 'avant-garde', some achieved greater recognition than others.

The leaking of some forms of academic explanation of disorder and not others into the vocabularies of the political agenda and common sense is at least in part due to this competition. This in turn has structured the social realities of the years that followed 1981 and 1985.

It would be impossible to map out with any great precision the formation of public knowledge in this way. However, to support the contention that the institutionalized nature of racial subordination is tied to the discursive field through which police practices are generated, it is useful to illustrate one of the key concepts through which the conflict between police and British black communities is manipulated, rationalized and reproduced.

POLICE/BLACK CLASHES, 'NO-GO AREAS' AND THE INVERSION OF HISTORY

'No-go area.' Attribute of an area impossible to enter (because of barricades etc.); to which entry is forbidden for specified persons, groups etc. e.g. *The Times* 24/5/72 'The UDA organised the Protestant "no-go" areas in Belfast last weekend.'

(OED Supplement 1976)

One of the central themes which dominated discussion of the St Paul's, Bristol, uprising of 1980 was the notion of the 'no-go area'. Media reportage frequently claimed that the local police had allowed the creation of such an area by withdrawing, albeit temporarily, from one part of the city at the height of the violence. Taking up an agenda that had thus been set principally by the tabloid press, the legitimacy of the concept was confirmed by parliamentary discussion of the events in St Paul's, particularly in the exchanges between the two relevant front-bench spokesmen, both former Secretaries of State for Northern Ireland. In the debate of 3 April 1980, Merlyn Rees, when making the principal contribution from the Labour Party, prefaced his speech with the comment: 'It is vital that there should never be "no-go" areas in this country' (*Hansard*, vol. 982, 3 April 1980: col. 667). Similarly, in parliamentary discussion of the Avon and Somerset Chief Constable's report on the St Paul's rioting, Rees opened with the statement that: 'I am inclined to accept the decision to regroup, though I dislike, from my past experience, "no-go" areas in whatever sense of the term' (*Hansard*, vol. 983, 3 April 1980: col. 973–4). Seizing on the prospect of a concept around which a consensual understanding of violent disorder could be built, William Whitelaw, then Home Secretary, promptly replied:

I am grateful to the right hon. Gentleman. He raises three points. From his experience he makes a major point about 'no-go' areas. So do I from my own experience. I am not prepared, and in no circumstances will be prepared, to contemplate 'no-go' areas in any part of this country or the United Kingdom. It is very important to say that, to be heard to say it, and for it to be realised that that will not happen in the future.

(*Hansard*, vol. 983, 3 April 1980: col. 974)

A phrase that had leaked from Ulster, which implied that there were parts of British cities which the police were unwilling or unable to patrol, was thus set to become part of the common vocabulary of political discourse, used throughout the 1980s in description of conflict between police and British black communities.

However, the repeated use of the term does not imply that the connotations associated with it remained constant throughout the decade. The emotive power of the term derives from a particular fear of civil disorder and the implicit reference to anarchy has remained constant, but the context in which the term was used has changed subtly but significantly through time.

In fact, description of the conflict between police and British black communities in terms of no-go areas goes back at least as far as the confrontations at the Notting Hill Carnival of 1976. Initially it was a descriptive categorization that rebuked police for their apparent failure to maintain the rule of 'law and order'. Hence, on 1 September 1976 there was a page one headline in the *Sun* 'IT'S NO TO NO-GO', accompanied by a story claiming that

> Metropolitan Police Commissioner Sir Robert Mark yesterday ruled out any suggestion of black no-go areas in London. Speaking in the aftermath of the Notting Hill riots he said firmly:
> 'There is no question of abdicating our responsibility. The Metropolitan Force will police every street in its district and will uphold the law. We are not going to buy illusory peace by watching decent black people being robbed by young black hooligans, even if it is to involve an element of risk going in to help them'.
>
> (*Sun*, ' September 1976)

Similarly, at the time of the events in St Paul's in 1980 much tabloid press reportage castigated the police for allowing the temporary existence of allegedly alien phenomenon of an area in a British city which violently disputed the policing prerogative. In the House of Commons, in the first parliamentary response to the disorders, the Home Secretary was asked:

> Did my right honourable friend hear a broadcast this morning by the chief constable, in which he admitted that for some hours last night there was a 'no-go' area for the police in Bristol. Will he assure the public that steps will be taken to ensure that such 'no-go' areas never occur again?
>
> (*Hansard*, vol. 983, 3 April 1980: col. 667)

In the 1980s the idiom of the 'no-go area' became a central theme in the description of the sort of spontaneous clashes that increasingly characterized specific places in London and elsewhere, similar to the 'front lines' already analysed.

Consequently, the term could cover both specific breakdowns in public order and a more general, almost quotidian, crisis of civil order, sometimes characterized as a 'slow riot' (e.g. Geoffrey Dear, *The Times* 29 February 1988: 'SLOW RIOT' FOMENTS AS ATTACKS ON POLICE RISE). The former analysis typified many of the responses to the disorders of 1985:

> We cannot have 'no-go' areas. You see what happened when for a few hours, a few hours only, part of one of our big cities is a 'no-go' area . . . you see the disasters which follow from that.
>
> (Douglas Hurd, 11 September 1985)

> Men in dreadlock hairstyles were out in force in the Villa Cross area where Monday's rioting erupted, but police denied that it had become an agreed 'no-go' area.
>
> (*The Times*, 12 September 1985)

> TERROR OF TOTTENHAM – SPECTRE OF THE NO-GO AREA IN ENGLAND.
>
> (*Daily Mail* headline, 8 October 1985)

The latter phenomenon can be illustrated by the example of the shopkeeper in Liverpool 8 who went so far as to take the Merseyside police to court for their caution in taking large-scale action in the area around Upper Parliament Street, Granby Street and Princess Boulevard: 'A Liverpool jeweller claimed that Merseyside's Chief Constable had created an unlawful "no-go" area in the riot zone which was a haven for criminals' (*The Times*, 31 October 1986).

The image of dark havens of criminality within the city is not novel, and contains echoes of some descriptions of Victorian London. Yet the story was important because it can be linked to the long tradition of dubious portraits of the immanent evils of city life (Williams 1973) and also more specifically and more recently the endemic, frequently melodramatic, lawlessness of inner-city Britain in the 1980s (Burgess 1984). The 'inner city' is represented as a 'new frontier', a place where civilization stops and anarchy begins.

Used in such a way the police are immediately placed on the defensive, seeking to justify past actions and possible failings; to deny the existence of these mythical places called 'no-go areas'. In the Liverpool case the local chief constable was reported in *The*

Times as saying that: 'The claim that Toxteth is a "no-go" area is not only unfair to residents but also to the police officers who patrol there' (Chief Constable Kenneth Oxford, 30 October 1986). In London Sir Kenneth Newman also was quick to rebut suggestions that there were such places: ' " NEWMAN RULES OUT NO-GO AREAS" ... Sir Kenneth Newman 'denied the existence of "no-go" areas where police feared to tread' (*Guardian* headline and story, 17 February 1987).

Nevertheless, a universal characteristic of language and all other sign systems is that the meaningful content of central terms can be inverted, manipulated in the process of signification; in this instance to connote not police incompetence but the primitive and naturally unpoliceable face of 1980s' Britain.

A new deployment of the term was seen in the early 1988 stories surrounding the emergence of alleged organized crime by 'The Yardies'. Early reports explicitly related the rationale for establishing Operation Lucy to a fear of nascent no-go areas. Hence a *Times* story that was headlined 'YARDIES "MAY SET UP NO-GO AREAS"' claimed that 'Yardies, the criminal gangs which originated in Jamaica, could establish no-go areas in British cities as a cover for their increasing cocaine trafficking, a police assessment says' (*The Times*, 8 February 1988). The possible existence of a no-go area, once evidence of policing failure, is now proof positive of the monstrous task facing the police-force. However, this protean symbolism does not arise out of nowhere. In order to understand the context in which the Metropolitan Police could now themselves use a term which they had once feared is to see how the police/black conflict has come to be rationalized as a manageable problem, digested by discourse.

It is here that the powerful nature of historical revisionism is revealed. For, of course, the 'reality' of so-called no-go areas has already been described. There are places where the conflict between police and black communities has become so historically mature that the regular challenges to the police/policed power relation and the consequent nature of policing in these particular places is qualitatively different from that in other parts of the same city. All Saints Road, Railton Road and Sandringham Road in the early 1980s would have topped the lists of many senior Met Officers asked to identify such places. It is also worth remembering Kenneth Newman's public reference to these same streets:

> Railton Road in Brixton, All Saints Road in Notting Hill and Sandringham Road in Hackney and so on. These are at the centre of areas where crime is at its worst, where drug dealing is intolerably overt, and where the racial ingredient is at its most potent.
> (K. Newman, 16 February 1987)

To repeat the substance of other work (Keith 1987), the defining characteristic of such locations is that national conflicts are locally realized. It is not that these are the places where police/black relations were worse than anywhere else, only that it is here where the policing prerogative was most frequently challenged.

Whether or not such localized social relations in space warrant categorization as 'no-go areas' is ultimately a meaningless and naïve question. The phrase is akin to any linguistic term which has an arbitrary referential property. What the phrase actually means is flexible within the constraints imposed by the anarchic reference at its heart. The term can symbolize either police failure or the enormity of the task facing the police-force and it is the struggle to decide which of these meanings will prevail that is more important than any isomorphic relationship between the term itself and 'the real world'. This struggle is conducted through the process of historical recording.

To get from the pejorative use of the no-go area epitomizing policing inadequacies to the Metropolitan Police prophecies of tomorrow's Britain requires three stages of reconstruction. Through these three stages policing problems are defined and rationalized within an orthodox vision of social consensus. It is necessary to forget history and then reinvent it, but only once the background chronology of more recent events has been suppressed in an intervening second stage.

Popular resistance to both the introduction of the British police-force and the practice of 'policing by consent' dates back a long way, as many of the revisionist police histories of the last decade or so have shown (Brogden 1982). The spatial realization of such resistance produced a series of historical precedents to the negotiated stand-offs that often characterized the front lines of the early 1980s. In those areas where opposition to the police presence was at its greatest, police:

Negotiated a complex, shifting, largely unspoken 'contract'.
They defined the activities they would turn a blind eye to, and
those which they would suppress, harass or control. This 'tacit
contract' between normal neighbourhood activities and police
objectives was sometimes oiled by corruption, but more often
secured by favours and friendship. This was the microscopic
basis of police legitimacy and it was a fragile basis at best.

(Ignatieff 1979: 444–5)

That such conflicts have tended to be written out of history by
most of the more conventional accounts of the British police (see
Reiner 1985a: 10–20) has inevitably contributed to the process of
historical amnesia. To mask the central contradictions of policing
always requires a major ideological exercise in the fiction of
consensus and the need for 'tacit contracts' is at variance with the
notion of a straightforward social contract based on the universal
acceptance of a police-service.

The ability of police discourse to transform major disturbances
into social scientific 'problems' of societal deprivation and crowd
psychology has already been analysed. The medical metaphors
most often used in such analysis are usefully ahistorical. It is by
turning civil disorder into a social problem, a societal blight
regularly witnessed in nascent form in the 'symbolic locations' of
conflict, that the historical context of unrest is suppressed. Once
this has occurred, the locational resistance of police operations,
the seeds of 'no-go area' descriptions, become a medium through
which the problem of civil unrest can be rationalized. Hence, in a
piece for *Police Journal*, a Bramshill lecturer suggests that:

In such areas as Bristol, a chief constable is placed in a most
invidious position. If he seeks to enforce the laws as they stand,
and rioting and disorder results because of a reaction by that
community, he may be accused of provoking the riot. If he does
nothing and turns a blind eye to what are often open and
flagrant breaches of the law, then he is accused by others of
operating double standards, and failing in his duty to uphold
the laws of the land.

(Vick 1982: 275)

Here there is frank description of the real problems of policing
without consent but significantly no reference to the history of
how consent was lost. Confrontation is a problem of policing but

it apparently stems from the refusal of unnamed groups to accept the rule of law.

The final stage of this process is to reinvent the 'no-go area', restore the history that was lost. In this process of reconstruction, Sir Kenneth Newman has provided an explicit 'police rationalization' (an official account) of the existence of 'symbolic locations' in sensitive parts of London where police actions are most frequently challenged, the streets he did not shy from naming. For Newman it was in these places that the challenge to police authority was most pronounced:

> This brand of destruction and hostility is at its height in certain parts of ethnic areas which have become a focal point for congregation and association by Black youths. In these locations confrontations with the police are deliberately engineered either to make a political point or to create a diversion in order to facilitate organised crime in relation to drugs or stolen property. If allowed to continue, locations with these characteristics assume a symbolic importance, a negative symbolism of the inability of police to maintain order. . . . The youths take a proprietorial posture in this location; they regard it as their territory. In general they will regard the police as intruders.
>
> (1983a: 9 and 1983b: 13)

Two connected themes provide the backbone for this conception of clashes on the front lines of London. The first is the notion of disorder as purely criminal activity. Rather than merely suppress time, Newman's statement goes further and turns time on its head, inverts chronology. Notwithstanding the long record of officially 'illegal' social activity in such places, history shows that some serious crime tends to exploit disorder, moving in on the collapse of policing by consent into the front line areas. Black 'challenges' to police action predate the very real major crime problems that grow up in these 'symbolic locations', they are not caused by that crime. The chronological inversion is an example of criminalization by area which simultaneously discredits the 'validity' of violent protest in symbolic locations by categorizing it as a form of criminal behaviour in the same class as street crime and drug-dealing.

The notion that 'all rioters are criminals' is a powerful

ideological classification that has obvious policing implications. It is only fair to Newman to acknowledge that as an individual he might not have concurred with such a simplistic equivalence, certainly Wells, at the time one of his closest Deputy Assistant Commissioner advisers, publicly contradicted this sort of classification (London Weekend Television, 11 October 1985). However, the refusal to acknowledge any element of protest in the actions of the 'rioters' was common within the Metropolitan Police Force.

It is important to differentiate between the individual and the nature of police discourse as a whole. The latter is characterized by a whole set of linguistic rules that render the questioning of police legitimacy contradictory, understandably almost unspeakable (Grimshaw and Jefferson 1987). Classification of violent disorder has to be squared with the vision of policing demanded by police discourse. In such a situation there is no attempt here to impugn the integrity or insult the intelligence of specific police-officers involved in such official conceptualizations, particularly given the less than admirable record of much 'academic social science' in exactly the same area.

The individual police-officer is placed in a relation to police discourse akin to that between agent and structure; the two are recursively tied to each other. In these circumstances there are necessary rules behind official rationalizations. The limits to police accounts of civil unrest are just one manifestation of these rules.

The second theme in the quotation from Newman's paper is one of territoriality. There is a very real difference between the ethological conception of the human 'territorial imperative' (Ardrey 1961) and the dramaturgical concept that individuals' behaviour will be conditioned by scene, a scene-setting process that will include the social sanctioning of violence in particular contexts (Marsh 1983). Both might be described as conceptions of 'territoriality', yet the former connotes a vision of human behaviour which is essentially pathological, or at best bestial, a powerful political transformation (Miller 1982). It is the contention here that the employment of the ethological concept of territoriality is often mistakenly used in the 'theoretical' analysis of police behaviour (e.g. Holdaway 1983 explicitly uses Ardrey's model), suggesting a misleadingly pathological view of police culture. It is also the contention that the connoted view of black culture implied by Newman employs an identical approach, an approach which incidentally devalues the form of location-specific black resistance by transforming the social into the natural (Barthes 1973), the rational act into a manifestation of animal nature.

Again, it is interesting and important to note that the lineage of Newman's remarks are much closer to a liberal social-science perspective than to a caricature of right reactionary law and order politics. This proximity was exemplified in an article written by *Guardian* journalist Stephen Cook in 1984, who, in a piece that reproduces much of the sympathetic but orthodox and predictable liberal vision of urban life in Britain, suggests that:

> What has developed, in my view, is essentially a conflict between police and blacks over occupation and control of the inner-city streets. It is like a tribal, territorial conflict, with strong overtones of sexual curiosity and jealousy, and fear and contempt of the other side's totems and ju-jus.
>
> (*Police Review*, 3 August 1984)

It is because this form of accounting and rationalization is so value-loaded that it remains important to be aware of the status of social science as one type of 'discourse' (Sayer 1984). Terms like '*Riot*', '*crime*' and '*territoriality*' may connote whole value systems and social orders, they do not exist simply as fixed objects open to study.

In this sense the phenomenon of academic appropriation of '*rioting*' outlined elsewhere (Keith 1987) is repeated by Newman: the 'explicandum' '*riot*' is determined by the preferred explanation of the phenomenon rather than vice versa. So, whilst holding back from any concession of the existence of 'no-go areas', Newman's account provides the explanatory framework through which such phenomena should be understood. If, of course, they were to develop in the future.

There can be no dialogue with 'criminals'. The claims of 'uprisings' to political substance are compromised by classification. Beyond this classification such criminal activity can either be put down to the deviant propensities of individuals, as the new right might prefer (see Lewis 1988), or one can look to liberal social science for rationalization.

KEEPING THE LID ON?

Reinforcing a central contention of this chapter that policing discourse is structured more by the tenets of liberal academic social science than by reactionary law and order politics, a central organizing metaphor of police discourse in the late 1980s has been 'the metaphor of the dustbin'. The notion that society delegates the police-force to 'keep the lid on' the cauldron of ills that is the modern inner city is both emotively persuasive and ideologically useful. It is a metaphor that has been used both inside and outside the police force to describe the genuinely difficult nature of the policing task, normally set against a list of social problems that need to be tackled (e.g. Wells 1987; Mark 1977).

As already suggested, this notion of discrete social problems is itself disingenuous; in refusing to tie various facets of urban deprivation to their societal context there is a danger that root causes are obscured by academic reification. The policing outcome of this sort of vision is also contradictory. Whilst in the vocabulary of 'keeping the lid on' the dustbin metaphor for British city life implicitly recognizes the injustice that is being legally enforced, there is also a refusal to address publicly the necessary ramifications that follow from the regulation of a disputed and institutionally racist social order. A real and recurrent difficulty all police face is how to enforce this unjust social order, but this task can barely be expressed in police discourse because such a vision cannot be reconciled with notions of policing by consent. Once again 'the fallacy of polite policing'.

Those who resist police actions must still take on the classification of 'criminals' by their necessary analytical position within a particular discursive field. Ultimately, it is not possible for individual police-officers publicly to transcend this discursive field, whatever their private opinions, for to do so would be to question the relationship between state and police that lies at the very heart of police legitimacy.

The selective amnesia which discredits violent conflict in 'symbolic locations' and 'front lines' exemplifies Foucault's notion of history as 'a mode of mobilising power'; the power of naming so crucial to the mapping of popular geographies or the common-sense territorialisation of the British city. There is no attempt here to romanticize or even to justify violence, only to prohibit classification of disorder as straightforwardly criminal or causally irrational. Memory of the history of particular places may differ between people who live in them and those that write official geographies of the city. It is not the purpose of this text to provide the counter memories to substantiate such alternative history, only to point to their existence.

When social relations in space are classified in terms of 'no-go areas' the phrase assumes connotations that are highly normative. The role of the medium of space is itself interpreted and deployed to rhetorical effect. This is not dissimilar to the passage in *Alice in Wonderland*, when, in the midst of a debate with Humpty Dumpty over the meaning of particular words, Alice is grumbling:

> 'I don't know what you mean by "glory,"' Alice said.
>
> Humpty Dumpty smiled contemptuously. 'Of course you don't – till I tell you. I meant "there's a nice knock-down argument for you!"'
>
> 'But "glory" doesn't mean "a nice knock-down argument,"' Alice objected.
>
> 'When I use a word,' Humpty Dumpty said in a rather scornful tone, 'it means just what I chose it to mean – neither more or less.'
>
> 'The question is,' said Alice, 'whether you can make words mean so many different things.'
>
> 'The question is,' said Humpty Dumpty, 'which is to be master – that's all.'

Sometimes this function was recognized explicitly. *Police Officer Magazine*, established in 1981 by the Superintendents' Association, included an opening editorial which included the statement that:

> On Sunday 13 November 1981 *'The Observer'* published a National Opinion Poll which, the newspaper says, 'Suggested that public confidence in the police is beginning to erode for the first time, especially among the young, and is not nearly as high as is popularly imagined.' If the poll is a true reflection of public opinion then 1982 should be a year in which the Police Service will intensify the efforts it is already making to put its house in order and to improve its professionalism. I hope this magazine has a part to play in that process.
>
> (*Police Officer Magazine*, December 1981)

Again, such relationships between rationalization and reality are not unusual. They merely serve to highlight the significance of police discourse and are cited here purely because of their relevance to the discursive rationalization of '*problems of race and racism*'.

One of the key concepts through which these rationalizations are constructed is through competing notions of police 'professionalism', of much current interest to debates on policing and police training that stem from attempts to define examples of good police practice. This in itself is not altogether a 'bad thing' but has remained a persistently problematic theme in much research on policing, most notably in the studies carried out on the Metropolitan Police Force by the Policy Studies Institute in the early 1980s and by Wolff Olins PR consultants in the late 1980s.

Attempts to define police professionalism cannot be seen as a socially neutral process. For it has to be said that professionalism in the police, as in all branches of the civil service, is in part a notion through which practices are standardized and consequently drained of any political or moral content. Out of the definitive uniting features about police discourse is the manner in which widely differing perceptions of police-work may co-exist in journals, in books and in social 'science', as long as the fundamental task of *policing* itself is not subjected to scrutiny. Significantly, if problems of the relations between police and black communities are cast solely in terms of notions of professionalism, then the core issues that underscore all policing in a multi-racist society are obscured rather than openly addressed. Yet it is in the arena of police discourse that precisely this sort of rationalization may be proffered.

Moreover, it is in these arenas of contestation that the reconstructions of reality may be generated which lend a sense to past and present. It has already been suggested that the process of proffering official memories and rationalizations performs a powerful role in the reproduction of social relations. Police discourse is one medium through which such power relations are exercised.

CONCLUSION

Banton's work in the 1970s was underwritten by academic 'expertise'. Commissioners such as Robert Mark and Kenneth

Newman have long recognised the value of media access, whilst a pronouncement by Lord Scarman invariably receives far greater publicity, and, in a real sense, exercises far greater power, than a differing opinion voiced in the editorial columns of *The Job*. As Foucault has suggested:

> Discourse that possesses an author's name is not to be immediately consumed and forgotten, neither is it accorded the momentary attention given to ordinary fleeting words. Rather, its status and its manner of reception are regulated by the culture in which it circulates.
>
> (Foucault 1977: 123)

The reason so many conspiratorial theories of police practice lack plausibility is that they fail to take on board the institutional complexity of the British police. Each group within the wider unit may speak with their own voice, even if they are not all received and heard with the same respect.

Even a very simplistic typology can be divided by hierarchy, function and geography. Each division in such a typology would have many sub-divisions. In terms of hierarchy, the *de facto* 'officer class' that is produced by Bramshill Police College has been subject to relatively little research. Often speaking through the columns of periodicals such as *Policing* and *Police Journal*, many who have passed through the Bramshill police graduate entry or the senior command course are frequently seen to hold very different opinions from other middle and senior management, not to mention the very different perspectives and objectives from the police rank and file. Chief constables, often using the institutional endorsement of ACPO (Association of Chief Police Officers), and media notables, often former policemen such as John Alderson and John Stalker, also have a real power to command particular attention. Yet the rank and file also now have the means and the will to enter into this same realm through Police Federation activity (see *Police*, *The Job*), as Tony Judge, editor of *Police* and former Labour Party councillor, has acknowledged:

> Ironically, many of us who were around in the days when the police was indeed a silent service, recall being criticised by such bodies as the NCCL for not speaking out and giving the public the benefit of police experience! It is the Federation's success as

a communicator which has made other pressure groups and some politicians, reach for their gags.

(*Policing* 1985, vol. 1: 308)

Yet this should not obscure the unities that homogenize different interest groups under the omnibus classification of policing discourse.

In short, police-forces are typical late twentieth-century bureaucracy standing in a specific relation to the state. Factionalism and patronage inevitably become part of managerial politics, whilst the multiplication of departmental divisions and subdivisions promotes institutional communication more akin to something out of Kafka than to a Weberian notion of bureaucratic rationalization.

A case in point might be taken from the various well-documented efforts that preoccupied certain senior officers and elements of the Metropolitan Police to discredit the Scarman inquiry at various times before, during and subsequent to the publication of the final report. The selective release of racially coded, disingenuously constructed crime statistics on 'mugging' in 1982, which occurred under the aegis of Assistant Commissioner Gilbert Kelland, was just one example. Yet to suggest that this move represented the united actions of the Metropolitan Police as a whole, and was not contentious inside as well as outside the force, would be misleading. A few years later, in what was widely seen at the time as a public snub to Kenneth Newman's attempt to discourage freemasonry in the Metropolitan Police: 'The Manor of St James's Lodge was founded by Brethren, all of whom had served as Police Officers in "C" or St James's District of the Metropolitan Police.' One of the original members is listed as W. Bro. Gilbert J. Kelland.

Any analysis of policing actions, particularly at the corporate or institutional level, that does not take on board these personal and departmental complexities and conflicting interests will inevitably lack plausibility.

To recognize that individuals acting in all integrity may purvey notions and explanations of society that are inadvertently iniquitous, dangerously policy prescriptive, is not to succumb to the reassuring vision of contemporary society as an essentially benevolent system, it is only to recognize the ideological power of particular rationalizations of violent conflict. In this hypothetical world, where Popper meets Pangloss, the legitimate tasks of the bureaucratic arms of the state are restricted to a neat array of 'social problems', discretely arrayed one apart from another.

In this context police discourse can assume the definitive characteristics of technocratic language (mystification), professionalism (over politics) and amnesia. Cast not so much as engineers of human souls as plumbers who must make do and mend, the police come to be represented, not unfairly, yet misleadingly, as one of many institutions holding together a confused and malfunctioning urban society.

On 9 September 1990 the Commissioner of the Metropolitan Police, Sir Peter Imbert, commented in a paper to the Howard League: 'the recent era when "law and order" was a party political issue seems to have almost passed'. *New realism* had arrived. The nature of institutional racism and racial criminalization could be forgotten. This systematic amnesia, constructed in police discourse representations of the nature of policing, has been endorsed by the politics of the Labour Party, anxious to disown the ostensibly difficult politics of policing a particular social order and to focus instead on the less contentious issues of service delivery and crime prevention, 'reifying crime and legitimising racism' (Keith and Murji 1990). *The problem* has reverted to one that echoes the disingenuous title of Robert Mark's collection of essays in 1977, that of 'Policing a Perplexed Society'. For black communities the outlook is ominous.

References

Ackroyd, C., Margolis, K., Rosenhead, J. and Shallice, T. (1977) *The Technology of Political Control*, Harmondsworth: Penguin.

ACPO/SEO (1986) *Liaison Between Police and Schools*, London: ACPO/SEO.

Advisory Committee on Police in Schools (1986) *Policing Schools*, London: Advisory Committee on Police in Schools.

AFFOR (1978) *Talking Blues*, Birmingham: AFFOR.

Alderson, J. (1984) *Law and Disorder*, London: Hamish Hamilton.

Anderton, J. (1981) 'The truth about the Moss Side meeting', *Police Review*, 18 September.

—— (1982) 'The reality of community policing', *Press Release* 12 March.

—— (1985) 'Community self-help in crime prevention', ACPO Conference Address, 7 June.

Aptheker, H. (1943) *American Negro Slave Revolts*, New York: International Publishers.

Arblaster, A. (1984) 'Police powers', *New Society*, 23 August.

Ardrey, R. (1961) *The Territorial Imperative*, London: Collins.

Arnold, D. (1977) 'The armed police and colonial rule in South India', *Modern Asian Studies* 11, 1: 101–27.

Arnott, H. (1990) 'Fortress Europe', *Poverty*, May.

Association of Chief Police Officers/Society of Education Officers (1986) *Liaison between Police and Schools*, London: ACPO/SEO.

Auletta, K. (1982) *The Underclass*, New York: Random House.

Bains, H.S. (1988) 'Southall Youth: an old-fashioned story', in P. Cohen and H.S. Bains (eds) *Multi-Racist Britain*, London: Mcmillan.

Banton, M. (1972) *Police Community Relations*, London: William Collins & Sons.

Barthes, R. (1973) *Mythologies*, London: Palladin.

Batta, I.D., Mawby, R.I. and McCulloch, J.W. (1978) 'Crime, social problems and Asian immigration: the Bradford experience', *International Journal of Contemporary Sociology* 18: 135–68.

Bayley, D.H. and Mendelson, H. (1969) *Minorities and The Police*, New York: Free Press.

Benn, M. (1985) 'Policing women', in J. Baxter and L. Koffman (eds) *Police: The Constitution and the Community*, Abingdon: Professional Books.

Benn, M. and Warpole, K. (1985) 'When the new policing brings terror to the home', *Guardian*, 6 December.

Benyon, J. (ed.) (1984) *Scarman and After*, Oxford: Pergamon.

Benyon, J. (1986) *A Tale of Failure: Race and Policing*, Policy Papers in Ethnic Relations no. 3, Warwick: University of Warwick.

—— (1987) 'Interpretations of civil disorder', in J. Benyon and J. Solomos (eds) *The Roots of Urban Unrest*, Oxford: Pergamon.

Benyon, J. and Solomos, J. (eds) (1987a) *The Roots of Urban Unrest*, Oxford: Pergamon.

Benyon, J. and Solomos, J. (1987b) 'The roots of urban unrest', in J. Benyon and J. Solomos (eds) *The Roots of Urban Unrest*, London: Pergamon.

Bergesen, A. (1982) 'Race riots of 1967: an analysis of police violence in Detroit and Newark', *Journal of Black Studies* 12, 3: 261–74.

Berkeley, G.E. (1969) *The Democratic Policeman*, Boston: Beacon Press.

Berlin, I. (1974) *Slaves Without Masters*, Oxford: Oxford University Press.

Bethnal Green and Stepney Trades Council (1978) *Blood on the Streets*, London: Bethnal Green and Stepney Trades Council.

Blauner, R. (1972) *Racial Oppression in America*, New York: Harper & Row.

Blom-Cooper, L. and Drabble, R. (1982) 'Police perception of crime', *British Journal of Criminology* 22, 1: 184–7.

Boss, P. (1967) *Social Policy and the Young Delinquent*, London: Routledge & Kegan Paul.

Bowes, S. (1966) *The Police and Civil Liberties*, London: Lawrence & Wishart.

Box, S. (1983) *Power, Crime and Mystification*, London: Tavistock.

—— (1987) *Recession, Crime and Punishment*, London: Macmillan.

Brewer, J. *et al.*, (1988) *The Police, Public Order and the State*, London: Macmillan.

Bridges, L. (1983a) 'Policing the urban wasteland', *Race and Class* 25, 2: 31–47.

—— (1983b) 'Extended views: the British Left and law and order', *Sage Race Relations Abstracts*, February: 19–26.

—— (1986) 'Beyond accountability: Labour and policing after the 1985 rebellions', *Race and Class* 27, 2: 45–61.

Brindley, J.M. (1982) 'Disruptive crowd behaviour – a psychological perspective', *Police Journal* LV: 28–39.

Brisbane, R.H. (1979) *The Black Vanguard: Origins of the Negro Social Revolution 1900–1960*, Valley Gorge, PA: The Judson Press.

Brogden, M. (1982) *The Police: Autonomy and Consent*, London: Academic Press.

Brogden, M., Jefferson, T. and Walklate, S. (1988) *Introducing Policework*, London: Unwin Hyman.

Brown, C. (1984) *Black and White Britain: The Third PSI Report*, London: Heinemann.

BSSRS (1985) *TECHNOCOP: New Police Technologies*, London: Free Association Books.

Bundred, S. (1982) 'Accountability and the metropolitan police', in D. Cowell, T. Jones and J. Young (eds) *Policing the Riots*, London: Junction Books.

Bunyan, T. (1982) 'The police against the people', *Race and Class* 22, 2/3: 153–71.

—— (1985) 'From Saltley to Orgreave via Brixton', *Journal of Law and Society* 12, 3: 293–305.

Burgess J. (1984) 'News from nowhere', in J. Burgess and R. Gold (eds) *Geography, The Media and Popular Culture*, London: Croom Helm.

Cain, M. and Sadigh, S. (1982) 'Racism, the police and community policing: a comment on the Scarman Report', *Journal of Law and Society* 9, 1: 87–102.

Campbell, D. (1987) 'Policing: a power in the land', *New Statesman*, 8 May.

Carr-Hill, R. and Drew D. (1988) 'Blacks, police and crime', in A. Bhat, R. Carr-Hill and S. Ohri (eds) *Britain's Black Population*, Aldershot: Gower.

Carter, T. (1986) *Shattering Illusions: West Indians in British Politics*, London: Lawrence & Wishart.

Cashmore, E. (1989) *United Kingdom?*, London: Allen and Unwin.

Cashmore, E. and Troyna, B. (eds) (1982) *Black Youth in Crisis*, London: Allen & Unwin.

Centre for Contemporary Cultural Studies (ed.) (1982) *The Empire Strikes Back*, London: Hutchinson.

Cesarani, D. (1990) 'The fear mongers within', *The Guardian*, 2 July.

Chigwada, R. (1989) 'The criminalization and imprisonment of black women', *Probation Journal*, September: 100–5.

Clark, K.B. (1965) *Dark Ghetto*, New York: Harper & Row.

Cohen, P. (1979) 'Policing the working class city', in B. Fine *et al.* (eds) *Capitalism and the Rule of Law*, London: Hutchinson.

—— (1988) 'The perversions of inheritance: studies in the making of multi-racist Britain', in P. Cohen and H.S. Bains (eds) *Multi-Racist Britain*, London: Macmillan.

Cooper, J.C. (1980) *The Police and the Ghetto*, Port Washington, NY: National University Publications.

Cox, B. (1975) *Civil Liberties in Britain*, Harmondsworth: Penguin.

Curry, L.D. (1981) *The Free Black in Urban America 1800–1850*, Chicago: Chicago University Press.

Davis, J. (1989) 'From "rookeries" to "communities": race, poverty and policing in London, 1850–1985', *History Workshop* 27: 66–86.

Dawes, N. (1972) 'Points for concern: police and black workers' *New Society*, 20 January.

Day, P. and Klein, R. (1987) *Accountabilities*, London: Tavistock.

Deakin, N. (1970) *Colour, Citizenship and British Society*, London: Panther.

Dear, G. (1972) 'Coloured immigrant communities and the police', *Police Journal*, April, XLV: 128–50.

—— (1985) *Handsworth/Lozells, September 1985: Report of the Chief Constable, West Midlands Police*, Birmingham: West Midlands Police.

Demuth, C. (1978) *'Sus', A Report on the Vagrancy Act 1824*, London: Runnymede Trust.

Department of Education and Science (1983) *Police Liaison with the Education Service*, London: HMSO.

Department of Environment (1988) *Action for Cities*, London: Department of Environment.

Detroit Police Department (1987) *Special Projects Department Annual Report*.

Douzinas, C. Homewood, S. and Warrington, R. (1988) 'The shrinking scope for public protest', *Index on Censorship*, 17, 8: 4–5.

Downes, D. and Ward, T. (1986) *Democratic Policing: Towards a Labour Party Policy on Police Accountability*, London: Labour Campaign for Criminal Justice.

Dugger, C. and Evans, C. (1989) *The Miami Herald*, 17 January.

Dummett, M. *et al.* (1980) *The Death of Blair Peach*, London: NCCL.

Dunhill, C. (1989) *The Boys in Blue: Women's Challenge to the Police*, London: Virago.

Dunn, J. and Fahy, T.A. (1987) 'Section 136 and the police', *Bulletin of the Royal College of Psychiatrists* II: 224–5.

—— and Fahy, T.A. 'Police admissions to a psychiatric hospital: demographic and clinical differences between ethnic groups', *British Journal of Psychiatry* 156: 373–8.

Durkheim, E. (1973) *The Division of Labour in Society*, Glencoe: Free Press.

Edelman, M. (1971) *Politics as Symbolic Action: Mass Arousal and Quiescence*, Chicago: Markham.

—— (1985) 'Political language and political reality', *Political Studies* xxiii: 10–19.

Erikson, K. (1966) *Wayward Puritans: A Study in the Sociology of Deviance*, New York: John Wiley.

Faligot, R. (1983) *Britain's Military Strategy in Ireland*, London: Zed Press.

Farrar, M. (1988) 'Chaos of carnival', *New Statesman & Society*, 5 August.

Farrington, D.P. and Bennett, T. (1981) 'Police cautioning of juveniles in London', *British Journal of Criminology* 21, 2: 123–35.

Faulkner, A. (1989) 'Women and Section 136 of the Mental Health Act 1983', in C. Dunhill (ed) *The Boys in Blue*, London: Virago.

Fine, B. and Miller, R. (eds) (1985) *Policing the Miners' Strike*, London: Macmillan.

Fogelson, R.M. (1971) *Violence as Protest: A Study of Riots in Ghettos*, New York: Doubleday Co.

Foucault, M. (1977) 'What is an author?', in *Language, Counter-Memory, Practice: Selected Essays and Interviews*, Oxford: Blackwell.

Franklin, J.H. (1974) *From Slavery to Freedom: A History of Negro Americans*, New York: Alfred Knopf.

Frazier, E.F. (1962) *Black Bourgeoisie*, New York: Collier.

Gaffney, J. (1987) 'Interpretations of Violence: The Handsworth Riots of 1985', *Policy Papers in Ethnic Relations*, No. 10, University of Warwick: Centre for Research in Ethnic Relations.

Gaskell, G. (1986) 'Black youth and the police', *Policing* 2, 1: 26–35.

Genovese, E.D. (1979) *From Rebellion to Revolution: Afro-American Slave Revolts in the Making of the Modern World*, Baton Rouge, Louisiana: Louisiana State University Press.

Gerber, D. (1976) *Black Ohio and the Color Line*, Urbana, Illinois: University of Illinois Press.

Geysels, F. (1990) 'Benelux, the forerunner of the European community in the field of free movement of persons across internal frontiers', *Police Journal*, April, 6: 338–55.

Gifford, Lord (1986) 'The Broadwater Farm Inquiry, London: Eaglehouse Press.

Gifford, Lord, Brown, W. and Bundey, R. (1989) *Loosen the Shackles: First Report of the Liverpool 8 Inquiry into Race Relations in Liverpool*, London: Karia Press.

Gilroy, P. (1982) 'The myth of black criminality', in M. Eve and D. Musson (eds) *The Socialist Register 1982*, London: Merlin.

—— (1983) 'Police and thieves', in Centre for Contemporary Cultural Studies (ed.) *The Empire Strikes Back*, London: Hutchinson.

—— (1987) *There Ain't No Black in the Union Jack*, London: Hutchinson.

Gilroy, P. and Sim, J. (1987) 'Law, order and the state of the Left', in P. Scraton (ed.) *Law, Order and the Authoritarian State*, Milton Keynes: Open University Press.

Glasgow, D. (1980) *The Black Underclass*, San Francisco, Ca: Jossey-Bass.

Glass, R. (1960) *Newcomers: The West Indians in London*, London: Allen & Unwin.

Gordon, P. (1985) *Policing Immigration: Britain's Internal Controls*, London: Pluto.

—— (1986) *Racial Violence and Harassment*, London: Runnymede Trust.

—— (1987) 'Community policing: towards the local police state?', in P. Scraton (ed) *Law, Order and the Authoritarian State*, Milton Keynes: Open University Press.

Graef, R. (1989) *Talking Blues*, London: William Collins & Sons.

Gramsci, A. (1971) *Selections from the Prison Notebooks*, London: Lawrence & Wishart.

Greater London Council (GLC) (1985) *Policing London*, 3, 16: 17–32.

Grimshaw, A.D. (1969) 'The case of racial violence in the United States', in A.D. Grimshaw (ed) *Racial Violence in the United States*, Chicago: Aldine Publishing Co.

Grimshaw, R. and Jefferson, T. (1987) *Interpreting Police Work*, London: Allen & Unwin.

Gutzmore, C. (1983) 'Capital, "black youth" and crime', *Race and Class*, 25, 2: 13–30.

Hackney National Union of Teachers (undated), *Police Out of Schools*, London: NUT.

Hall, R. (1985) *Ask Any Woman*, Bristol: Falling Wall Press.

Hall, S. (1987) 'Urban unrest in Britain', in J. Benyon and J. Solomos (eds) *The Roots of Urban Unrest*, Oxford: Pergamon.

—— (1988a) 'Popular-democratic vs authoritarian populism: two ways of "taking democracy seriously"', in S. Hall (ed.) *The Hard Road to Renewal*, London: Verso.

—— (1988b) 'Authoritarian populism: a reply to Jessop *et al.*', in S. Hall (ed.) *The Hard Road to Renewal*, London: Verso.

Hall, S., Critcher, C., Clarke, J., Jefferson, T. and Roberts, B. (1978) *Policing the Crisis*, London: Macmillan.

Hanmer, J., Radford, J. and Stanko, E. (1989) *Women, Policing and Male Violence*, London: Routledge.

Harrison, P. (1983) *Inside the Inner City*, Harmondsworth: Penguin.

HCRC (1983) *Policing in Hackney: A Record of HCRE's Experience – 1978–1982*, London: Hackney CRE.

Heaven, O. and Mars, M. (1989) 'Black women targeted', in C. Dunhill (ed.) *The Boys in Blue*, London: Virago.

Helmreich, W.T. (1983) *The Black Crusaders*, New York: Harper & Row.

Henry, H.M. (1968) *The Police Control of the Slave in South Carolina*, New York: Negro University Press.

Her Majesty's Inspectorate (1989) *Annual Report of the Chief Inspector of Constabulary*, London: HMSO.

Hill, M.J. and Issacharoff, R.M. (1971) *Community Action and Race Relations*, Oxford: Oxford University Press.

Hillyard, P. (1987) 'The normalization of special powers: from Northern Ireland to Britain', in P. Scraton (ed.) *Law, Order and the Authoritarian State*, Milton Keynes: Open University Press.

Hillyard, P. and Percy-Smith, J. (1988) *The Coercive State*, London: Fontana.

Hobsbawm, E. (1989) *Politics for a Rational Left*, London: Verso.

Hogg, R. (1988) 'Taking crime seriously: left realism and Australian criminology', in M. Findlay and R. Hogg (eds) *Understanding Crime and Criminal Justice*, Sydney, NSW: The Law Book Company.

Holdaway, S. (1977) 'Changes in urban policing', *British Journal of Sociology*, 28, 2: 119–35.

—— (1983) *Inside the British Police*, Oxford: Blackwell.

Hollingsworth, M. (1986) *The Press and Political Dissent*, London: Pluto.

Holmes, C. (1979) *Anti-Semitism in British Society, 1976–1939*, London: Edward Arnold.

Home Office (1981) *Racial Attacks*, London: HMSO.

—— (1989) *Inter Departmental Racial Attacks Group Report*, London: HMSO.

Hope, T. and Shaw, M. (eds) (1988) *Communities and Crime Reduction*, London: HMSO.

Horton, C. and Smith, D.J. (1988) *Evaluating Police Work*, London: Policy Studies Institute.

Hough, J.M. and Heal, K.H. (1979) 'Police effectiveness: some popular misconceptions', *Home Office Research Bulletin*, 7, London: Home Office.

Hough, M. and Mayhew, P. (1983) *The British Crime Survey: First Report*, Home Office Research Study, 76, London: HMSO.

Howe, D. (1988) *From Bobby to Babylon*, London: Race Today Publications.

Humphry, D. (1972) *Police Power and Black People*, London: Panther.

Humphry, D. and John, G. (1971) *Because They're Black*, London: Pelican.

Hunte, J. (1965) *Nigger Hunting in England?*, London: West Indian Standing Conference.

Ignatieff, M. (1979) 'Police and the people: the birth of Mr Peel's blue locusts', *New Society*, 30 August.

Independent Committee of Inquiry (1989) *Policing in Hackney 1945–1984: A Report Commissioned by the Roach Family Support Committee*, London: Karia Press/Roach Family Support Committee.

Ineichen, B., Harrison, G. and Morgan, H.G. (1984) 'Psychiatric hospital admissions in Bristol', *British Journal of Psychiatry*, 145: 600–4.

Inner London Education Authority (1986) *Police in Schools: A Discussion Paper*, London: Inner London Education Authority.

Institute of Race Relations (1979) *Police Against Black People*, London: Institute of Race Relations.

—— (1987) *Policing Against Black People*, London: Institute of Race Relations.

James, S. (ed.) *Strangers and Sisters: Women, Race and Immigration*, Bristol: Falling Wall Press.

Jefferson, T. (1987a) 'Controversies around police powers and accountability', Open University, Block D310.3., *Delivering Justice*, Milton Keynes: Open University Press.

—— (1987b) 'Beyond paramilitarism', *British Journal of Criminology* 27, 1: 47–53.

—— (1988) 'Race, crime and policing: empirical, theoretical and methodological issues', *International Journal of the Sociology of Law* 16: 521–9.

—— (1990) *The Case Against Paramilitary Policing*, Milton Keynes: Open University Press.

Jefferson, T. and Grimshaw, R. (1984), *Controlling the Constable: Police Accountability in England and Wales*, London: Muller.

Jefferson, T., Walker, M.A. and Senevirate, M. (1990) 'Ethnic minorities, crime and criminal justice', in D. Downes (ed.) *Crime and Criminal Justice*, London: Macmillan.

Jessop, B., Bonnett, K., Bromley, S. and Ling, T. (1984) 'Authoritarian populism, two nations and Thatcherism', *New Left Review* 147: 32–60.

John, G. (1985) 'The trials of Jackie Berkeley', *Race Today*, May/June.

Johnson, B., Baker, J.E., Foster, M.D. and Cooper, H.A. (1969) 'East St. Louis Riots: Report of the special committee authorized by Congress to investigate the East St. Louis Riots', in A. Grimshaw (ed.) *Racial Violence in the United States*, Chicago: Aldine Publishing Company.

Joint Council for the Welfare of Immigrants (1989) *Unequal Migrants: The European Community's Unequal Treatment of Migrants and Refugees*, Policy Papers in Ethnic Relations no. 13, Warwick: University of Warwick.

Jones, T., McLean, B. and Young, J. (1986) *The Islington Crime Survey: Crime Victimization and Policing in Inner City London*, Aldershot: Gower.

Jordan, W.D. (1974) *The White Man's Burden*, Oxford: Oxford University Press.

Joshua, H. and Wallace, T. (1983) *To Ride the Storm: The 1980 Bristol Riot and the State*, London: Heinemann.

Judge, A. (1974) 'The police and the coloured communities: a police view', *New Community*, III, 3: 199–204.

Karnig, A. and Welch, S. (1980) *Black Representation and Urban Policy*, Chicago: University of Chicago Press.

Katz, J. (1980) *From Prejudice to Destruction: Anti-Semitism, 1700–1933*, Cambridge, Mass.: Harvard University Press.

Keith, M. (1987) ' "Something happened": the problems of explaining the 1980 and 1981 riots in British cities', in P. Jackson (ed.) *Race and Racism*, London: Unwin Hyman.

—— (1989) 'Riots as a "social problem" in British cities', in D.T. Herbert and D.M. Smith (eds) *Social Problems and the City*, Oxford: Oxford University Press.

Keith, M. and Murji, K. (1990) 'Reifying crime, legitimising racism: policing, local authorities and left realism', unpublished paper.

Kerner, O. (1968) *Report of the National Advisory Commission on Civil Disorders*, New York: Bantam Books.

Kettle, M. (1980) 'The politics of policing and the policing of politics', in P. Hain (ed.) *Policing the Police*, Vol. 2, London: J. Calder.

Kettle, M. and Hodges, L. (1982) *Uprising: The Police, the People and the Riots in Britain's Cities*, London: Pan Books.

Kettle, M. and Shirley, J. (1983) 'Revolution at the Yard', *Sunday Times*, 6 November.

Kinsey, R. (1984) *Merseyside Crime Survey: 1st Report*, Liverpool: Police Committee Support Unit.

Kinsey, R., Lea, J. and Young, J. (1986) *Losing the Fight Against Crime*, Oxford: Basil Blackwell.

Knopf, T.A. (1975) *Rumors, Race and Riots*, New Brunswick NJ: Transaction Books.

Kolenzo, E. (1984) 'Police in schools', in ALTARF, *Challenging Racism*, London: ALTARF.

Kuo, W. (1973) 'Mayoral influence on urban policy-making', *American Journal of Sociology*, 79: 28–62.

Kusmer, K.L. (1976) *A Ghetto Takes Shape: Black Cleveland 1870–1930*, Urbana, Illinois: University of Illinois Press.

Lambert, J. (1970) *Crime, Police and Race Relations: A study in Birmingham*, London: Oxford University Press.

—— (1984) 'The crisis in policing', in P. Norton (ed.) *Law and Order and British Politics*, Aldershot: Gower.

Landau, S. (1981) 'Juveniles and the police', *British Journal of Criminology*, 21, 1: 27–46.

Landau, S. and Nathan, G. (1983) 'Selecting delinquents for cautioning in the London Metropolitan area', *British Journal of Criminology* 28, 2: 128–49.

Lea, J. and Young, J. (1984) *What Is To Be Done About Law and Order?*, Harmondsworth: Penguin.

Leavy, W. (1982) 'Hail to the chiefs', *Ebony*, November: 115–20.

Leinen, S. (1984) *Black Police, White Society*, New York: New York University Press.

Leon, C. (1989) 'From Dad's army to Cinderella Service? The recruitment and deployment of special constables', British Criminology Conference, July.

Levenson, H. (1981) 'Democracy and the police', *Poly Law Review*, 6, 2: 41–51.

Lewis, R. (1988) *Anti-Racism: A Mania Exposed*, London: Quartet.
Locke, H. (1969) *The Detroit Riot of 1967*, Detroit: Wayne University Press.
Loveday, B. (1988) 'Joint boards and the local accountability of the police in the metropolitan areas', INGLOV, University of Birmingham.
McCabe, S. and Wallington, P. with Alderson, J., Gostin, L. and Mason, C. (1988) *The Police, Public Order and Civil Liberties*, London: Routledge.
MacDonald, K. (1976) 'A police state in Britain?', *New Society*, 9 January.
McGovern, D. and Cope, R. (1987) 'First psychiatric admission rates of first and second generation Afro-Caribbeans', *Social Psychiatry*, 22: 139–49.
McNee, D. (1983) *McNee's Law*, London: William Collins & Sons.
Maguire, M. and Pointing, J. (eds) (1988) *Victims of Crime*, Milton Keynes: Open University Press.
Mainwaring-White, S. (1983) *The Policing Revolution*, Brighton: Harvester Press.
Mark, R. (1977) *Policing a Perplexed Society*, London: Allen & Unwin.
Marsh, P. (ed) (1983) *Aggression and Violence*, Oxford: Basil Blackwell.
Marshall, P. (1975) 'Urban stress and policing', in J. Brown and G. Howes (eds) *The Police and the Community*, Farnborough: Saxon House.
Marshall, T. (1943) 'The Gestapo in Detroit', *Crisis*, 50, 8: 232–3.
Mawby, R. (ed) (1987) *Policing Britain*, Plymouth: Plymouth Polytechnic.
Mayor's Commission on Conditions in Harlem (1936) 'The complete Harlem riot report', *The New York Amsterdam News*, 18 July.
Memmi, A. (1990) *The Colonizer and the Colonized*, London: Earthscan Books.
Mendez, G.A. (1983) 'The role of race and ethnicity in the incidence of police use of deadly force', National Urban League *Annual Report*, 114–15.
Mentor, I. (1988) 'The long arm of education: a review of recent documents on police/school liaison', *Critical Social Policy*, 21: 68–77.
Merricks, F.R. (1970) 'The development of community relations in the Metropolitan police', *Police Journal*, January, XLIII: 29–35.
Metropolitan Police (1985) *Police in Schools – A Fresh Approach*, London: Metropolitan Police.
—— (1986) *Public Order Review – Civil Disturbances, 1981–85*, London: Metropolitan Police.
Miles, R. (1987) *Capitalism and Unfree Labour*, London: Tavistock.
Miller, J. (1982) *States of Mind*, London: BBC.
Miller, P. and Rose, N. (1986) *The Power of Psychiatry*, London: Polity Press.
Morgan, J. (1987) *Conflict and Order*, Oxford: Oxford University Press.
Morgan, R. (1989) 'Criminal Justice', in M. McCarthy (ed.) *The New Politics of Welfare: An Agenda for the 1990s*, London: Macmillan.
Morris, T. (1989) *Crime and Criminal Justice since 1945*, Oxford: Blackwell.
NACRO (1986) *Black People and the Criminal Justice System*, London: NACRO.
—— (1989) *Race and Criminal Justice: A Way Forward*, London: NACRO.
Nairn, T. (1979) 'The future of the British crisis', *New Left Review* 113/114: 43–69.

Nandy, D. (1967) 'An illusion of competence', in A. Lester and N. Deakin (eds) *Policies for Racial Equalities*, London: Fabian Society.

Narine, D. (1988) 'Top Cops', *Ebony*, May: 132–6.

NCCL (1980) *Southall 23 April 1979*, London: NCCL.

Negrine, R. (1989) *Politics and the Mass Media in Britain*, London: Routledge.

Nelson, W. and Meranto, P. (1977) *Electing Black Mayors*, Columbus, Oh.: Ohio State University Press.

Newham Monitoring Project (1989) *Into the 1990s: From Strength to Strength*, London: NMP Publications.

Newman, Sir K. (1983a) 'Policing and social policy in multi-ethnic areas in Europe', paper given at Cambridge Cropwood Conference.

—— (1983b) 'Public order in free societies', address to *European Atlantic Group*, 24 October.

—— (1983c) 'Policing London Post-Scarman', Sir George Bean Memorial Lecture.

Niederhoffer, A. (1975) 'Authoritarian police personality', in J. Skolnick and T. Gray (eds) *Police in America*, Boston: Little, Brown & Associates.

Northam, G. (1988) *Shooting in the Dark*, London: Faber & Faber.

Norton-Taylor, R. (1990) *In Defence of the Realm? The Case for Accountable Security Services*, London: Civil Liberties Trust.

NUT (1986) *Guidelines on Police School Liaison*, London: NUT.

Oliver, I. (1987) *Police, Government and Accountability*, London: Macmillan.

Owen, R. and Dynes, M. (1989) *The Times Guide to 1992*, London: Times Books.

Palmer, S. (1988) *Police and Protest in England and Ireland, 1780–1850*, Cambridge: Cambridge University Press.

Parker, S. and Kleiner, R. (1970) 'Status position, mobility and ethnic identification of the negro', in M. Goldschmid (ed.) *Black Americans and White Racism*, New York: Holt, Reinhart & Winston.

Patterson, S. (1965) *Dark Strangers*, Harmondsworth: Penguin.

Phillips, S. and Cochrane, R. (1986) 'Schools Liaison', *Policing*, 2, 1: 68–82.

Phipps, A. (1988) 'Ideologies, political parties and victims of crime', in M. Maguire and J. Pointing (eds) *Victims of Crime*, Milton Keynes: Open University Press.

Pilger, J. (1990) 'The dismantling of freedom', *Manchester Evening News*, 19 March.

Piliavin, I. and Briar, S. (1964) 'Police encounters with juveniles', *American Journal of Sociology*, 70: 206–14.

Platt, S. (1986) 'Return to Broadwater Farm', *New Socialist*, April.

Player, E. (1989) 'Women and crime in the city', in D. Downes (ed.) *Crime in the City*, London: Macmillan.

Police Monitoring and Research Group (1987) 'Mental Health Act and the policing of women', *Policing London*, 26, March/April.

Policy Studies Institute (1983) *The Police and People in London*, Vols I–IV, London: Policy Studies Institute.

Pope, D.W. (1985) 'Developments and problems in police–community relations', in J.R. Thacharah (ed.) *Contemporary Policing*, London: Sphere.

Porter, B. and Dunn, M. (1984) *The Miami Riot of 1980*, Lexington: D.C. Heath & Company.

Pulle, S. (1973) *Police–Immigrant Relations in Ealing*, London: Runnymede Trust.

Rabinowitz, H.N. (1980) *Race Relations in the South 1865–1890*, Urbana, Illinois: University of Illinois Press.

Ramdin, R. (1987) *The Making of the Black Working Class in Britain*, Aldershot: Gower.

Reed, A. (1986) *The Jesse Jackson Phenomenon*, New Haven: Yale University Press.

Reiner, R. (1980) 'Forces of disorder', *New Society*, 10 April.

—— (1983) 'The politicisation of the police in Britain' in M. Punch (ed.) *Control in the Police Organisation*, Cambridge, Mass.: MIT Press.

—— (1985a) *The Politics of the Police*, Brighton: Wheatsheaf.

—— (1985b) 'Police and race relations', in J. Baxter and L. Koffman (eds) *Police: The Constitution and the Community*, Abingdon: Professional Books.

—— (1989a) 'The politics of police research in Britain', in M. Weatheritt (ed.) *Police Research: Some Future Prospects*, Aldershot: Gower.

—— (1989b) 'Whatever happened to police accountability?', *SAMIZDAT*, May/June.

Review Panel into Handsworth Rebellions of 1985 (1986) *A Different Reality*, West Midlands Council.

Rex, J. (1987) 'Life in the ghetto', in J. Benyon and J. Solomos (eds) *The Roots of Urban Unrest*, Oxford: Pergamon.

—— (1988) *The Ghetto and the Underclass*, Aldershot: Avebury/Gower.

Rich, P.B. (1986) *Race and Empire in British Politics*, Cambridge: Cambridge University Press.

Rich, W.C. (1989) *Coleman Young and Detroit Politics*, Detroit: Wayne State University Press.

Richmond, A.H. (1961) *The Colour Problem*, Harmondsworth: Penguin.

Roach, L. (1978) 'The Metropolitan Police community relations branch', *Police Studies*, September.

Robson, B. (1988) *Those Inner Cities*, Oxford: Clarendon Press.

Rock, P. (1988) 'Governments, victims and policies in two countries', *British Journal of Criminology*, 28, 1: 44–66.

Rohrer, R. (1981) 'Police open fire on civilians', *New Statesman*, 17 July.

Rook, C. (1979) *The Hooligan Nights*, Oxford: Oxford University Press.

Rose, D. (1989) 'The bitter question of racial violence', *Guardian*, 13 December.

Rudwick, E.M. (1964) *Race Riot at East St. Louis, July 2 1917*, Carbondale, Illinois: Southern University Press.

Runnymede Trust (1989) *Fortress Europe? The Meaning of 1992*, London: Runnymede Trust.

Said, E. (1979) *Orientalism*, London: Penguin.

Saltzstein, G.H. (1989) 'Black mayors and police policies' *Journal of Politics*, 51, 3 (August): 525–44.

Sashidharan, S.P. (1988) 'Blacks and madness in society', *Guardian*, 31 October.

Savage, S. (1989) 'Crime control, the law and the community', *Talking Politics*, 21, 3: 12–15.

Sayer, A. (1984) *Methods in Social Science*, London: Hutchinson.

Schaffer, E. (1980) *Community Policing*, London: Croom Helm.

Scarman, Lord (1981) *The Brixton Disorders 10–12 April 1981: Report of an Inquiry by the Rt Hon. The Lord Scarman*, London: HMSO.

Scott, E.J. (1920) *Negro Migration During the War*, New York: Arnos Press (reprinted 1969).

Scott, S. and Dickens, A. (1989) 'Police and the professionalization of rape', in C. Dunhill (ed.) *The Boys in Blue*, London: Virago.

Scraton, P. (1985) *The State of the Police*, London: Pluto.

—— (1987) 'Unreasonable force: policing, punishment and marginalization', in P. Scraton (ed.) *Law, Order and the Authoritarian State*, Milton Keynes: Open University Press.

Sher, A. (1989) *Freedom of Protest, Public Order and the Law*, Oxford: Basil Blackwell.

Sherman, L.W. (1983) 'Reducing police gun use: critical events, administrative policy and organizational changes', in M. Punch (ed.) *Control in the Police Organization*, Cambridge, Mass.: MIT Press.

Sim, J. (1982) 'Scarman: The police counter-attack', in M. Eve and D. Musson (eds) *The Socialist Register 1982*, London: Merlin Press.

Sim, J., Scraton, P. and Gordon, P. (1987) 'Crime, the state and critical analysis', in P. Scraton (ed.) *Law, Order and the Authoritarian State*, Milton Keynes: Open University.

Sington, D. (1966) 'The policeman and the immigrant', *New Society*, 24 February.

Sivanandan, A. (1976) *Race, Class and the State: The Black Experience in Britain*, Race and Class Pamphlet, No. 1, London: Institute of Race Relations.

—— (1983) *A Different Hunger*, London: Pluto.

—— (1988) 'The new racism', *New Statesman & Society*, 4 November.

Skolnick, J.H. (1975) *Justice Without Trial*, New York: John Wiley.

Skolnick, J.H. and Bayley, D.H. (1986) *The New Blue Line*, New York: Free Press.

Skolnick, R. (1969) *The Politics of Protest*, New York: Simon & Schuster.

Smith, D.J. (1983) *A Survey of Londoners*, Police and People in London vol. 1, London: Policy Studies Institute.

—— (1987) 'Policing and urban unrest', in J. Benyon and J. Solomos (eds) *The Roots of Urban Unrest*, London: Pergamon.

Smith, D.J. and Gray, J. (1983) *The Police in Action*, Police and People in London, vol. IV, London: Policy Studies Institute.

—— (1985) *Police and People in London: The PSI Report*, Aldershot: Gower.

Solomos, J. (1986) *Riots, Urban Protest and Social Policy: The Interplay of Reform and Social Control*, Policy Papers in Ethnic Relations, Warwick: University of Warwick.

—— (1988) *Black Youth, Racism and the State*, Cambridge: Cambridge

University Press.

—— (1989) *Race and Racism in Contemporary Britain*, London: Macmillan.

Spare Rib (1990) *Communities of Resistance Challenge Fortress Europe*, no. 212, May.

State Research Bulletin (1980) *Policing the 1980s: The Iron Fist*, London: State Research.

Stephens, M. (1988) *Policing*, Brighton: Harvester.

Stevens, P. and Willis, C. (1979) *Race, Crime and Arrests*, Home Office Research Study no. 58, London: HMSO.

Storch, R. (1976) 'The policeman as domestic missionary', *Journal of Social History* 9, 4: 481–510.

Swift, R. and Gilley, S. (1985) *The Irish in the Victorian City*, London: Croom Helm.

Swigert, V.L. and Farrell, R.A. (eds) (1977) *Deviance and Social Control*, Glenview, Illinois: University of Illinois Press.

Taylor, I. (1981) *Law and Order: Arguments for Socialism*, London: Macmillan.

Thackrah, J. (1985) 'Reactions to terrorism and riots', in J. Thackrah (ed) *Contemporary Policing*, London: Sphere.

Thatchell, P. (1983) *Battle for Bermondsey*, London: Heretic Books.

Thompson, E.P. (1979) *The Secret State*, London: IRP.

Thompson, K. (1988) *Under Siege*, London: Penguin.

Thornton, P. (1989) *Decade of Decline: Civil Liberties in the 1980s*, London: NCCL.

Trevizias, E. (1983) 'Crowd dynamics and the prevention and control of collective disorders', *Police Journal*, LVI: 142–63.

Trotter, J.W. (1985) *Black Milwaukee*, Urbana, Illinois: University of Illinois Press.

Troyna, B. and Smith, D.I. (1983) *Racism, School and the Labour Market*, Leicester: National Youth Bureau.

Tuck, M. and Southgate, P. (1981) *Ethnic Minorities, Crime and Policing*, Home Office Research Study No. 70, London: HMSO.

Tuttle, W.M. (1970) *Race Riot: Chicago in the Red Summer of 1919*, New York: Atheneum.

Upton, J.N. (1984) *A Social History of 20th Century Urban Riots*, Bristol, Ind.: Wyndham Hall Press.

van Dijk, T. (1988) *News Analysis: Case Studies of International and National News in the Press*, New Jersey: Lawrence Erlbaum.

Vick, C.F.J. (1982) 'Ideological responses to the riots', *Police Journal*, LV: 262–78.

Visher, C. (1983) 'Gender police arrest decisions and notions of chivalry', *Criminology*, 21: 5–27.

Vorhaus, G. (1984) *Police in the Classroom*, Middlesex: Hillingdon Legal Resource Centre.

Waddington, P.A.J. (1984) 'Conservativism, dogmatism and authoritarianism in British police officers: a comment', *Sociology*, 16: 4.

—— (1987) 'Towards paramilitarism', *British Journal of Criminology* 27, 1: 37–46.

—— (1988) *Arming an Unarmed Police*, London: Police Foundation.

—— (1989) 'Riot control, minimum force and the British police tradition', Paper delivered at the British Criminology Conference, Bristol, July.

Wainwright, H. (1987) *Labour: A Tale of Two Parties*, London: Hogarth.

Walker, M. (1986) *A Report To The Manchester City Council Police Monitoring Unit*, unpublished report.

Walker, M.A. (1987) 'Interpreting race and crime statistics', *Journal of the Royal Statistical Society*, A, 150, part 1: 39–56.

Walker, M., Jefferson, T. and Senevirate, M. (1989) 'Race and criminal justice in a provincial city', unpublished paper presented to British Criminology Conference, Bristol Polytechnic, July.

Walklate, S. (1989) *Victimology: the Victim and the Criminal Justice Process*, London: Unwin Hyman.

Weeks, J. (1990) 'The £1 billion bill for Europol', *Police*, April.

Wells, R. (1987) 'The will and the way to move forward in policing', in J. Benyon and J. Solomos (eds) *The Roots of Urban Unrest*, London: Pergamon.

Williams, B. (1985) *The Making of the Manchester Jewry, 1740–1875*, Manchester: Manchester University Press.

Williams, R. (1973) *The Country and the City*, London: Chatto & Windus.

Willis, C. (1983) *The Use, Effectiveness and Impact of Police Stop and Search Powers*, London: Home Office Research Unit.

Willmot, P. (ed.) *Policing and the Community*, London: Policy Studies Institute.

Woman of Broadwater Farm, The (1989) 'Into our homes', in C. Dunhill (ed.) *The Boys in Blue*, London: Virago.

Wood, F.G. (1970) *Black Scare: The Racist Response to Emancipation and Reconstruction*, Berkeley, CA: University of California Press.

Yette, S. (1971) *The Choice*, New York: G.P. Putnam's Sons.

Zander, M. (1985) *The Police and Criminal Evidence Act*, London: Sweet & Maxwell.

Zimring, F.E. (1976) 'Making the punishment fit the crime', *Hastings Centre Report*, 6 December.

Name index

Ackroyd, C. 30, 40
ACPO/SEO 162
AFFOR 113
Alderson, J. 196, 198, 212
Anderton, J. 12, 13, 109, 117, 198
Aptheker, H. 66–7
Arblaster, A. 33
Ardrey, R. 207
Arnold, D. 29
Arnott, H. 133
Auletta, K. 174

Bains, H.S. 181, 185
Baker, E. 140
Banton, M. 192–4, 211
Barthes, R. 208
Batta, I.D. 180
Bayley, D.H. 100
Benn, M. 134, 142
Bennett, T. 180
Benyon, J. 46, 177, 181, 186
Bergesen, A. 81
Berkeley, G.E. 109
Berkeley, J. 140
Berlin, I. 70–1
Bethnal Green and Stepney
    Trades Council 113
Birch, R. 125
Blakelock, K. 7, 48
Blauner, R. 89–90
Blom-Cooper, L. 180
Boss, P. 156
Bowes, S. 26
Box, S. 12, 13

Brewer, J. 19
Briar, S. 180
Bridges, L. 34, 123, 178
Brindley, J.M. 197
Brisbane, R.H. 78
Brogden, M.: account of police
    work 168; on Home Office 38;
    on police accountability 110;
    on police expenditure 13, 14;
    on politicization of police 39;
    on public attitudes 18; on
    police prejudice 135; on
    policing by consent 197, 204
Brown, C. 181
Brown, L.P. 87–8, 100, 101, 103,
    104
BSSRS 29, 30
Bundred, S. 115
Bunyan, T. 16, 29
Bunyard, R. 10
Burgess, J. 202

Cain, M. 180
Callaghan, J. 173, 176
Campbell, D. 112
Carr-Hill, R. 154
Carter, R. 96
Carter, T. 6, 153–4, 158
Cashmore, E. 11, 23
Cesarani, D. 16
Chigwada, R. 6, 145, 148
Clark, K.B. 76–7
Cochrane, K. 26
Cohen, P. 167, 169–73, 175, 185

Subject index